PRACTICAL USES FOR GARFIELD'S HAIRBALLS

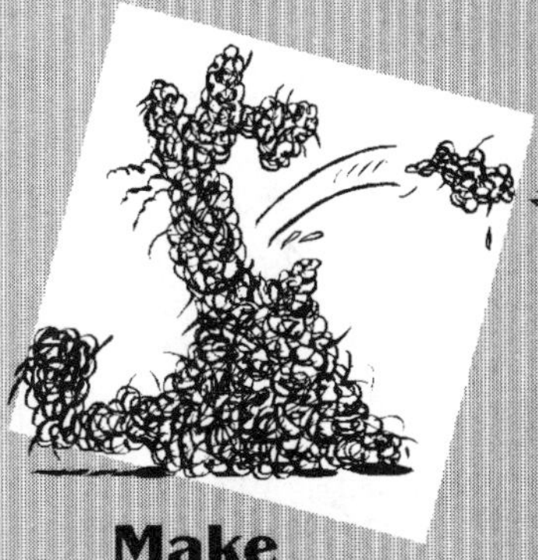

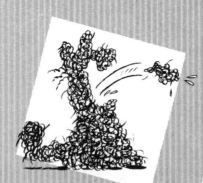

Make Another Cat

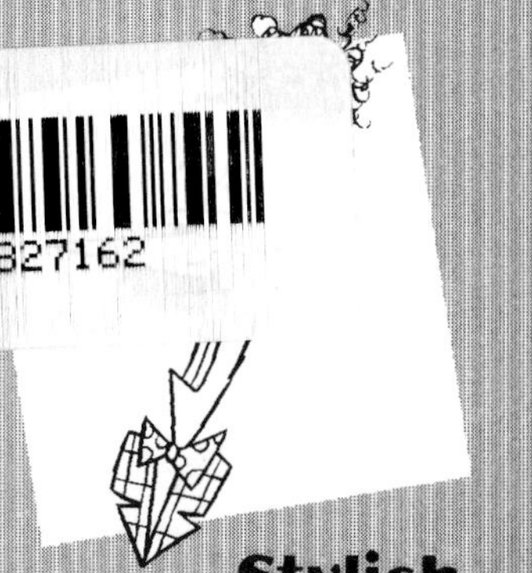

Stylish Toupees

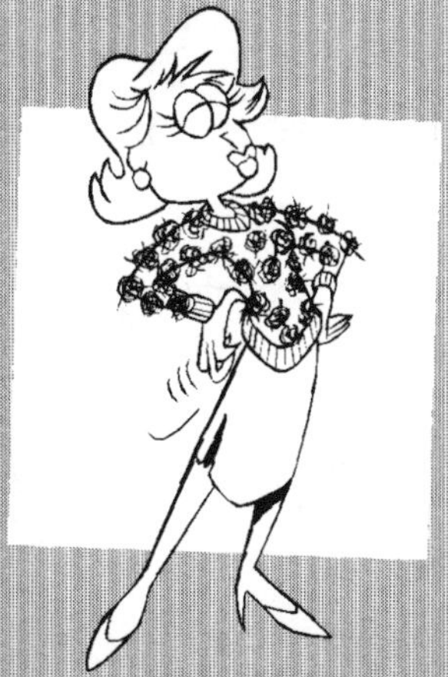

Uniq
Sweaters

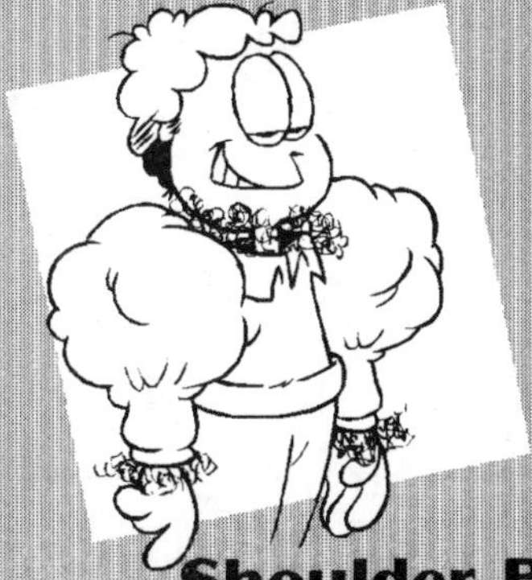

Shoulder Pads

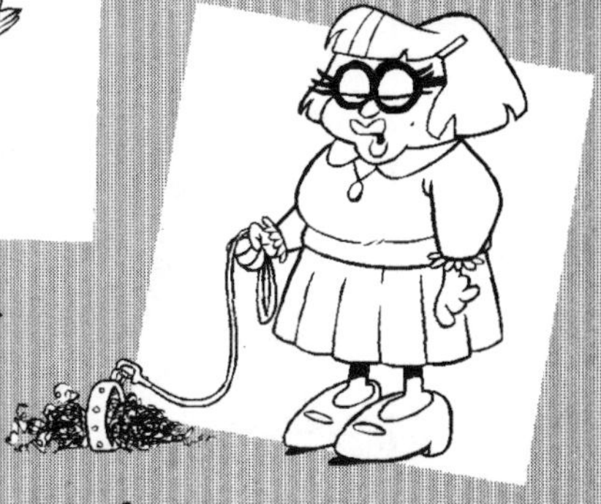

Maintenance-Free Pets

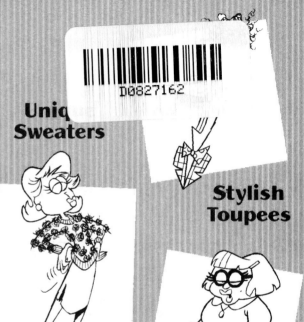

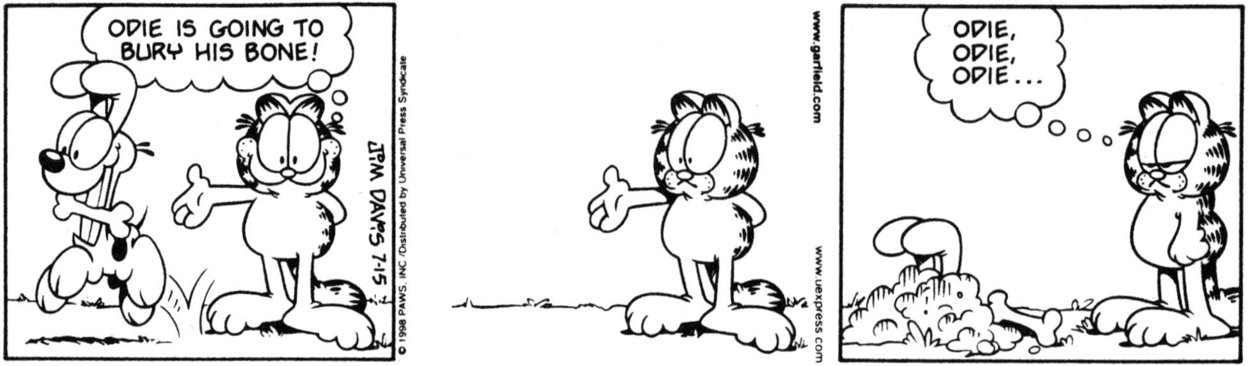
ODIE IS GOING TO BURY HIS BONE!
JIM DAVIS 7-15
© 1998 PAWS, INC./Distributed by Universal Press Syndicate
www.garfield.com
www.uexpress.com
ODIE, ODIE, ODIE...

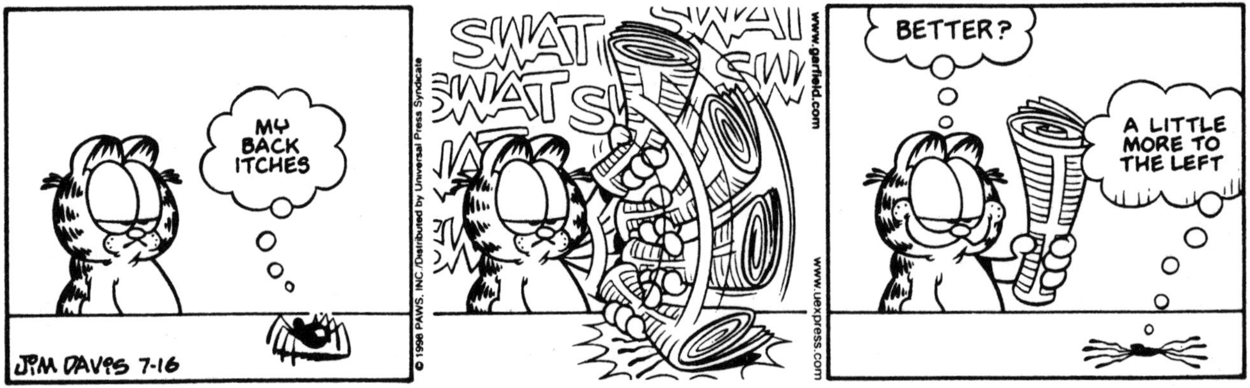
MY BACK ITCHES
JIM DAVIS 7-16
© 1998 PAWS, INC./Distributed by Universal Press Syndicate
SWAT SWAT SWAT
www.garfield.com
www.uexpress.com
BETTER?
A LITTLE MORE TO THE LEFT

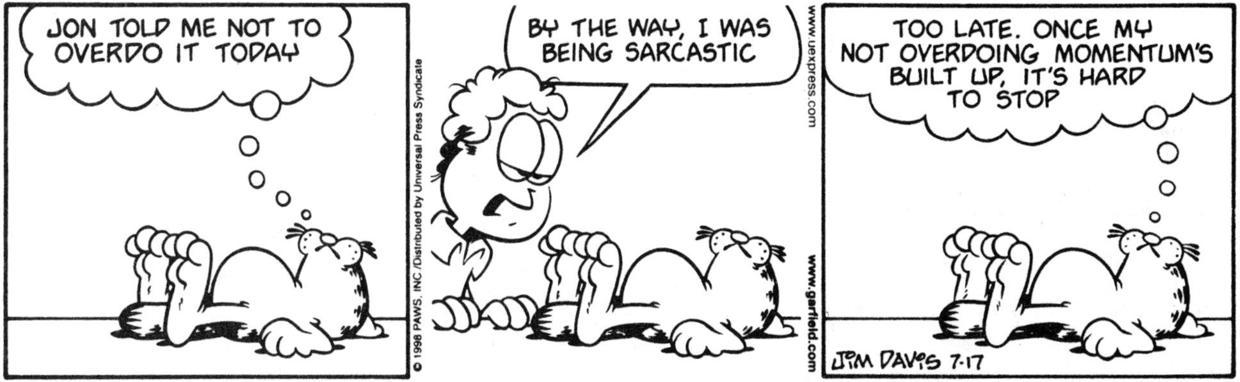
JON TOLD ME NOT TO OVERDO IT TODAY
BY THE WAY, I WAS BEING SARCASTIC
TOO LATE. ONCE MY NOT OVERDOING MOMENTUM'S BUILT UP, IT'S HARD TO STOP
JIM DAVIS 7-17
© 1998 PAWS, INC./Distributed by Universal Press Syndicate
www.uexpress.com
www.garfield.com

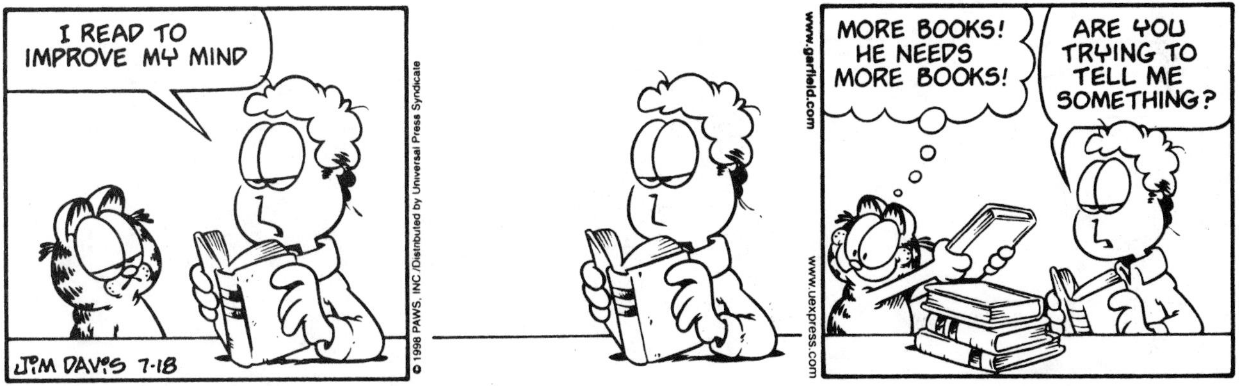
I READ TO IMPROVE MY MIND
MORE BOOKS! HE NEEDS MORE BOOKS!
ARE YOU TRYING TO TELL ME SOMETHING?
JIM DAVIS 7-18
© 1998 PAWS, INC./Distributed by Universal Press Syndicate
www.garfield.com
www.uexpress.com

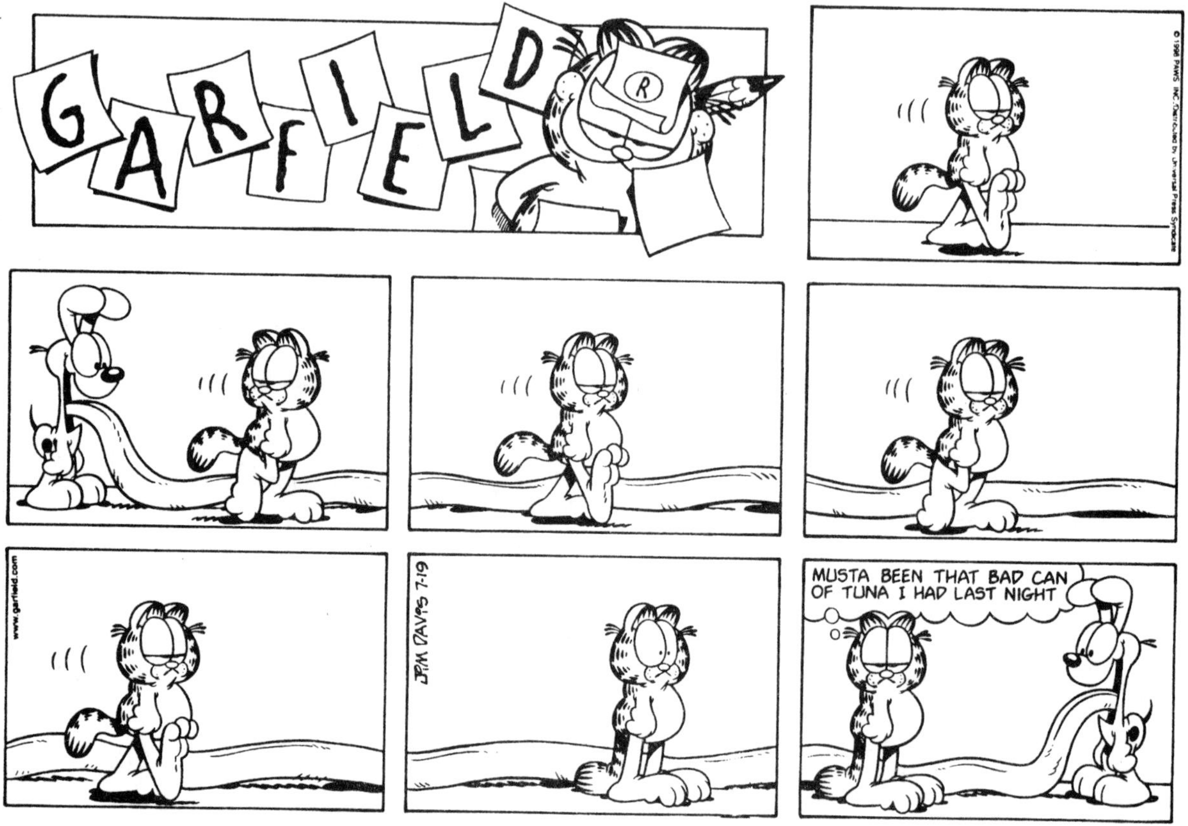
GARFIELD®
© 1998 PAWS, INC. Distributed by Universal Press Syndicate
www.garfield.com
JPM DAVPS 7-19
MUSTA BEEN THAT BAD CAN OF TUNA I HAD LAST NIGHT

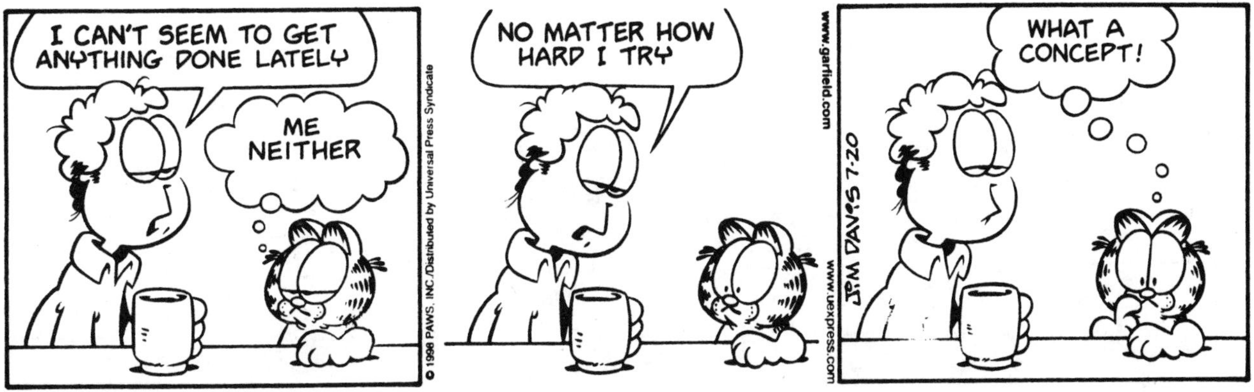
I CAN'T SEEM TO GET ANYTHING DONE LATELY
ME NEITHER
NO MATTER HOW HARD I TRY
WHAT A CONCEPT!
JIM DAVIS 7-20
© 1998 PAWS, INC./Distributed by Universal Press Syndicate
www.garfield.com
www.uexpress.com

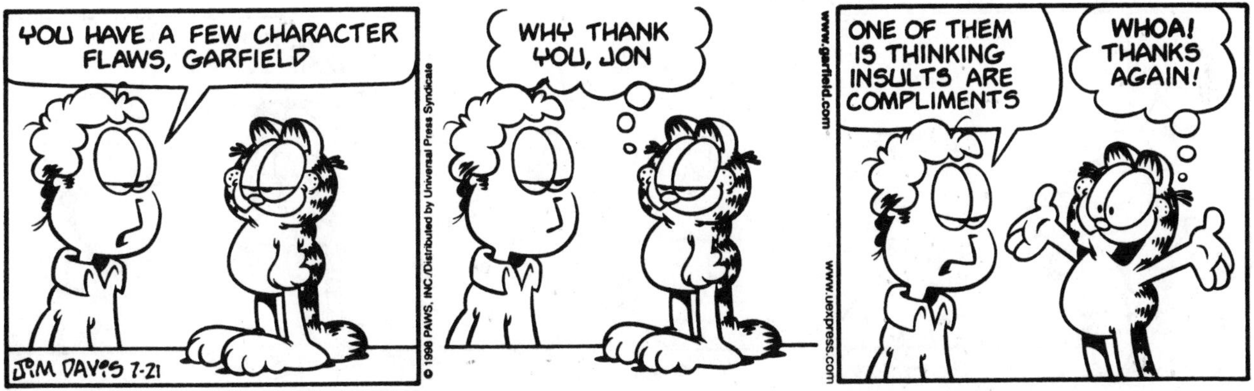
YOU HAVE A FEW CHARACTER FLAWS, GARFIELD
WHY THANK YOU, JON
ONE OF THEM IS THINKING INSULTS ARE COMPLIMENTS
WHOA! THANKS AGAIN!
JIM DAVIS 7-21
© 1998 PAWS, INC./Distributed by Universal Press Syndicate
www.garfield.com
www.uexpress.com

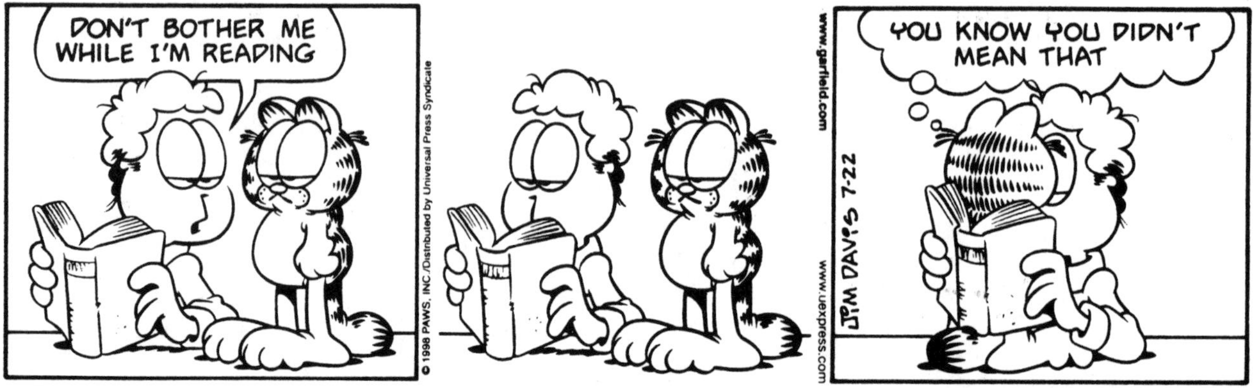
DON'T BOTHER ME WHILE I'M READING
YOU KNOW YOU DIDN'T MEAN THAT
JIM DAVIS 7-22
© 1998 PAWS, INC./Distributed by Universal Press Syndicate
www.garfield.com
www.uexpress.com

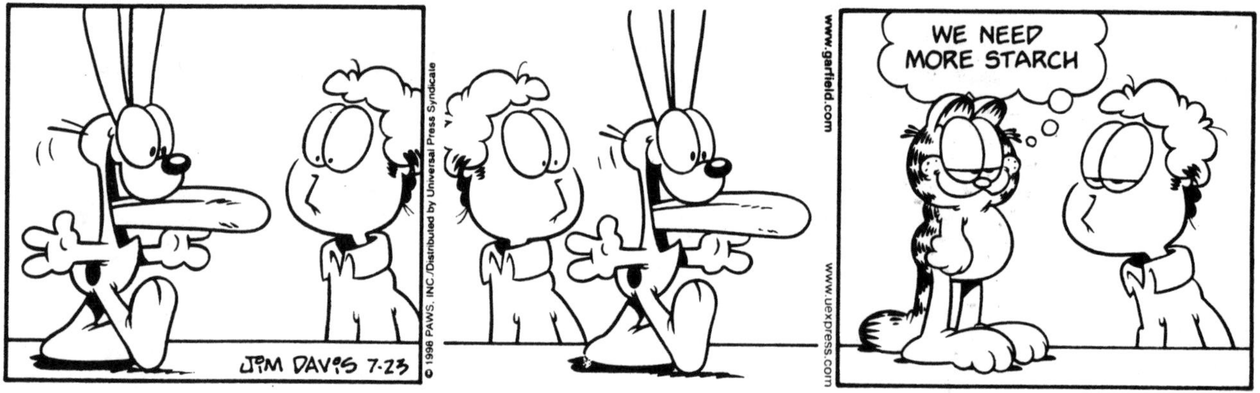
WE NEED MORE STARCH
JIM DAVIS 7-23
© 1998 PAWS, INC./Distributed by Universal Press Syndicate
www.garfield.com
www.uexpress.com

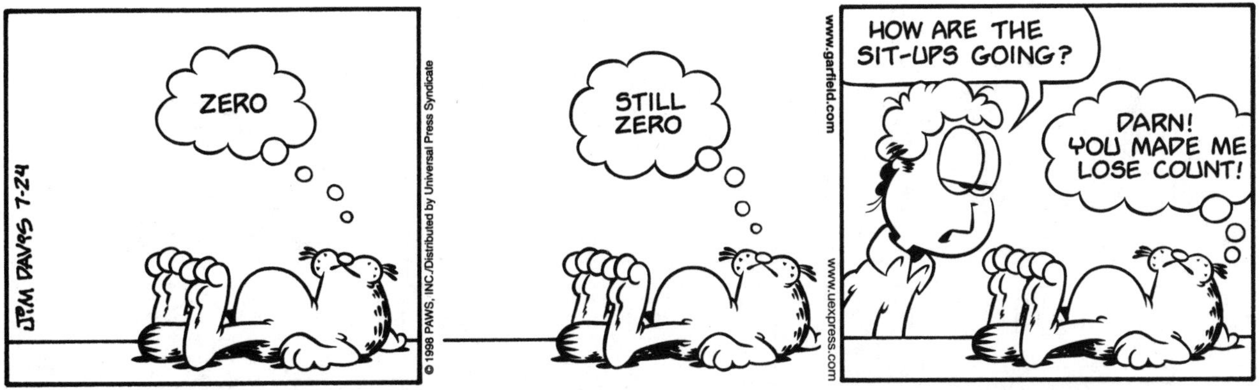
ZERO
JIM DAVIS 7-24
© 1998 PAWS, INC./Distributed by Universal Press Syndicate
STILL ZERO
www.garfield.com
www.uexpress.com
HOW ARE THE SIT-UPS GOING?
DARN! YOU MADE ME LOSE COUNT!

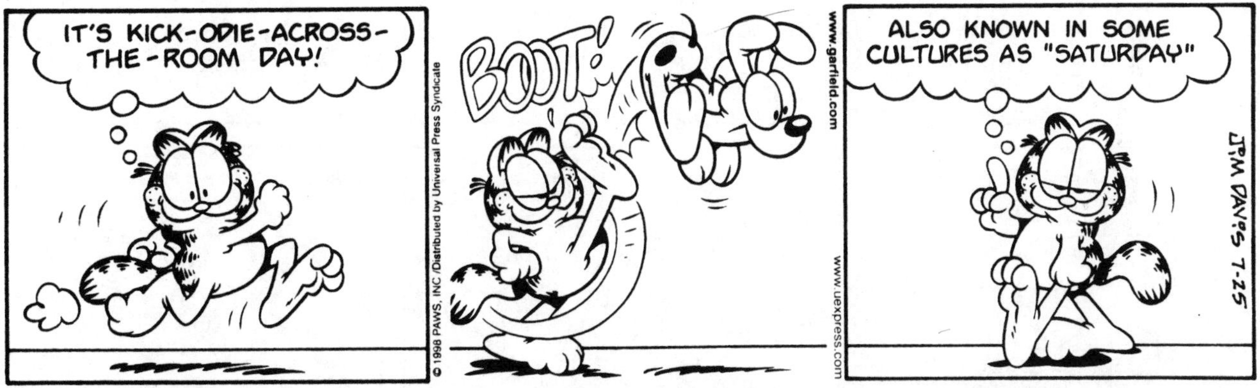
IT'S KICK-ODIE-ACROSS-THE-ROOM DAY!
© 1998 PAWS, INC /Distributed by Universal Press Syndicate
BOOT!
www.garfield.com
www.uexpress.com
ALSO KNOWN IN SOME CULTURES AS "SATURDAY"
JIM DAVIS 7-25

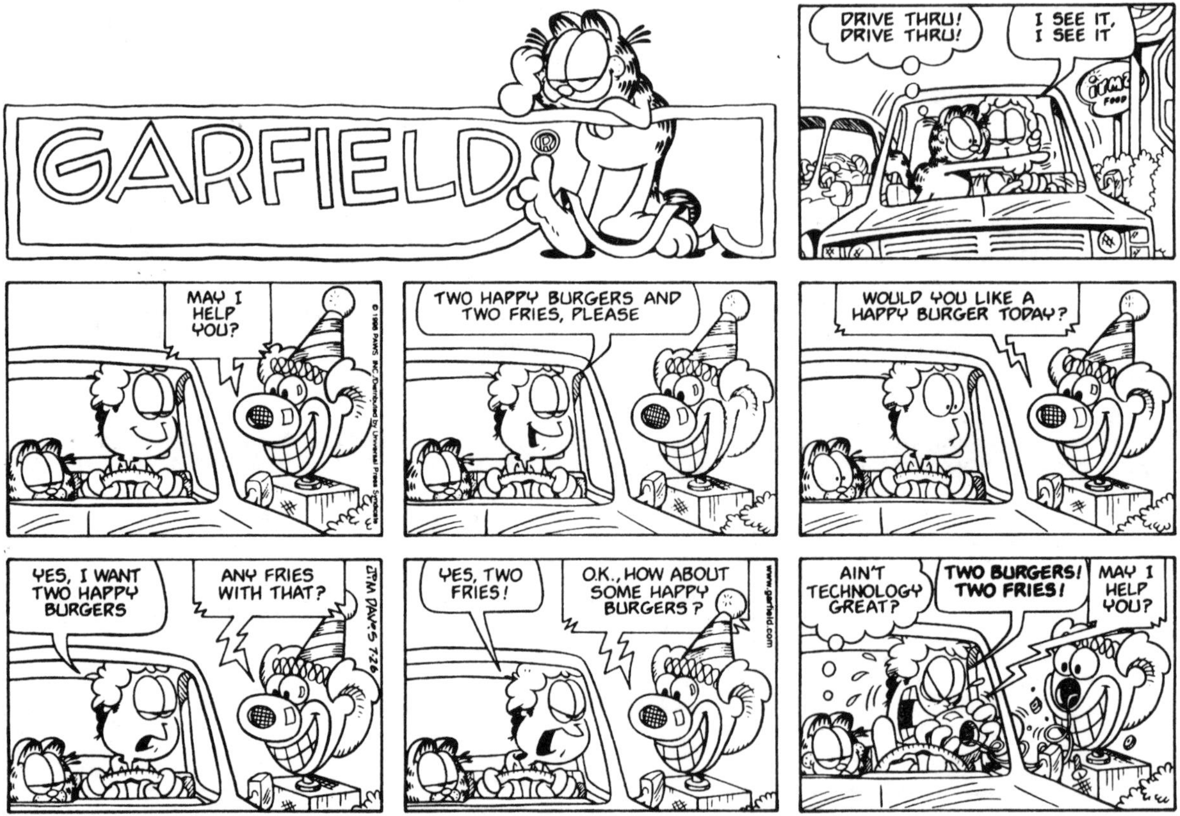
GARFIELD®
DRIVE THRU! DRIVE THRU!
I SEE IT, I SEE IT
MAY I HELP YOU?
© 1998 PAWS, INC./Distributed by Universal Press Syndicate
TWO HAPPY BURGERS AND TWO FRIES, PLEASE
WOULD YOU LIKE A HAPPY BURGER TODAY?
YES, I WANT TWO HAPPY BURGERS
ANY FRIES WITH THAT?
JIM DAVIS 7-26
YES, TWO FRIES!
O.K., HOW ABOUT SOME HAPPY BURGERS?
www.garfield.com
AIN'T TECHNOLOGY GREAT?
TWO BURGERS! TWO FRIES!
MAY I HELP YOU?

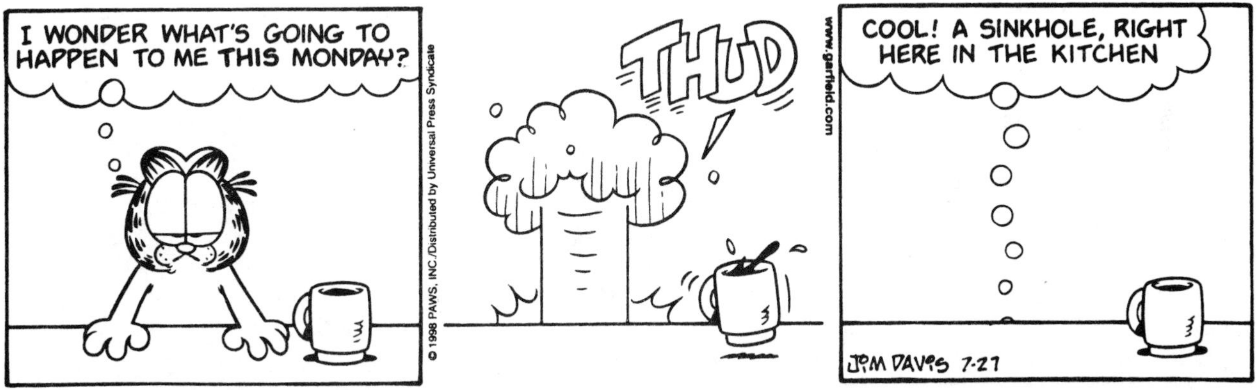
I WONDER WHAT'S GOING TO HAPPEN TO ME THIS MONDAY?
© 1998 PAWS, INC./Distributed by Universal Press Syndicate
THUD
www.garfield.com
COOL! A SINKHOLE, RIGHT HERE IN THE KITCHEN
JIM DAVIS 7-27

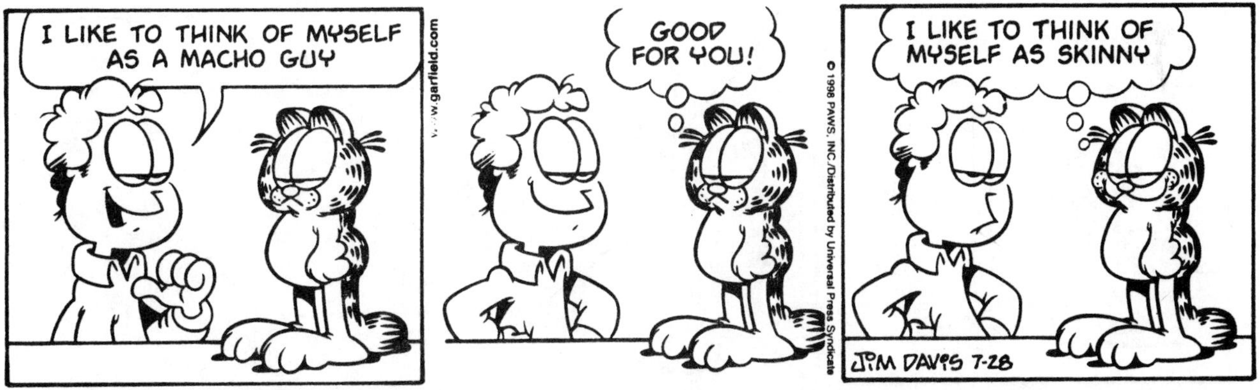
I LIKE TO THINK OF MYSELF AS A MACHO GUY
GOOD FOR YOU!
© 1998 PAWS, INC./Distributed by Universal Press Syndicate
I LIKE TO THINK OF MYSELF AS SKINNY
JIM DAVIS 7-28

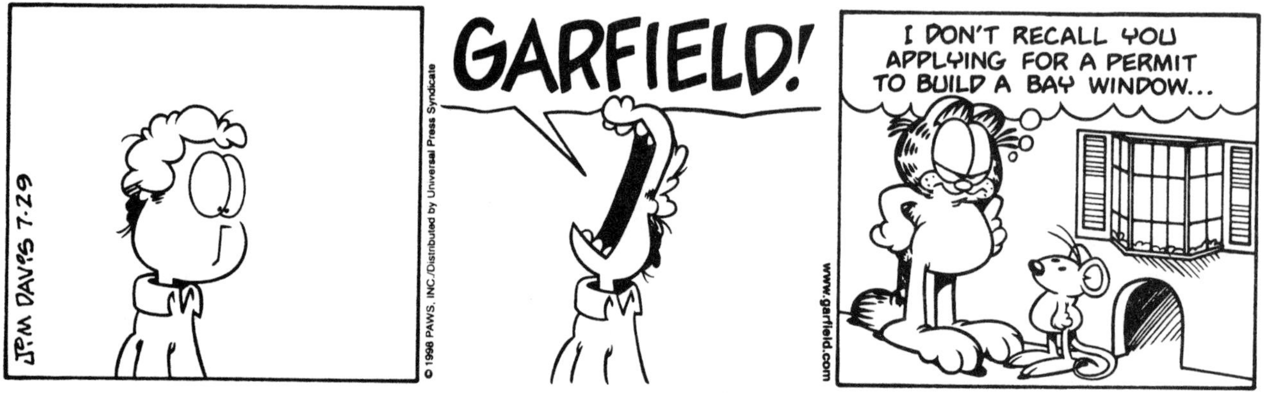
JIM DAVIS 7·29
GARFIELD!
I DON'T RECALL YOU APPLYING FOR A PERMIT TO BUILD A BAY WINDOW...
© 1998 PAWS, INC./Distributed by Universal Press Syndicate
www.garfield.com

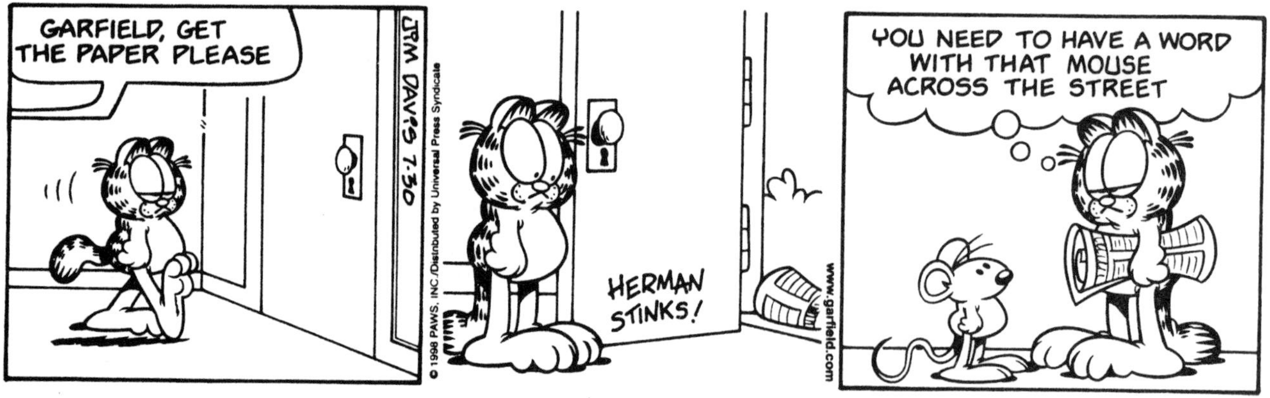
GARFIELD, GET THE PAPER PLEASE
JIM DAVIS 7·30
HERMAN STINKS!
YOU NEED TO HAVE A WORD WITH THAT MOUSE ACROSS THE STREET
© 1998 PAWS, INC./Distributed by Universal Press Syndicate
www.garfield.com

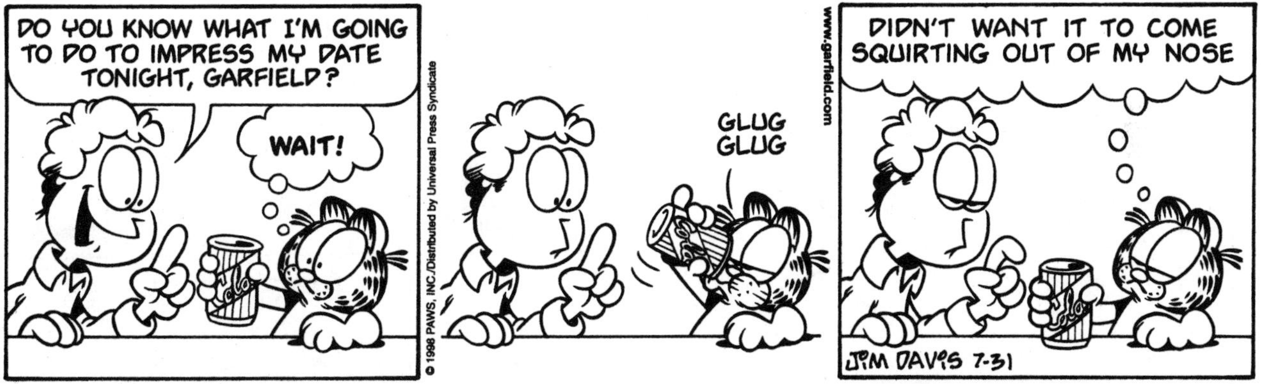
DO YOU KNOW WHAT I'M GOING TO DO TO IMPRESS MY DATE TONIGHT, GARFIELD?
WAIT!
© 1998 PAWS, INC./Distributed by Universal Press Syndicate
GLUG GLUG
www.garfield.com
DIDN'T WANT IT TO COME SQUIRTING OUT OF MY NOSE
JIM DAVIS 7-31

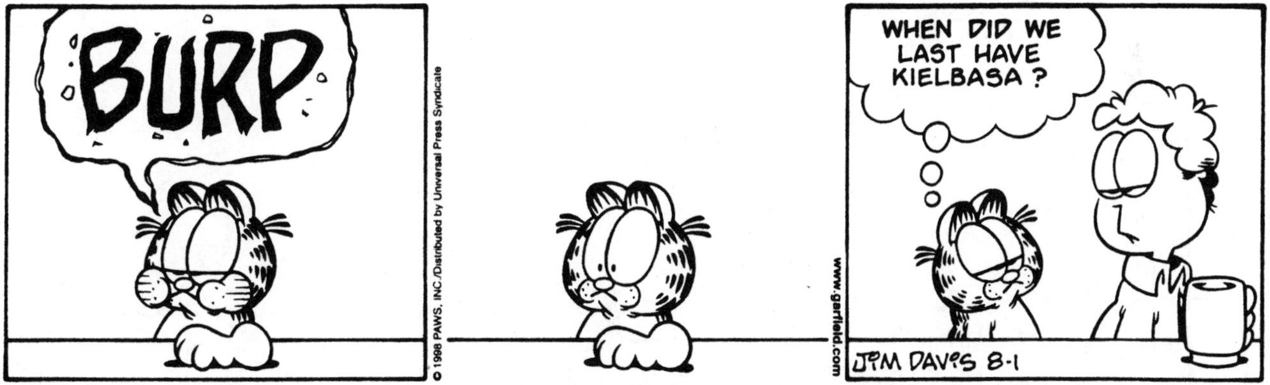
BURP
© 1998 PAWS, INC./Distributed by Universal Press Syndicate
www.garfield.com
WHEN DID WE LAST HAVE KIELBASA?
JIM DAVIS 8-1

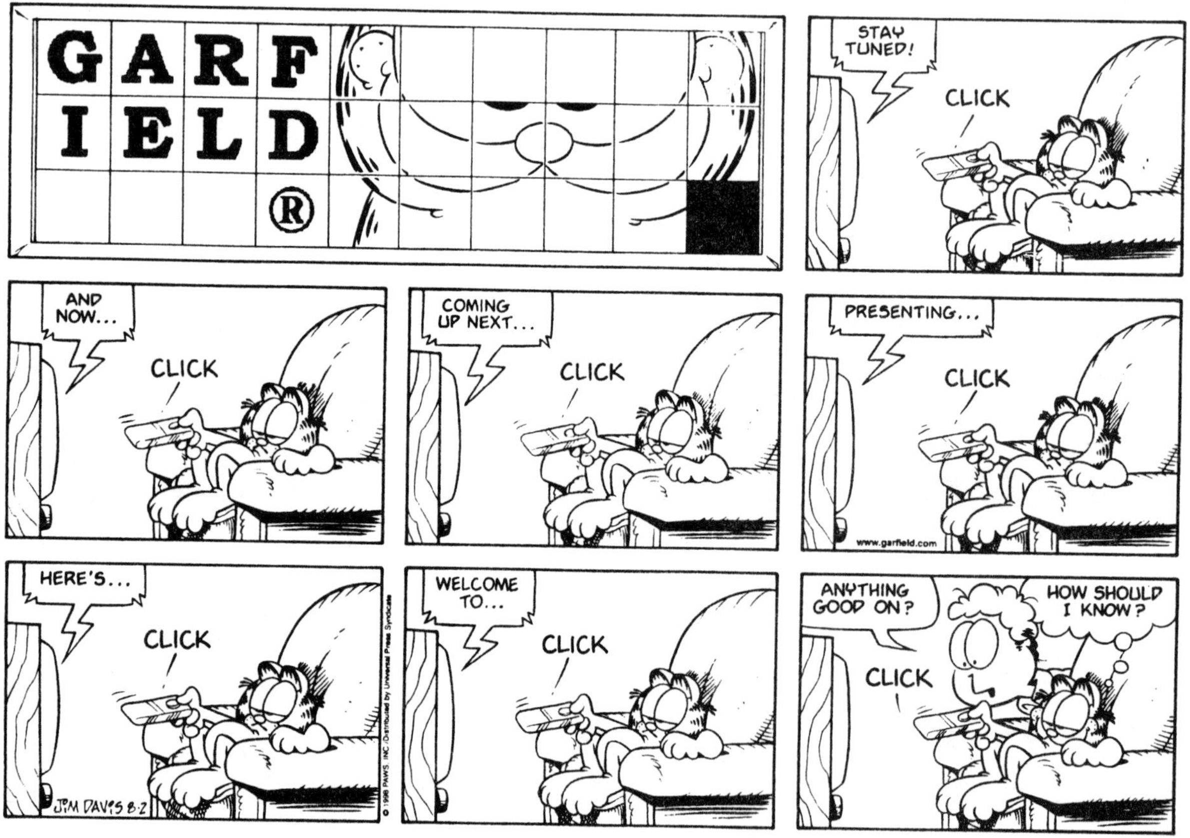
GARFIELD®
STAY TUNED!
CLICK
AND NOW...
CLICK
COMING UP NEXT...
CLICK
PRESENTING...
CLICK
www.garfield.com
HERE'S...
CLICK
JIM DAVIS 8-2
© 1998 PAWS, INC./Distributed by Universal Press Syndicate
WELCOME TO...
CLICK
ANYTHING GOOD ON?
CLICK
HOW SHOULD I KNOW?

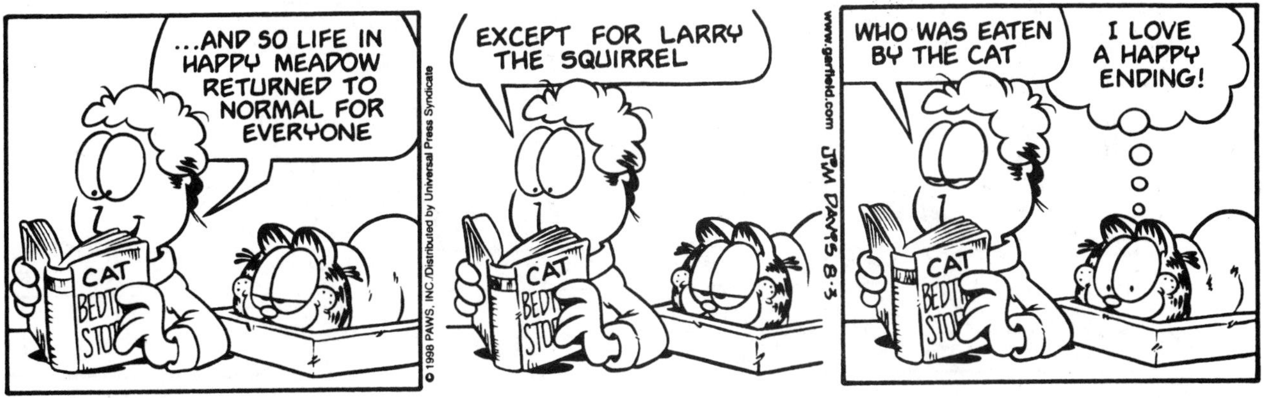
...AND SO LIFE IN HAPPY MEADOW RETURNED TO NORMAL FOR EVERYONE
EXCEPT FOR LARRY THE SQUIRREL
WHO WAS EATEN BY THE CAT
I LOVE A HAPPY ENDING!
CAT BEDTI STOR
JIM DAVIS 8-3
www.garfield.com

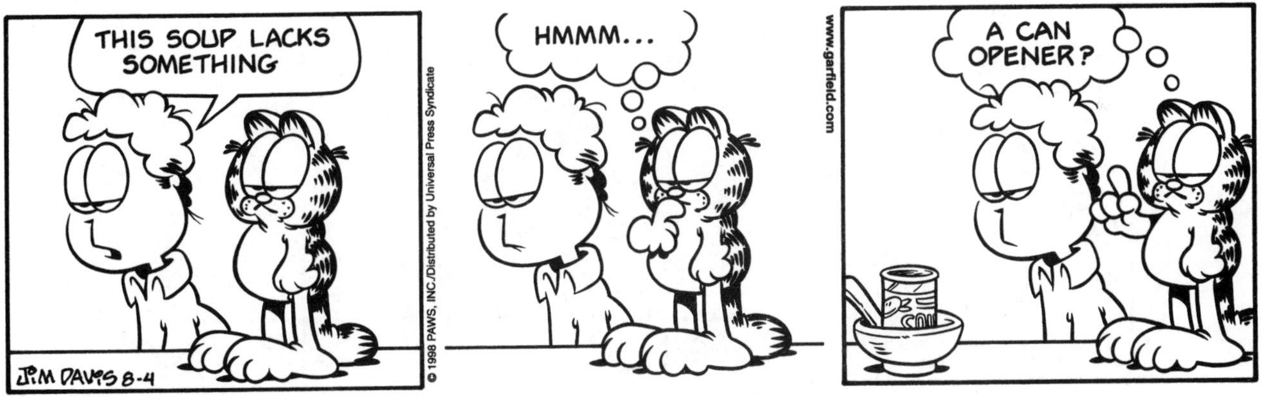
THIS SOUP LACKS SOMETHING
HMMM...
A CAN OPENER?
JIM DAVIS 8-4
www.garfield.com

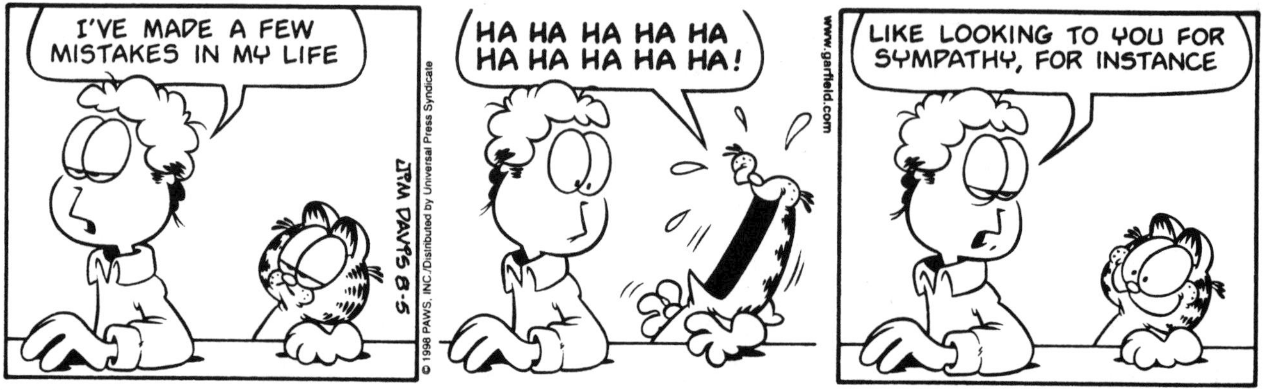
I'VE MADE A FEW MISTAKES IN MY LIFE
HA HA HA HA HA HA HA HA HA HA!
LIKE LOOKING TO YOU FOR SYMPATHY, FOR INSTANCE
JIM DAVIS 8-5
© 1998 PAWS, INC./Distributed by Universal Press Syndicate
www.garfield.com

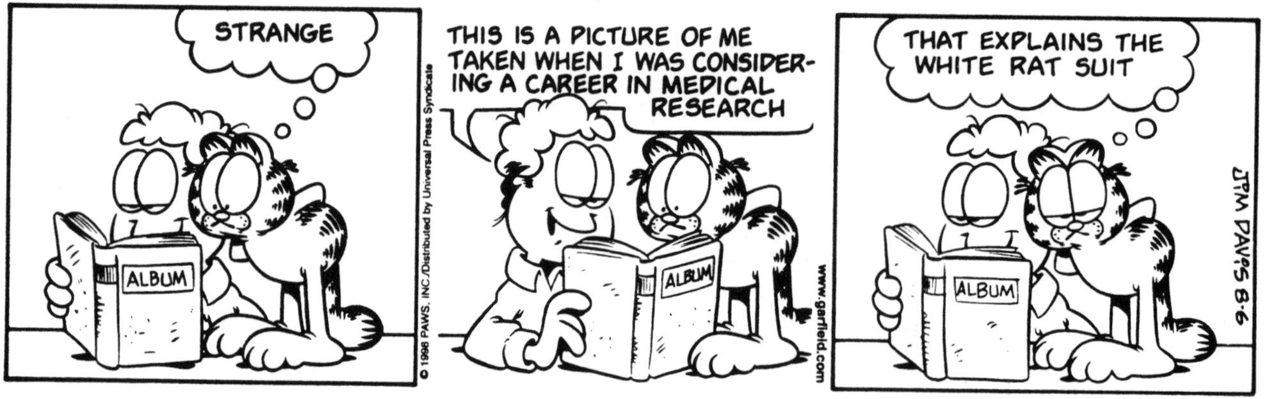
STRANGE
ALBUM
THIS IS A PICTURE OF ME TAKEN WHEN I WAS CONSIDER-ING A CAREER IN MEDICAL RESEARCH
ALBUM
THAT EXPLAINS THE WHITE RAT SUIT
ALBUM
JIM DAVIS 8-6
© 1998 PAWS, INC./Distributed by Universal Press Syndicate
www.garfield.com

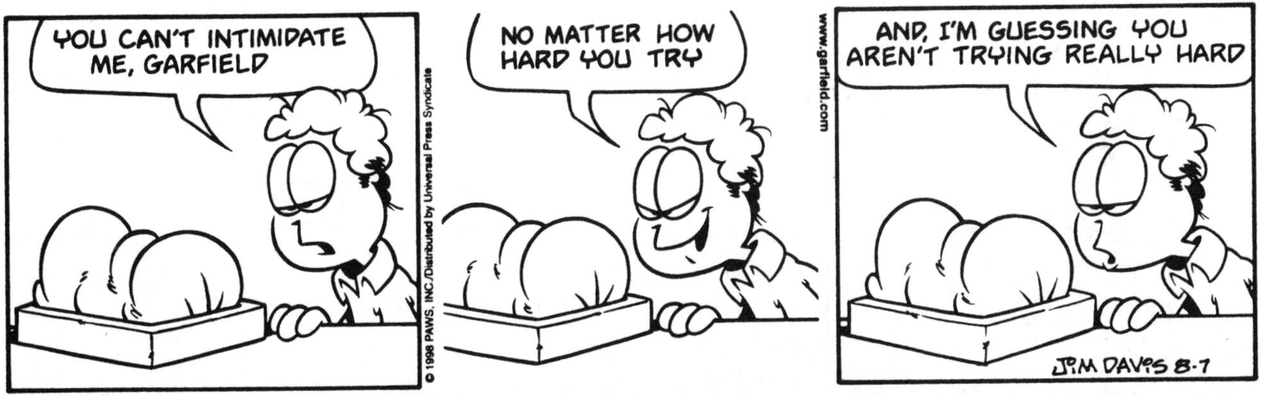
YOU CAN'T INTIMIDATE ME, GARFIELD
NO MATTER HOW HARD YOU TRY
AND, I'M GUESSING YOU AREN'T TRYING REALLY HARD
JIM DAVIS 8-7

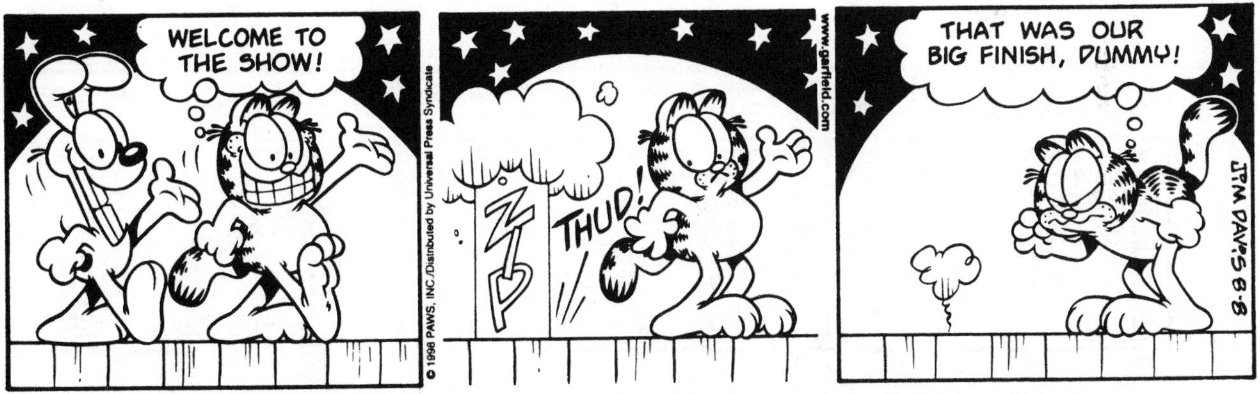
WELCOME TO THE SHOW!
ZIP
THUD!
THAT WAS OUR BIG FINISH, DUMMY!
JIM DAVIS 8-8

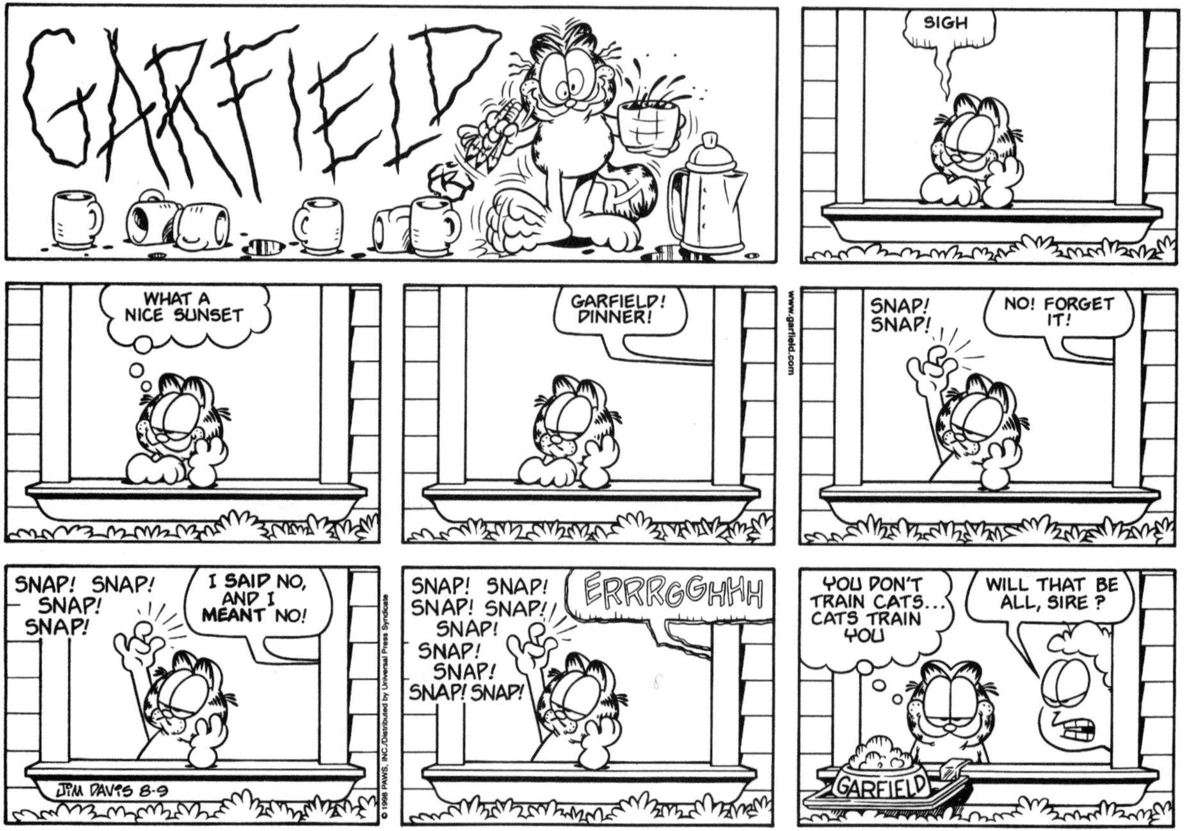
GARFIELD
SIGH
WHAT A NICE SUNSET
GARFIELD! DINNER!
SNAP! SNAP!
NO! FORGET IT!
SNAP! SNAP! SNAP! SNAP!
I SAID NO, AND I MEANT NO!
JIM DAVIS 8-9
© 1998 PAWS, INC./Distributed by Universal Press Syndicate
SNAP! SNAP! SNAP! SNAP! SNAP! SNAP! SNAP! SNAP! SNAP!
ERRRGGHHH
YOU DON'T TRAIN CATS... CATS TRAIN YOU
WILL THAT BE ALL, SIRE ?
GARFIELD
www.garfield.com

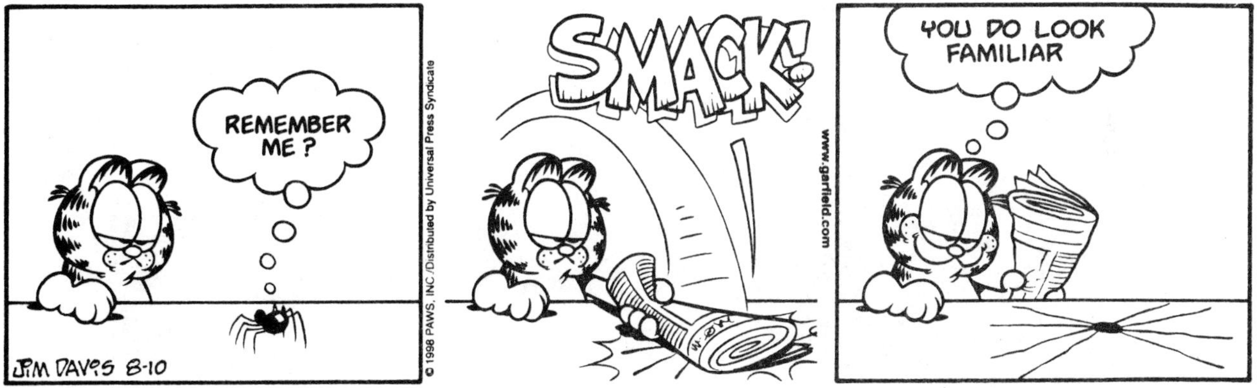
REMEMBER ME ?
JIM DAVIS 8-10
© 1998 PAWS, INC./Distributed by Universal Press Syndicate
SMACK!
www.garfield.com
YOU DO LOOK FAMILIAR

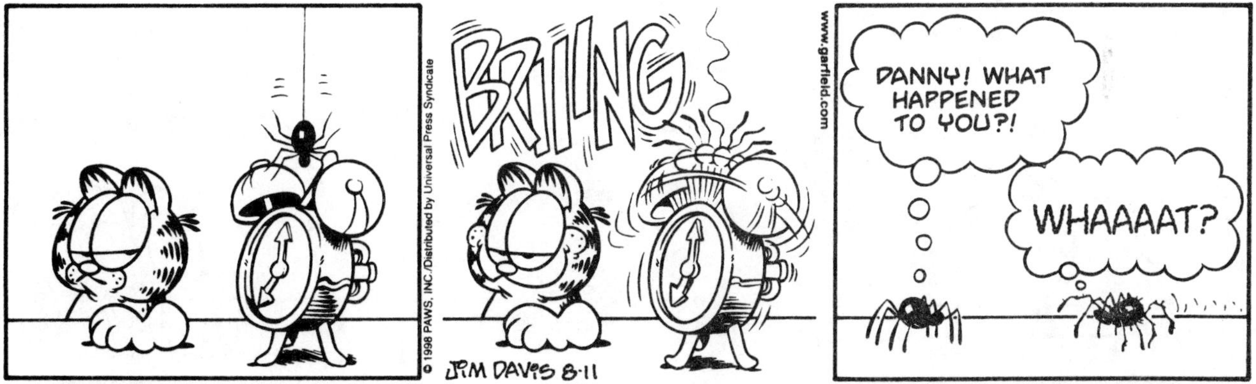
© 1998 PAWS, INC./Distributed by Universal Press Syndicate
BRIING
JIM DAVIS 8-11
www.garfield.com
DANNY! WHAT HAPPENED TO YOU?!
WHAAAAT?

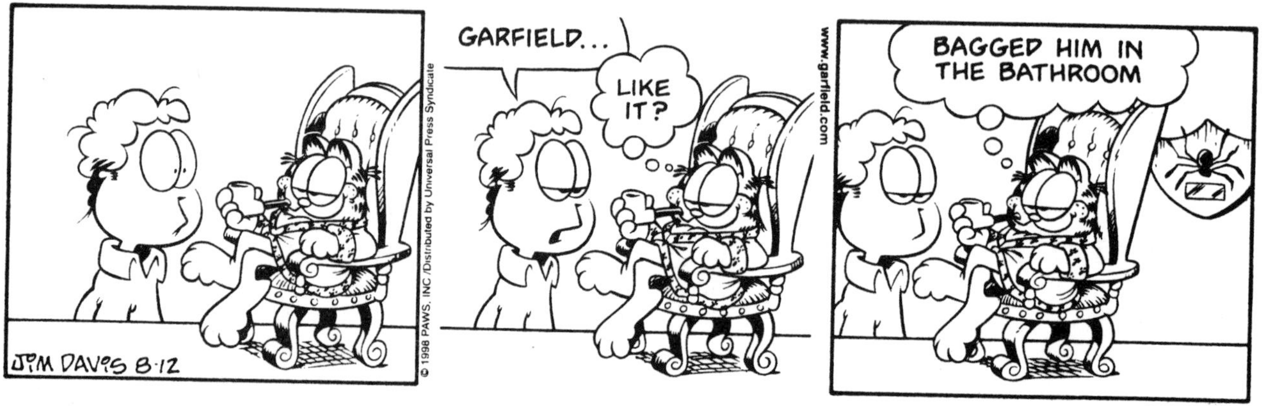
JIM DAVIS 8-12
© 1998 PAWS, INC./Distributed by Universal Press Syndicate
GARFIELD...
LIKE IT?
www.garfield.com
BAGGED HIM IN THE BATHROOM

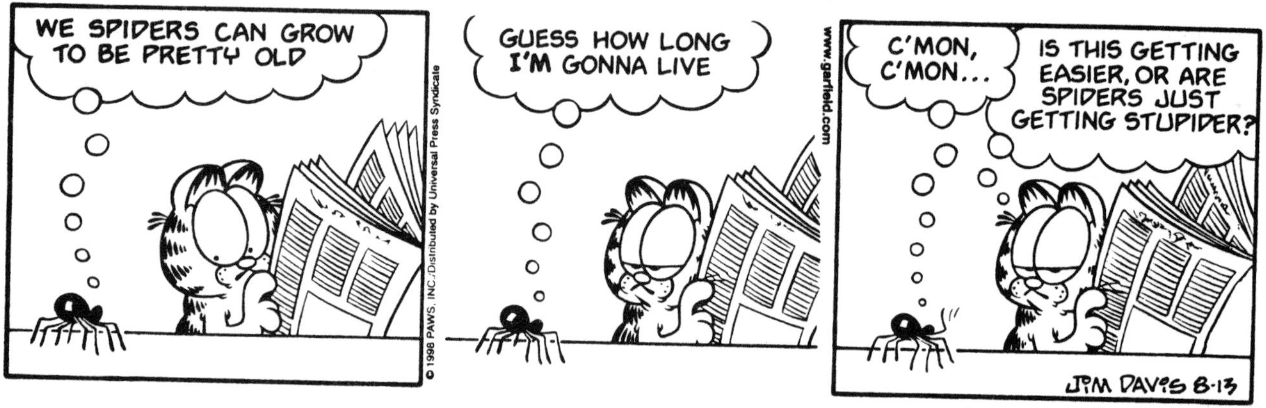
WE SPIDERS CAN GROW TO BE PRETTY OLD
© 1998 PAWS, INC./Distributed by Universal Press Syndicate
GUESS HOW LONG I'M GONNA LIVE
www.garfield.com
C'MON, C'MON...
IS THIS GETTING EASIER, OR ARE SPIDERS JUST GETTING STUPIDER?
JIM DAVIS 8-13

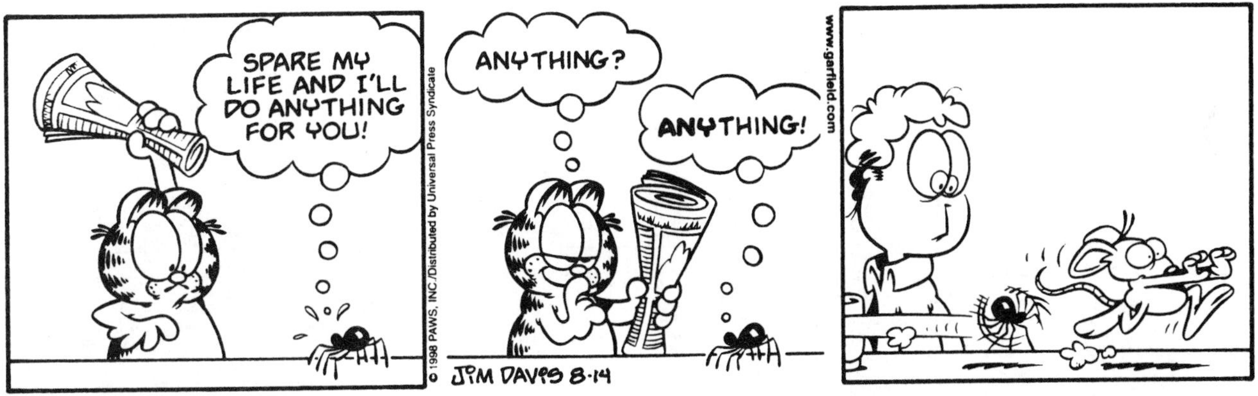
SPARE MY LIFE AND I'LL DO ANYTHING FOR YOU!
ANYTHING?
ANYTHING!
© 1998 PAWS, INC./Distributed by Universal Press Syndicate
JIM DAVIS 8-14
www.garfield.com

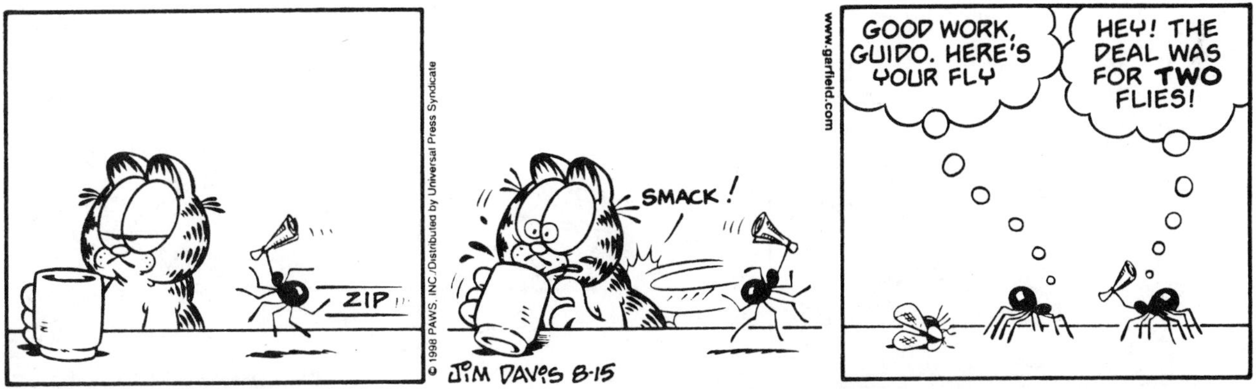
ZIP
SMACK!
© 1998 PAWS, INC./Distributed by Universal Press Syndicate
JIM DAVIS 8-15
www.garfield.com
GOOD WORK, GUIDO. HERE'S YOUR FLY
HEY! THE DEAL WAS FOR TWO FLIES!

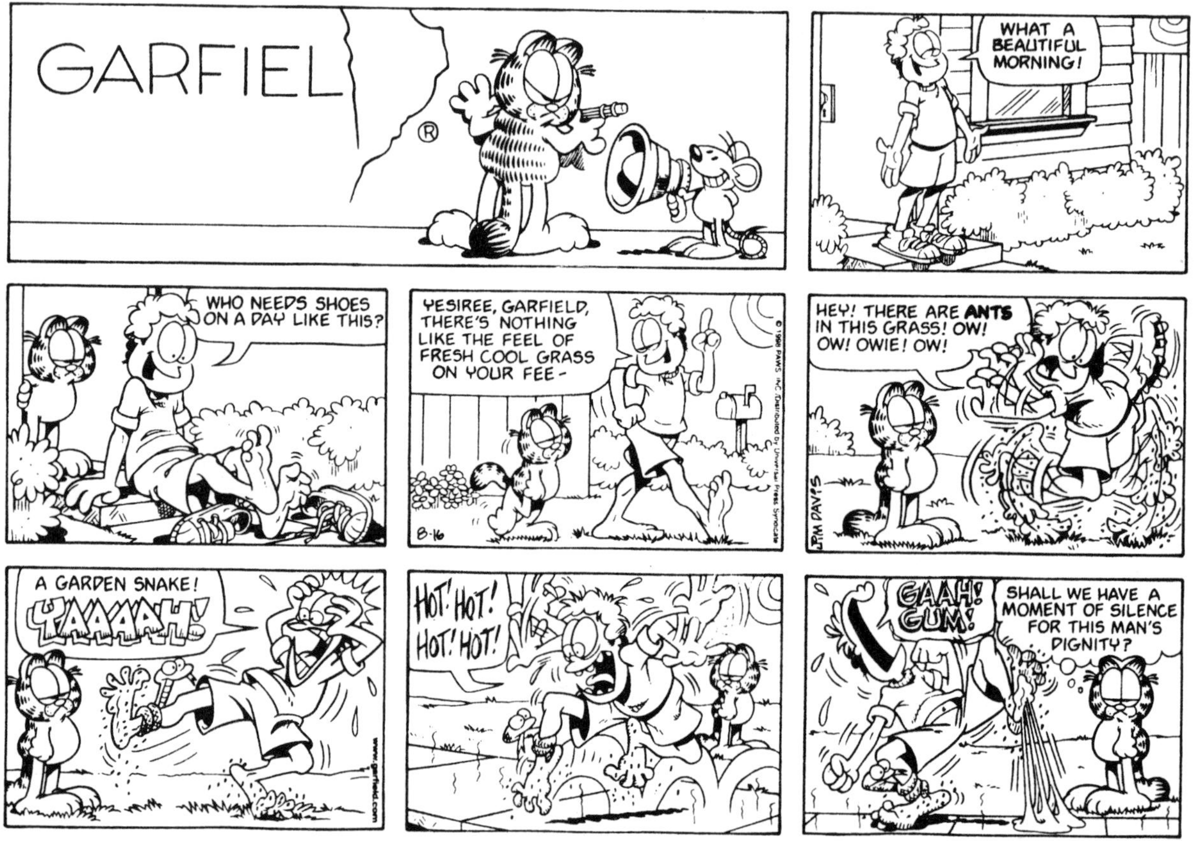
GARFIEL
®
WHAT A BEAUTIFUL MORNING!
WHO NEEDS SHOES ON A DAY LIKE THIS?
YESIREE, GARFIELD, THERE'S NOTHING LIKE THE FEEL OF FRESH COOL GRASS ON YOUR FEE-
© 1998 PAWS, INC./Distributed by Universal Press Syndicate
8-16
HEY! THERE ARE **ANTS** IN THIS GRASS! OW! OW! OWIE! OW!
JPM DAVIS
A GARDEN SNAKE!
YAAAAH!
www.garfield.com
HOT! HOT! HOT! HOT!
GAAH! GUM!
SHALL WE HAVE A MOMENT OF SILENCE FOR THIS MAN'S DIGNITY?

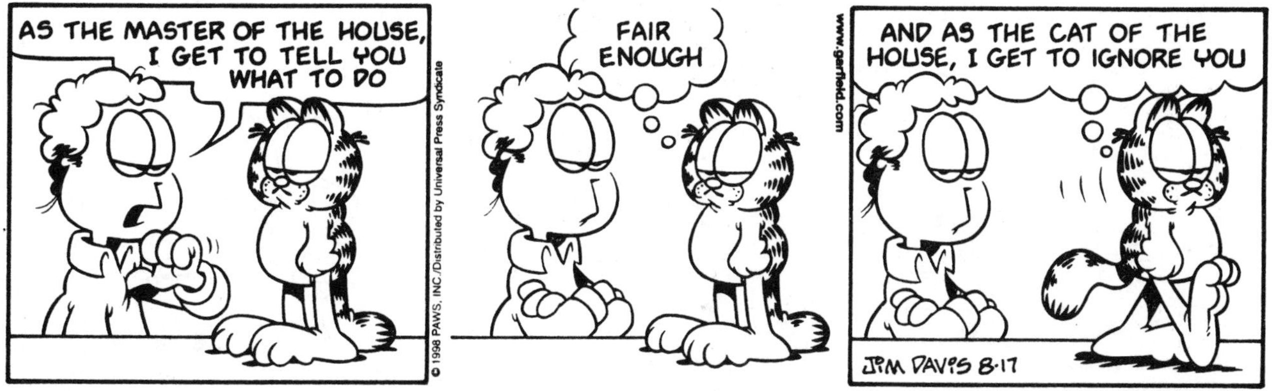
AS THE MASTER OF THE HOUSE, I GET TO TELL YOU WHAT TO DO
FAIR ENOUGH
AND AS THE CAT OF THE HOUSE, I GET TO IGNORE YOU
© 1998 PAWS, INC./Distributed by Universal Press Syndicate
www.garfield.com
JIM DAVIS 8-17

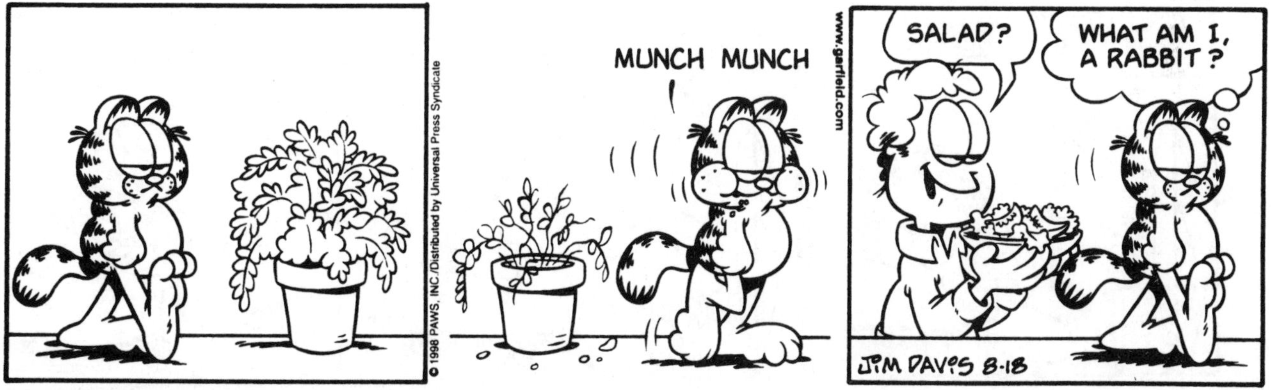
MUNCH MUNCH
SALAD?
WHAT AM I, A RABBIT?
© 1998 PAWS, INC./Distributed by Universal Press Syndicate
www.garfield.com
JIM DAVIS 8-18

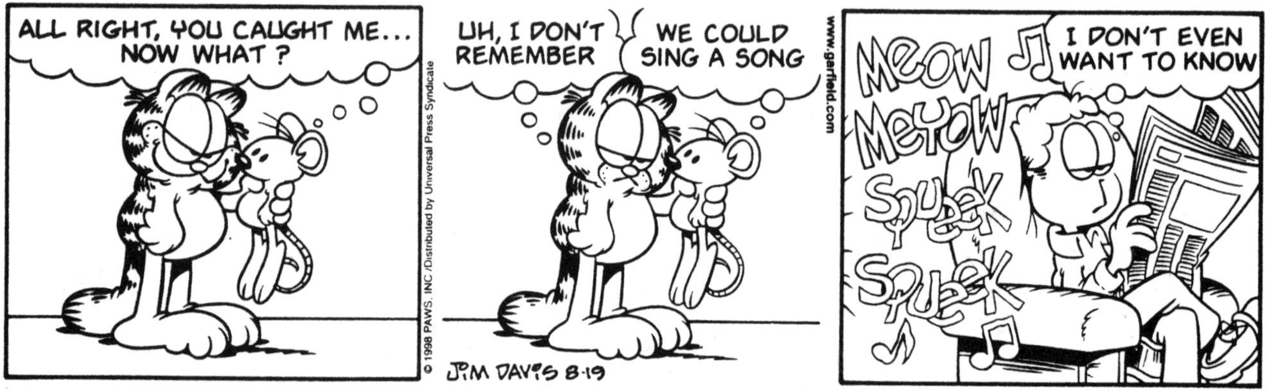
ALL RIGHT, YOU CAUGHT ME... NOW WHAT ?
UH, I DON'T REMEMBER
WE COULD SING A SONG
MEOW
MEYOW
SQUEEK
SQUEEK
I DON'T EVEN WANT TO KNOW
© 1998 PAWS, INC./Distributed by Universal Press Syndicate
JIM DAVIS 8-19
www.garfield.com

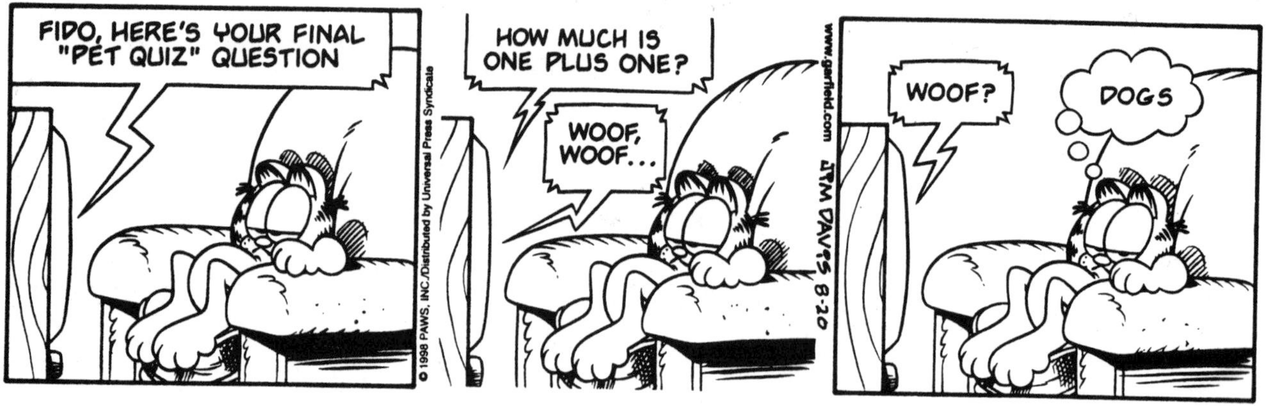
FIDO, HERE'S YOUR FINAL "PET QUIZ" QUESTION
HOW MUCH IS ONE PLUS ONE?
WOOF, WOOF...
WOOF?
DOGS
© 1998 PAWS, INC./Distributed by Universal Press Syndicate
JIM DAVIS 8-20
www.garfield.com

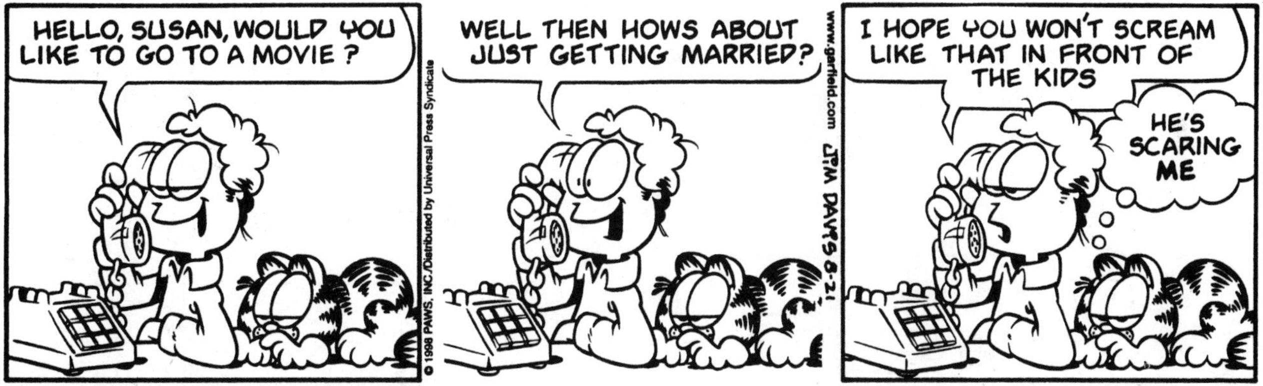
HELLO, SUSAN, WOULD YOU LIKE TO GO TO A MOVIE ?
© 1998 PAWS, INC./Distributed by Universal Press Syndicate
WELL THEN HOWS ABOUT JUST GETTING MARRIED?
www.garfield.com
JIM DAVIS 8-21
I HOPE YOU WON'T SCREAM LIKE THAT IN FRONT OF THE KIDS
HE'S SCARING ME

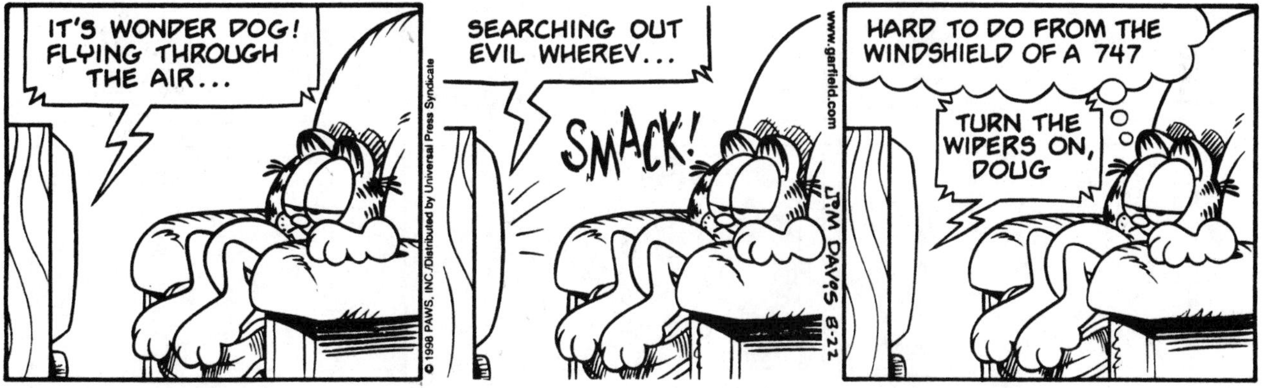
IT'S WONDER DOG! FLYING THROUGH THE AIR...
© 1998 PAWS, INC./Distributed by Universal Press Syndicate
SEARCHING OUT EVIL WHEREV...
SMACK!
www.garfield.com
JIM DAVIS 8-22
HARD TO DO FROM THE WINDSHIELD OF A 747
TURN THE WIPERS ON, DOUG

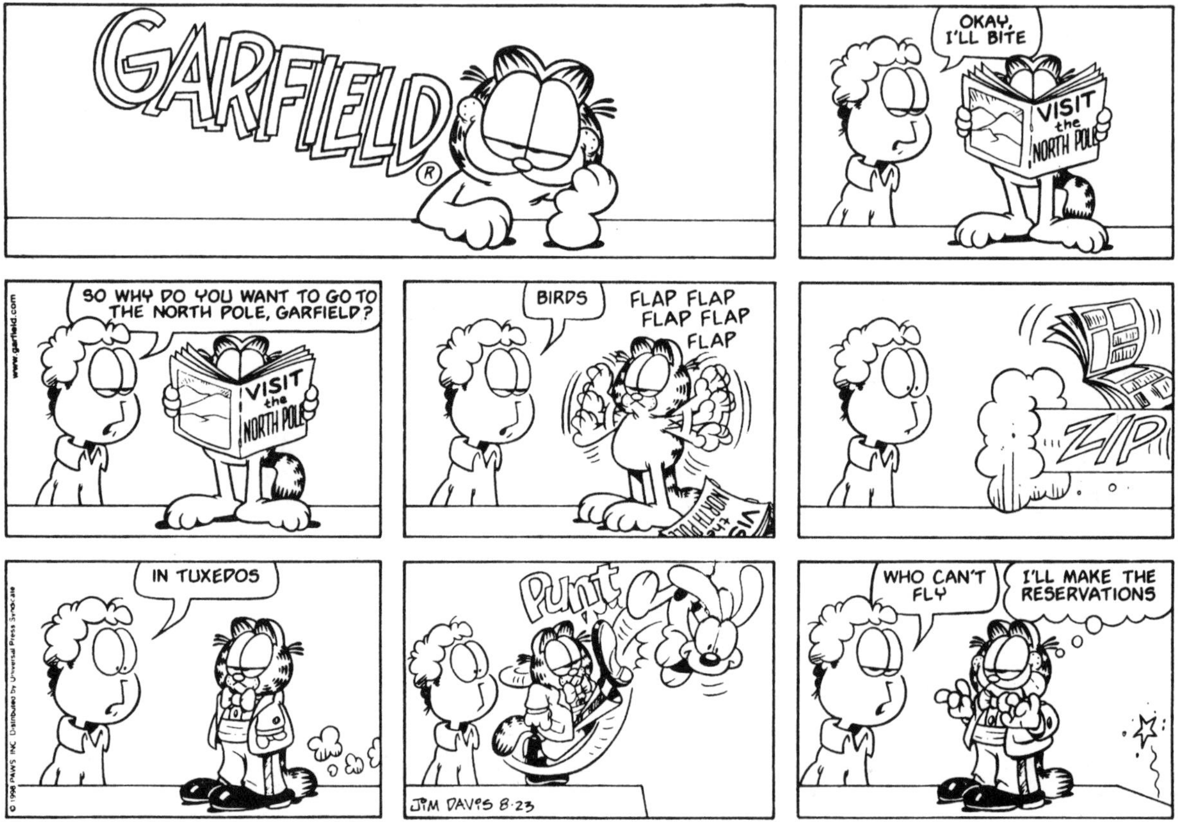
GARFIELD®
OKAY, I'LL BITE
VISIT the NORTH POLE
SO WHY DO YOU WANT TO GO TO THE NORTH POLE, GARFIELD?
www.garfield.com
BIRDS
FLAP FLAP FLAP FLAP FLAP
ZIP
IN TUXEDOS
© 1998 PAWS INC Distributed by Universal Press Syndicate
PUNT
JIM DAVIS 8-23
WHO CAN'T FLY
I'LL MAKE THE RESERVATIONS

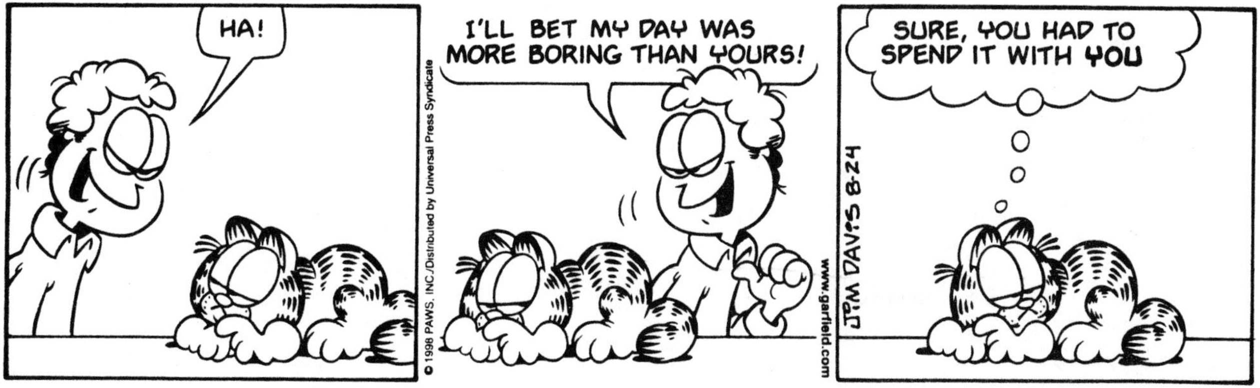
HA!
I'LL BET MY DAY WAS MORE BORING THAN YOURS!
SURE, YOU HAD TO SPEND IT WITH YOU
© 1998 PAWS, INC./Distributed by Universal Press Syndicate
www.garfield.com
JIM DAVIS 8-24

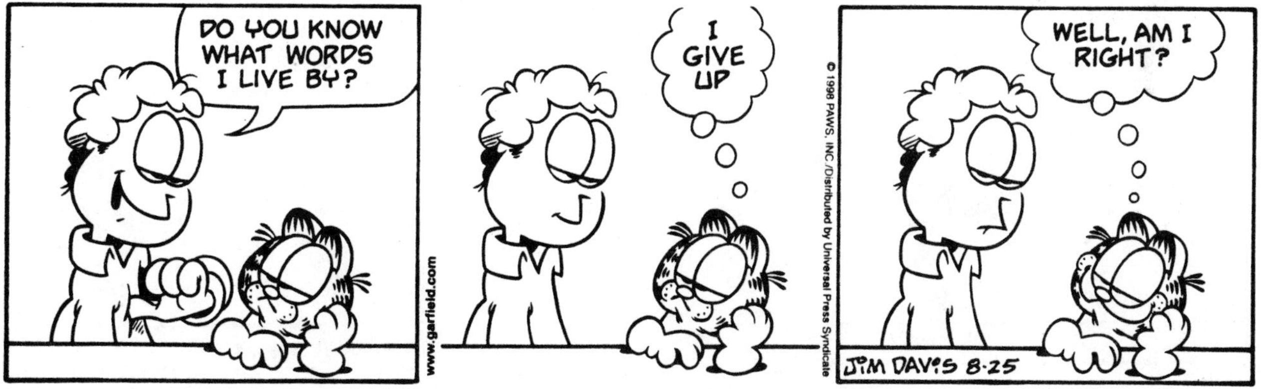
DO YOU KNOW WHAT WORDS I LIVE BY?
I GIVE UP
WELL, AM I RIGHT?
www.garfield.com
© 1998 PAWS, INC./Distributed by Universal Press Syndicate
JIM DAVIS 8-25

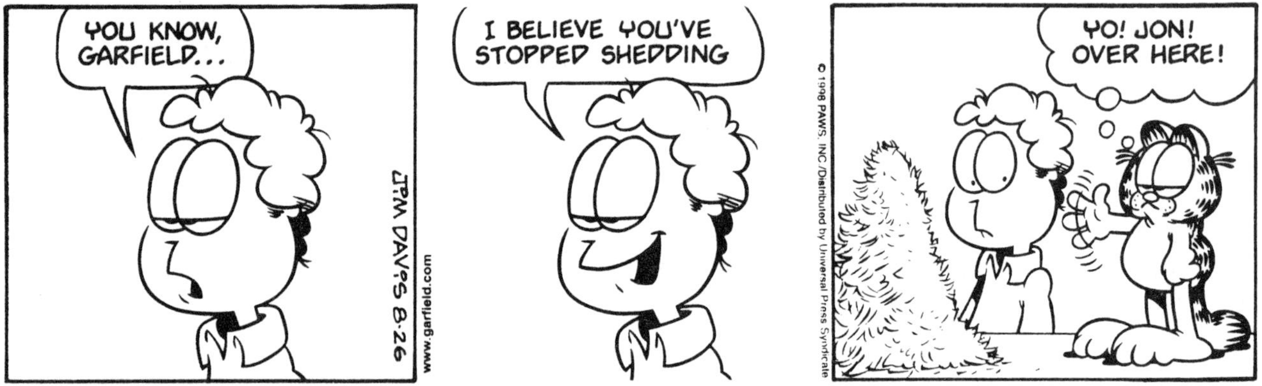

YOU KNOW, GARFIELD...
JIM DAVIS 8-26
www.garfield.com
I BELIEVE YOU'VE STOPPED SHEDDING
© 1998 PAWS, INC./Distributed by Universal Press Syndicate
YO! JON! OVER HERE!

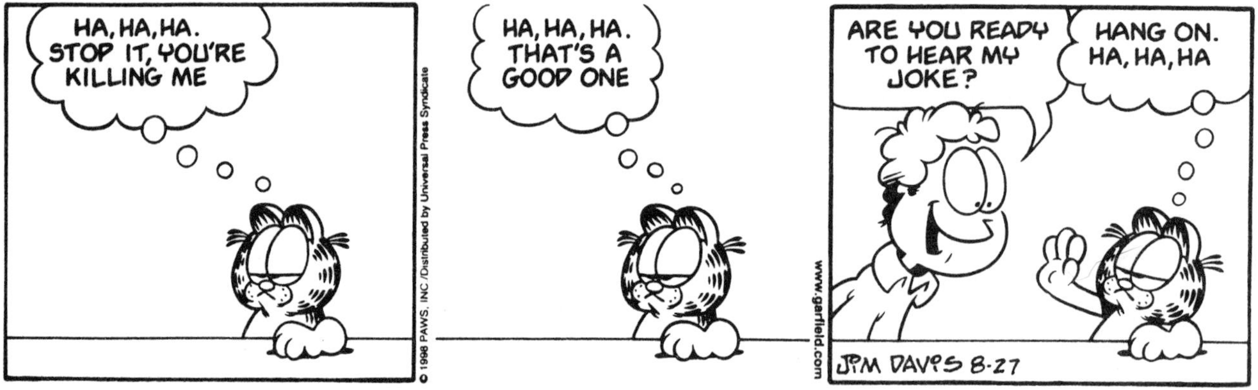

HA, HA, HA. STOP IT, YOU'RE KILLING ME
© 1998 PAWS, INC./Distributed by Universal Press Syndicate
HA, HA, HA. THAT'S A GOOD ONE
www.garfield.com
ARE YOU READY TO HEAR MY JOKE?
HANG ON. HA, HA, HA
JIM DAVIS 8-27

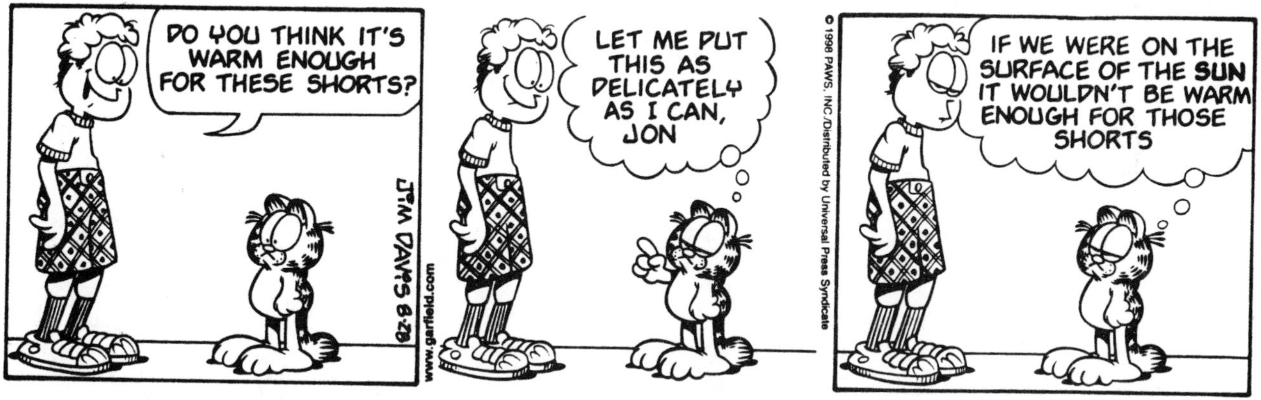
DO YOU THINK IT'S WARM ENOUGH FOR THESE SHORTS?
JIM DAVIS 8-28
www.garfield.com
LET ME PUT THIS AS DELICATELY AS I CAN, JON
© 1998 PAWS, INC./Distributed by Universal Press Syndicate
IF WE WERE ON THE SURFACE OF THE SUN IT WOULDN'T BE WARM ENOUGH FOR THOSE SHORTS

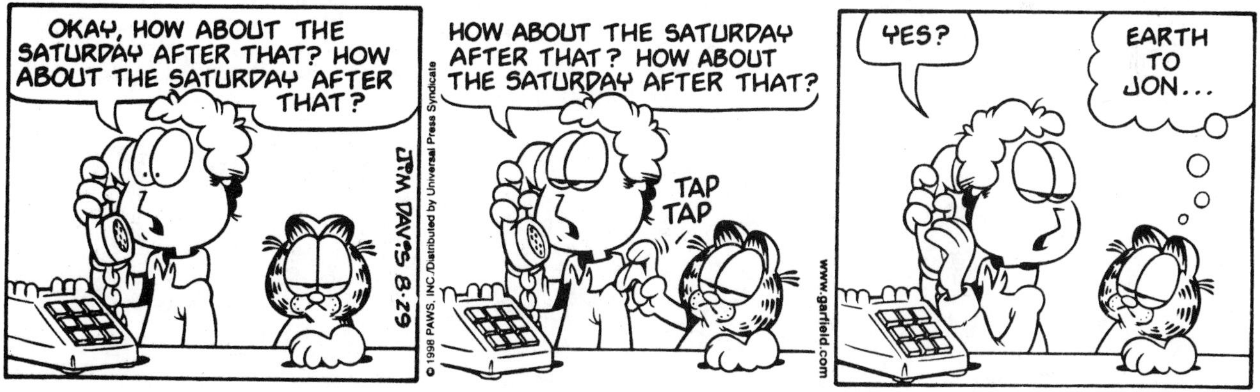
OKAY, HOW ABOUT THE SATURDAY AFTER THAT? HOW ABOUT THE SATURDAY AFTER THAT?
JIM DAVIS 8-29
© 1998 PAWS, INC./Distributed by Universal Press Syndicate
HOW ABOUT THE SATURDAY AFTER THAT? HOW ABOUT THE SATURDAY AFTER THAT?
TAP TAP
www.garfield.com
YES?
EARTH TO JON...

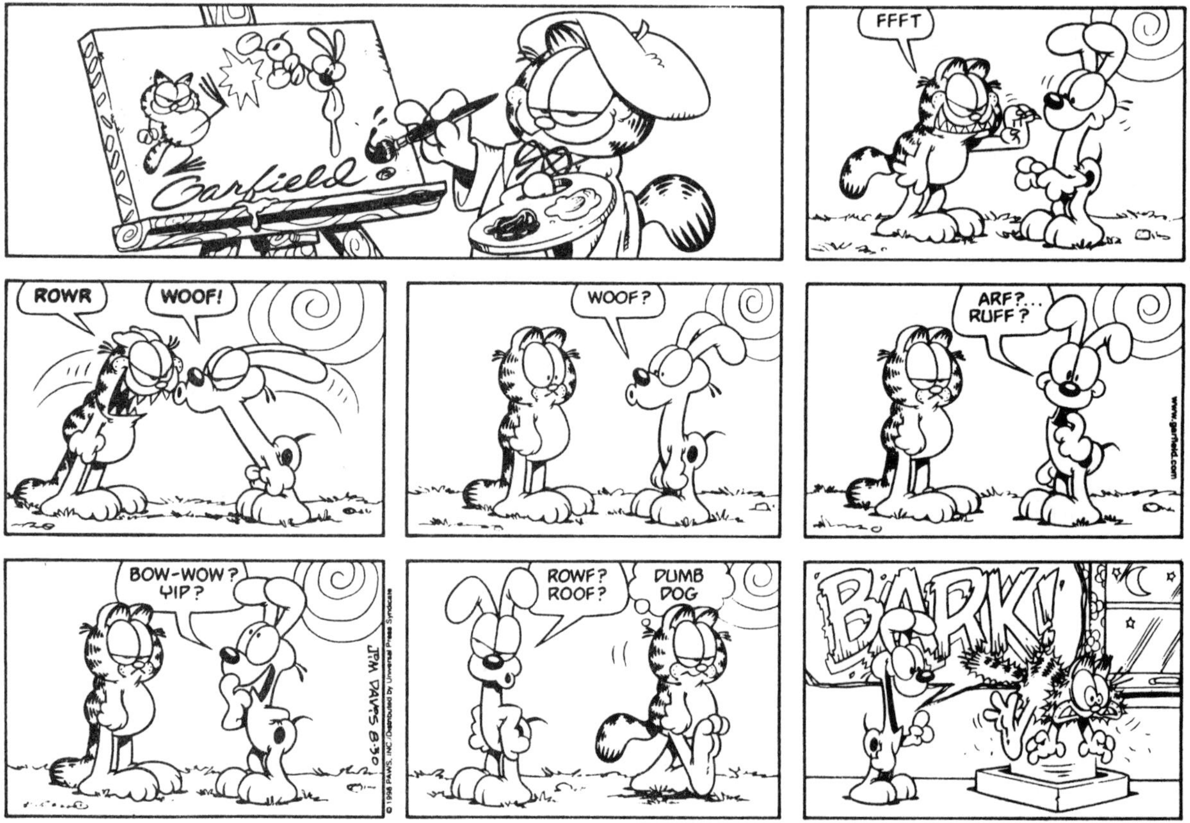
Garfield
FFFT
ROWR
WOOF!
WOOF?
ARF?... RUFF?
www.garfield.com
BOW-WOW? YIP?
JPM DAVIS 8-30
© 1998 PAWS, INC./Distributed by Universal Press Syndicate
ROWF? ROOF?
DUMB DOG
BARK!

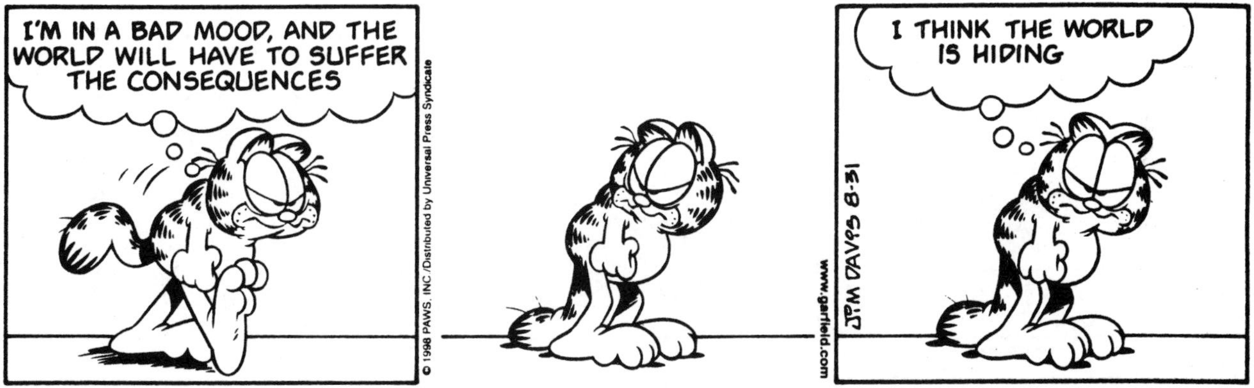
I'M IN A BAD MOOD, AND THE WORLD WILL HAVE TO SUFFER THE CONSEQUENCES
I THINK THE WORLD IS HIDING
© 1998 PAWS, INC /Distributed by Universal Press Syndicate
JIM DAVIS 8-31
www.garfield.com

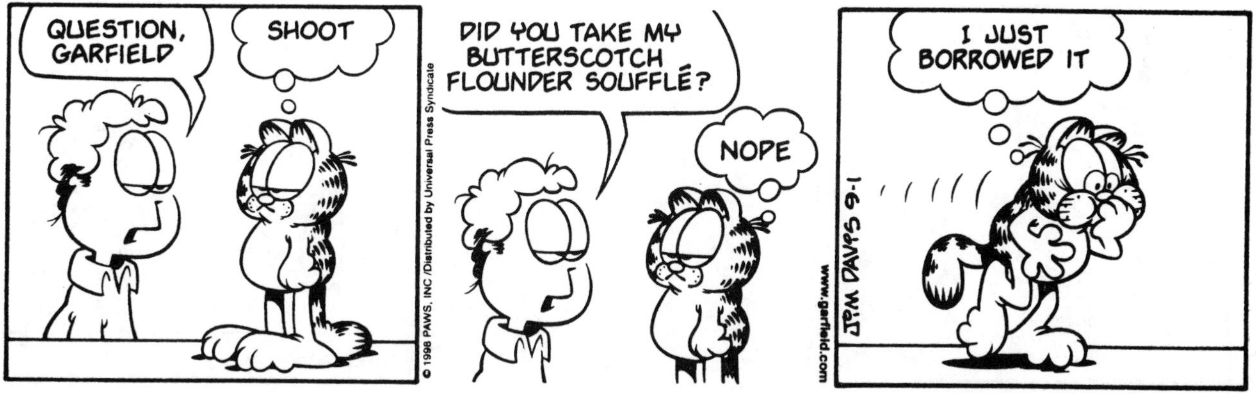
QUESTION, GARFIELD
SHOOT
DID YOU TAKE MY BUTTERSCOTCH FLOUNDER SOUFFLÉ?
NOPE
I JUST BORROWED IT
© 1998 PAWS, INC /Distributed by Universal Press Syndicate
JIM DAVIS 9-1
www.garfield.com

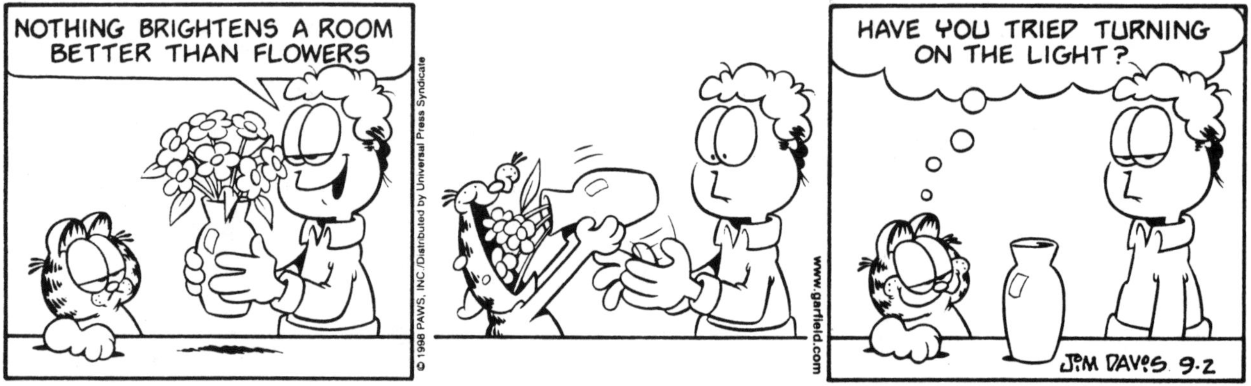
NOTHING BRIGHTENS A ROOM BETTER THAN FLOWERS
HAVE YOU TRIED TURNING ON THE LIGHT?
JIM DAVIS 9-2

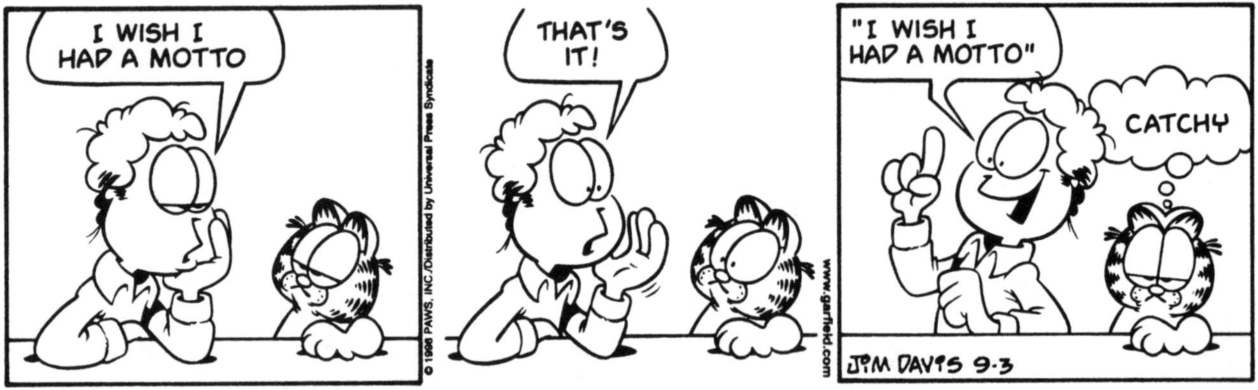
I WISH I HAD A MOTTO
THAT'S IT!
"I WISH I HAD A MOTTO"
CATCHY
JIM DAVIS 9-3

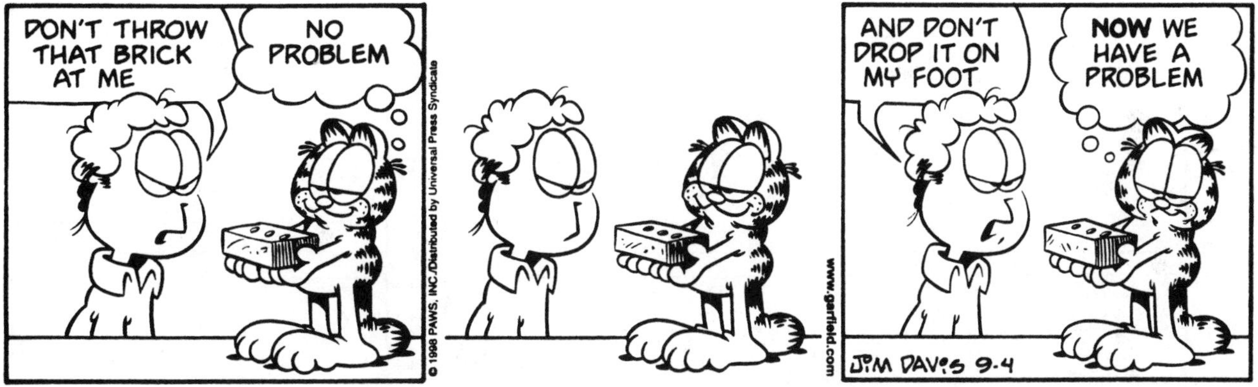
DON'T THROW THAT BRICK AT ME
NO PROBLEM
© 1998 PAWS, INC./Distributed by Universal Press Syndicate
www.garfield.com
AND DON'T DROP IT ON MY FOOT
NOW WE HAVE A PROBLEM
JIM DAVIS 9-4

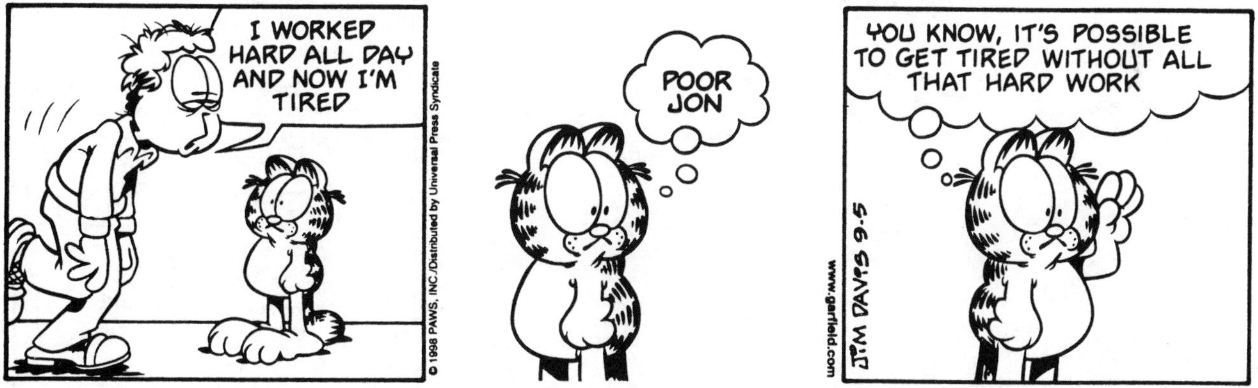
I WORKED HARD ALL DAY AND NOW I'M TIRED
© 1998 PAWS, INC./Distributed by Universal Press Syndicate
POOR JON
www.garfield.com
JIM DAVIS 9-5
YOU KNOW, IT'S POSSIBLE TO GET TIRED WITHOUT ALL THAT HARD WORK

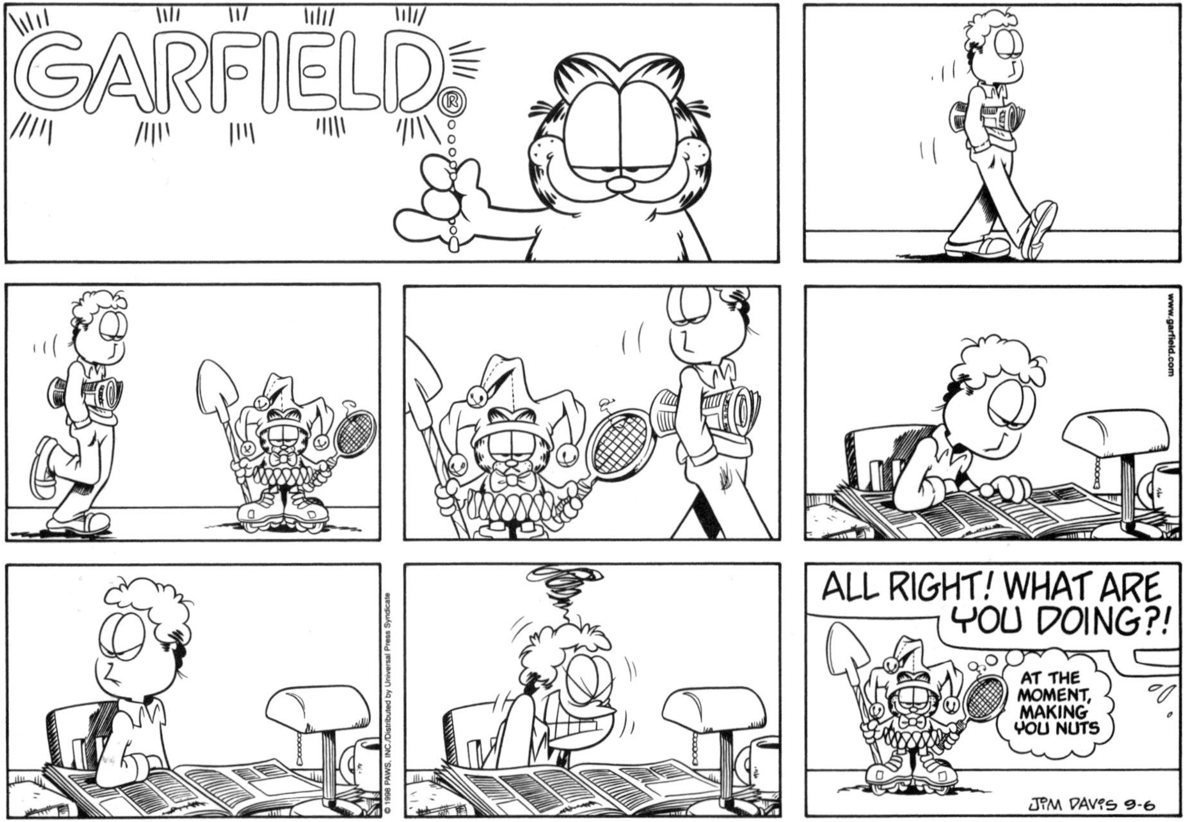
GARFIELD®
www.garfield.com
© 1998 PAWS, INC./Distributed by Universal Press Syndicate
ALL RIGHT! WHAT ARE YOU DOING?!
AT THE MOMENT, MAKING YOU NUTS
JIM DAVIS 9-6

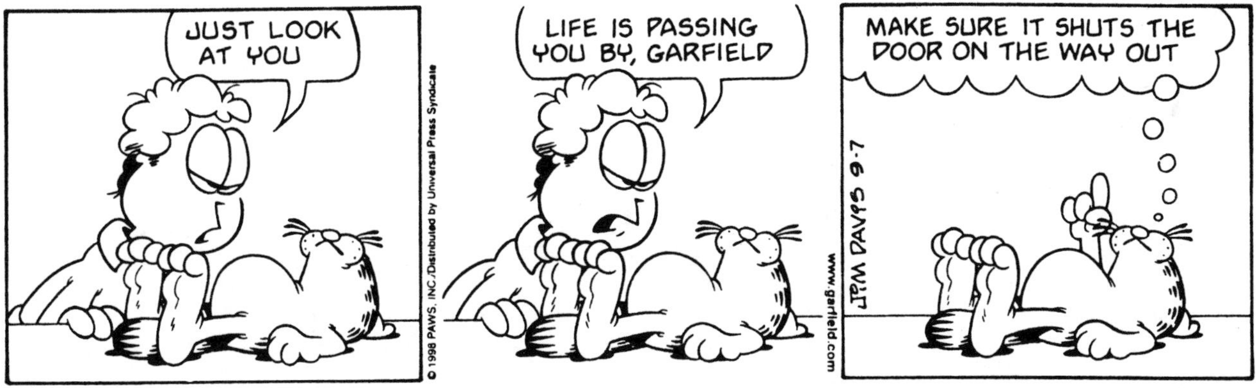
JUST LOOK AT YOU
LIFE IS PASSING YOU BY, GARFIELD
MAKE SURE IT SHUTS THE DOOR ON THE WAY OUT
© 1998 PAWS, INC./Distributed by Universal Press Syndicate
www.garfield.com
JIM DAVIS 9-7

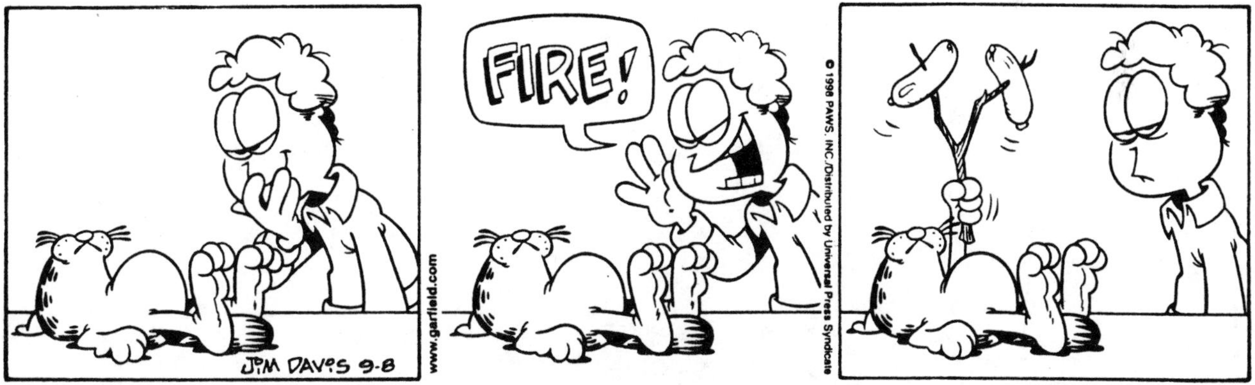
JIM DAVIS 9-8
www.garfield.com
FIRE!
© 1998 PAWS, INC./Distributed by Universal Press Syndicate

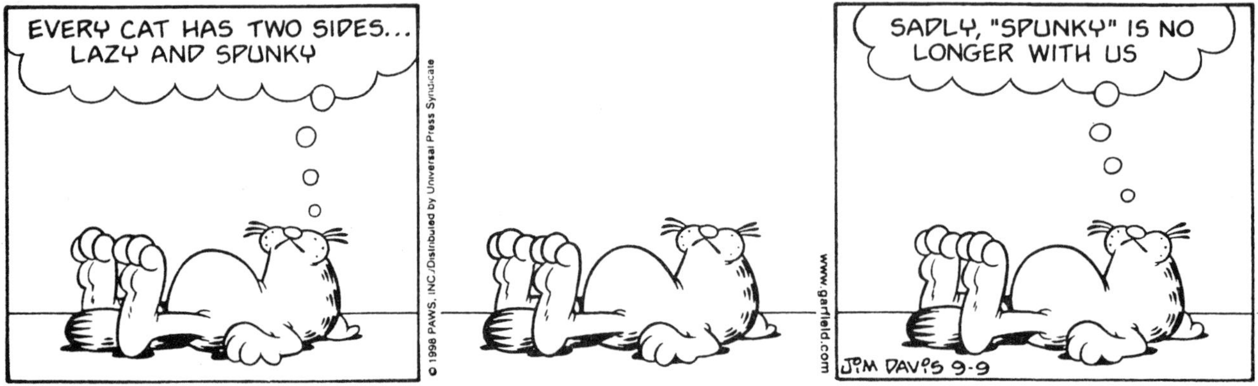
EVERY CAT HAS TWO SIDES... LAZY AND SPUNKY
SADLY, "SPUNKY" IS NO LONGER WITH US
© 1998 PAWS, INC./Distributed by Universal Press Syndicate
www.garfield.com
JIM DAVIS 9-9

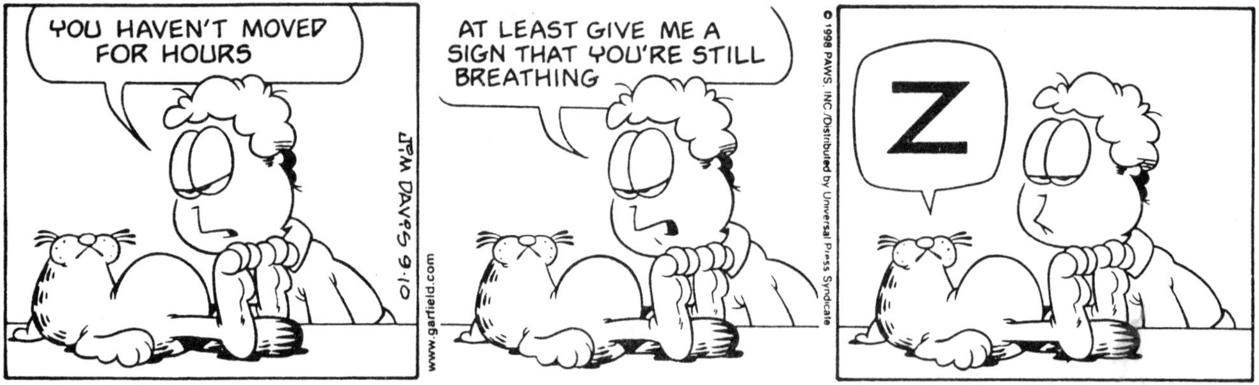
YOU HAVEN'T MOVED FOR HOURS
AT LEAST GIVE ME A SIGN THAT YOU'RE STILL BREATHING
Z
JIM DAVIS 9-10
www.garfield.com
© 1998 PAWS, INC./Distributed by Universal Press Syndicate

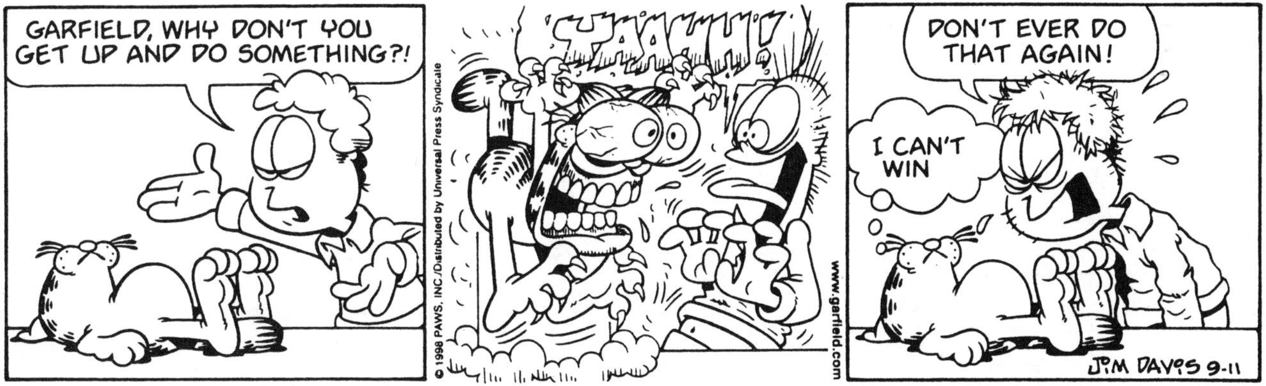
GARFIELD, WHY DON'T YOU GET UP AND DO SOMETHING?!
YAAHH!
DON'T EVER DO THAT AGAIN!
I CAN'T WIN
© 1998 PAWS, INC./Distributed by Universal Press Syndicate
www.garfield.com
JIM DAVIS 9-11

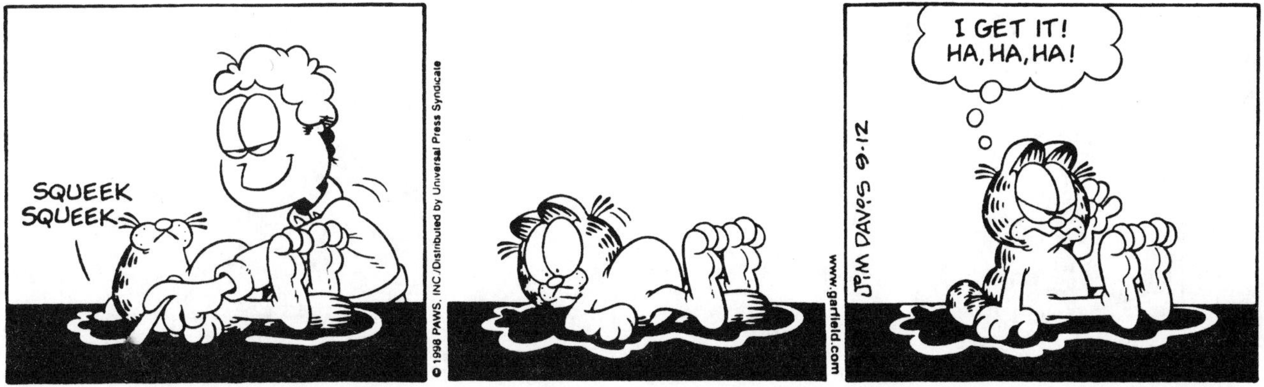
SQUEEK SQUEEK
I GET IT! HA, HA, HA!
© 1998 PAWS, INC./Distributed by Universal Press Syndicate
www.garfield.com
JIM DAVIS 9-12

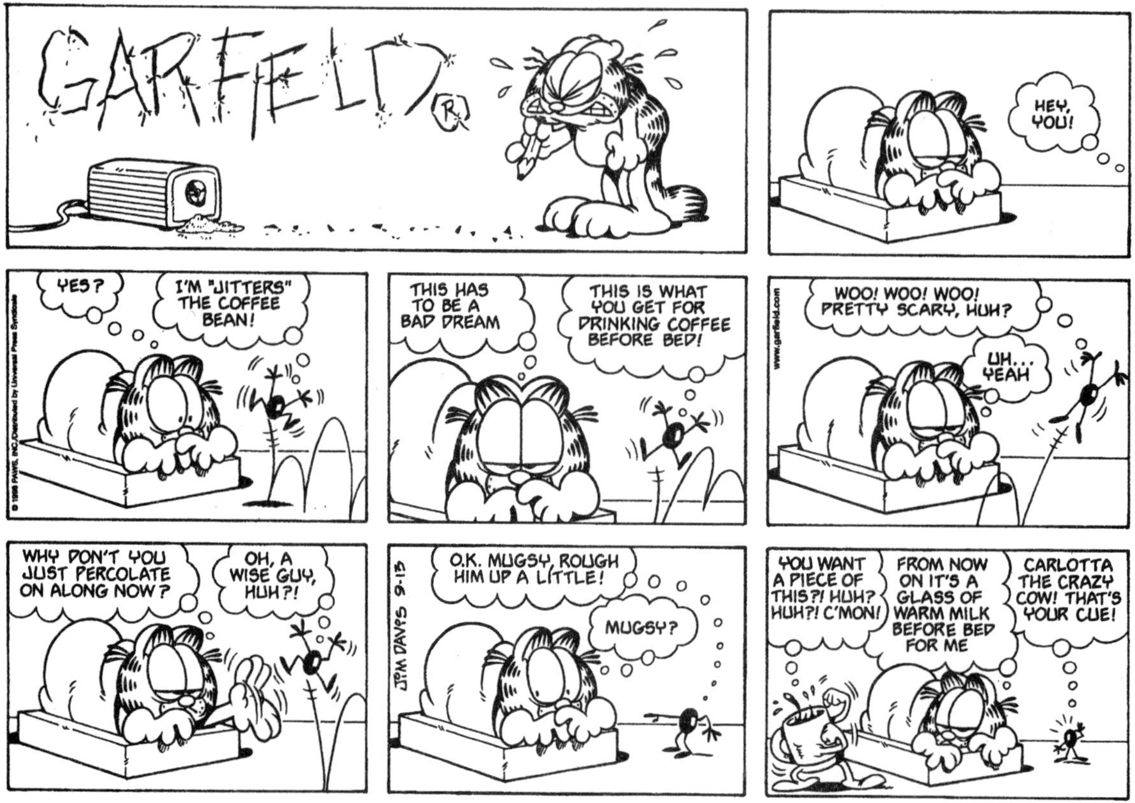
GARFIELD®
HEY, YOU!
YES?
I'M "JITTERS" THE COFFEE BEAN!
© 1998 PAWS, INC./Distributed by Universal Press Syndicate
THIS HAS TO BE A BAD DREAM
THIS IS WHAT YOU GET FOR DRINKING COFFEE BEFORE BED!
www.garfield.com
WOO! WOO! WOO! PRETTY SCARY, HUH?
UH... YEAH
WHY DON'T YOU JUST PERCOLATE ON ALONG NOW?
OH, A WISE GUY, HUH?!
JIM DAVIS 9-13
O.K. MUGSY, ROUGH HIM UP A LITTLE!
MUGSY?
YOU WANT A PIECE OF THIS?! HUH? HUH?! C'MON!
FROM NOW ON IT'S A GLASS OF WARM MILK BEFORE BED FOR ME
CARLOTTA THE CRAZY COW! THAT'S YOUR CUE!

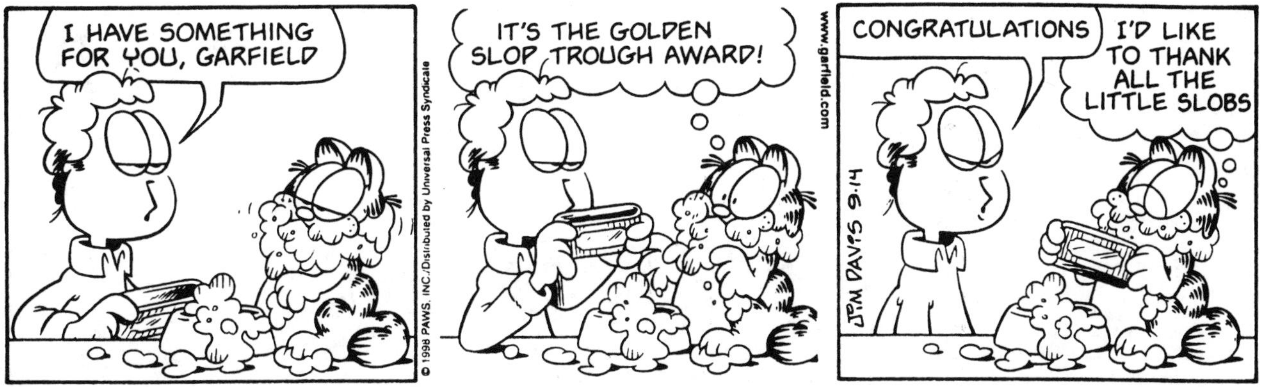
I HAVE SOMETHING FOR YOU, GARFIELD
IT'S THE GOLDEN SLOP TROUGH AWARD!
CONGRATULATIONS
I'D LIKE TO THANK ALL THE LITTLE SLOBS
© 1998 PAWS, INC./Distributed by Universal Press Syndicate
www.garfield.com
JPM DAVPS 9·14

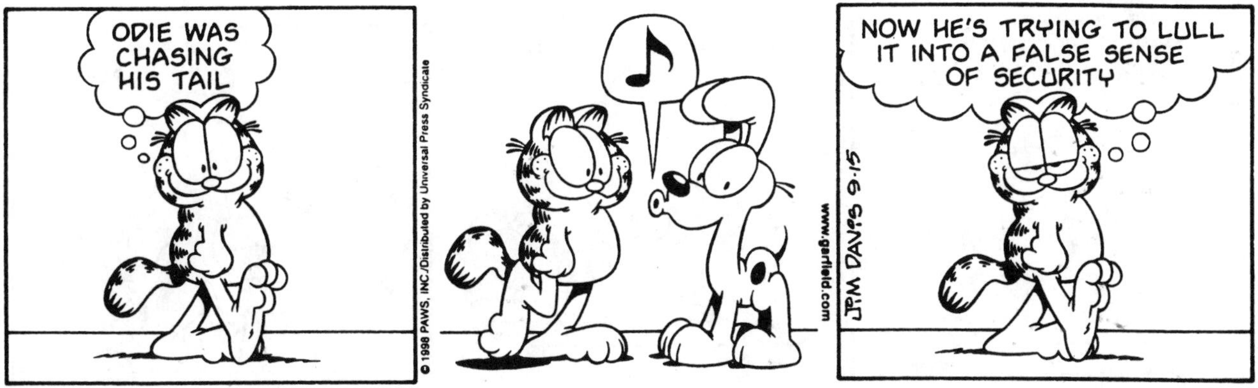
ODIE WAS CHASING HIS TAIL
♪
NOW HE'S TRYING TO LULL IT INTO A FALSE SENSE OF SECURITY
© 1998 PAWS, INC./Distributed by Universal Press Syndicate
www.garfield.com
JPM DAVPS 9·15

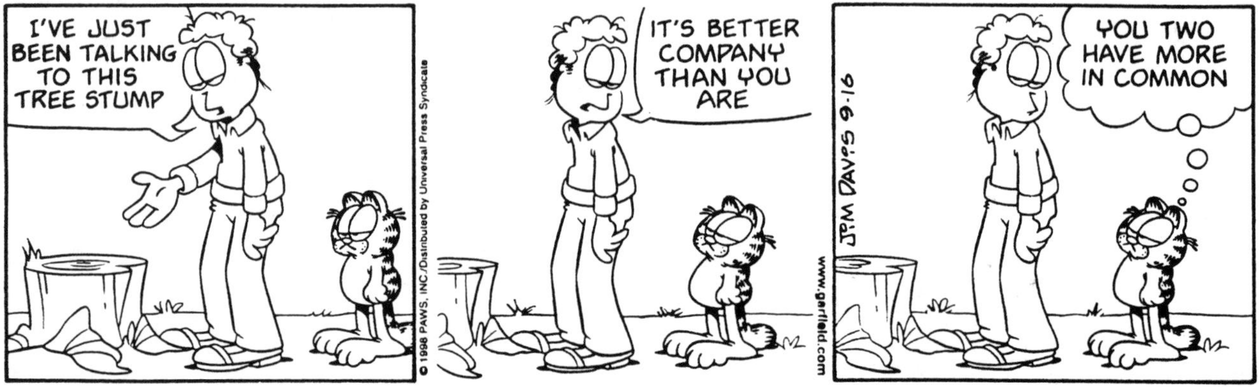
I'VE JUST BEEN TALKING TO THIS TREE STUMP
© 1998 PAWS, INC./Distributed by Universal Press Syndicate
IT'S BETTER COMPANY THAN YOU ARE
www.garfield.com
JIM DAVIS 9-16
YOU TWO HAVE MORE IN COMMON

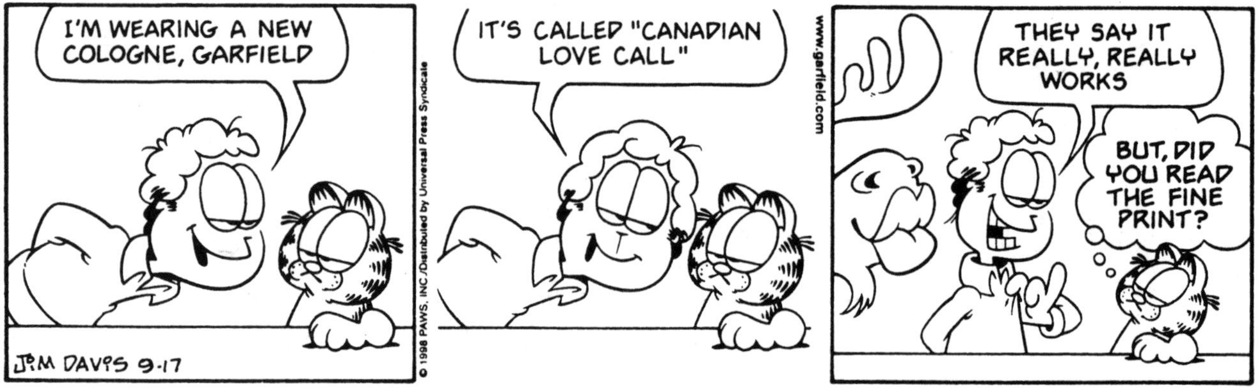
I'M WEARING A NEW COLOGNE, GARFIELD
JIM DAVIS 9-17
© 1998 PAWS, INC./Distributed by Universal Press Syndicate
IT'S CALLED "CANADIAN LOVE CALL"
www.garfield.com
THEY SAY IT REALLY, REALLY WORKS
BUT, DID YOU READ THE FINE PRINT?

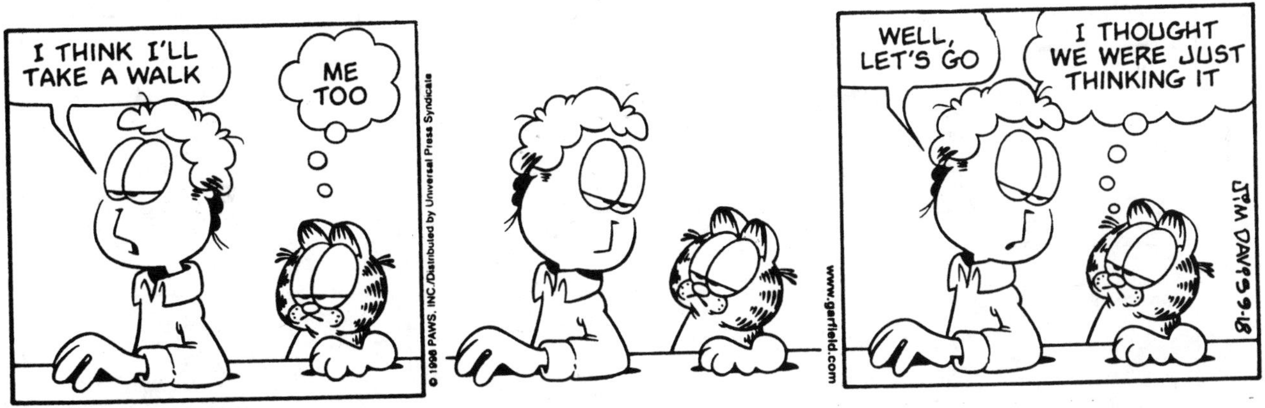
I THINK I'LL TAKE A WALK
ME TOO
© 1998 PAWS, INC./Distributed by Universal Press Syndicate
www.garfield.com
WELL, LET'S GO
I THOUGHT WE WERE JUST THINKING IT
JPM DAVIS 9-18

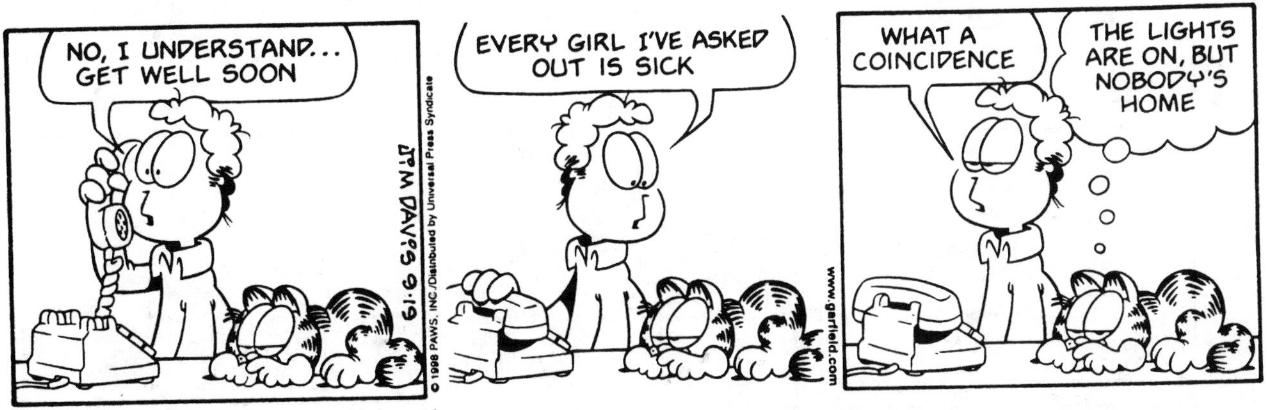
NO, I UNDERSTAND... GET WELL SOON
JPM DAVIS 9-19
© 1998 PAWS, INC./Distributed by Universal Press Syndicate
EVERY GIRL I'VE ASKED OUT IS SICK
www.garfield.com
WHAT A COINCIDENCE
THE LIGHTS ARE ON, BUT NOBODY'S HOME

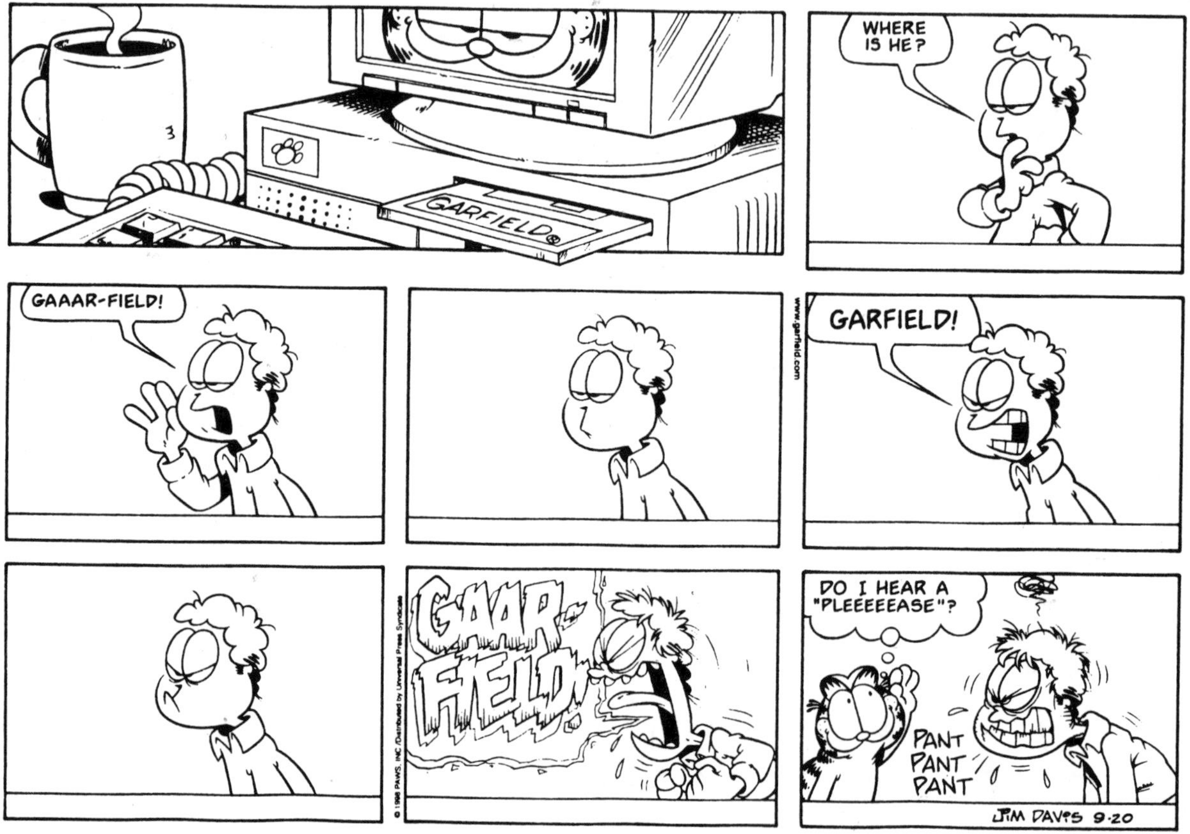
GARFIELD®
WHERE IS HE?
GAAAR-FIELD!
www.garfield.com
GARFIELD!
© 1998 PAWS, INC./Distributed by Universal Press Syndicate
GAAR-FIELD!
DO I HEAR A "PLEEEEEASE"?
PANT PANT PANT
JIM DAVIS 9·20

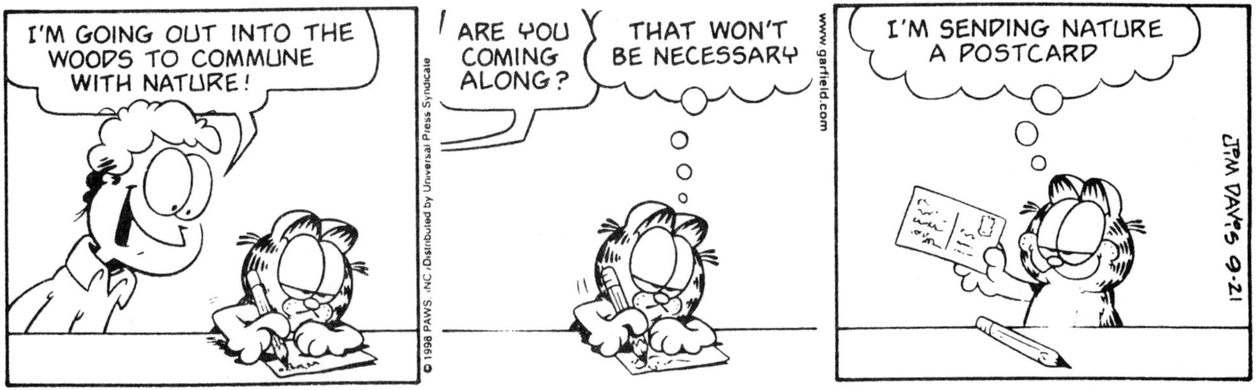
I'M GOING OUT INTO THE WOODS TO COMMUNE WITH NATURE!
ARE YOU COMING ALONG?
THAT WON'T BE NECESSARY
I'M SENDING NATURE A POSTCARD
© 1998 PAWS, INC./Distributed by Universal Press Syndicate
www.garfield.com
JIM DAVIS 9-21

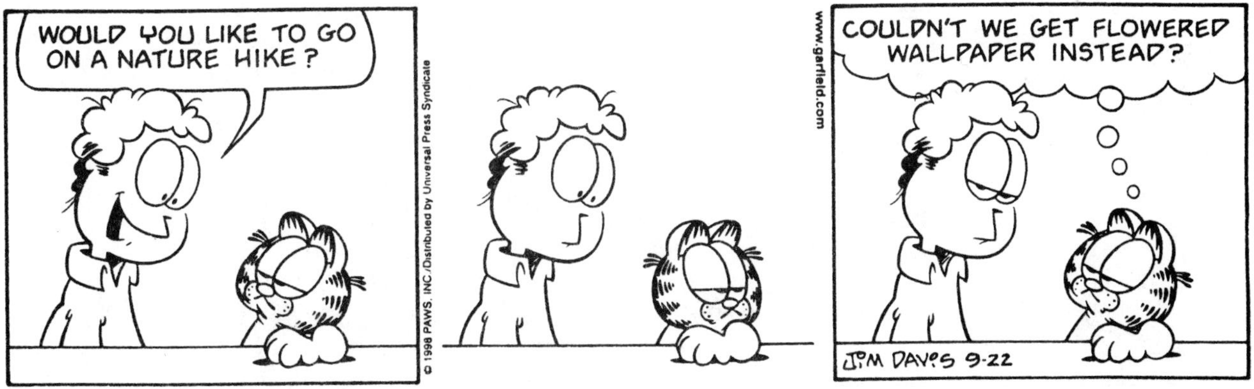
WOULD YOU LIKE TO GO ON A NATURE HIKE?
COULDN'T WE GET FLOWERED WALLPAPER INSTEAD?
© 1998 PAWS, INC./Distributed by Universal Press Syndicate
www.garfield.com
JIM DAVIS 9-22

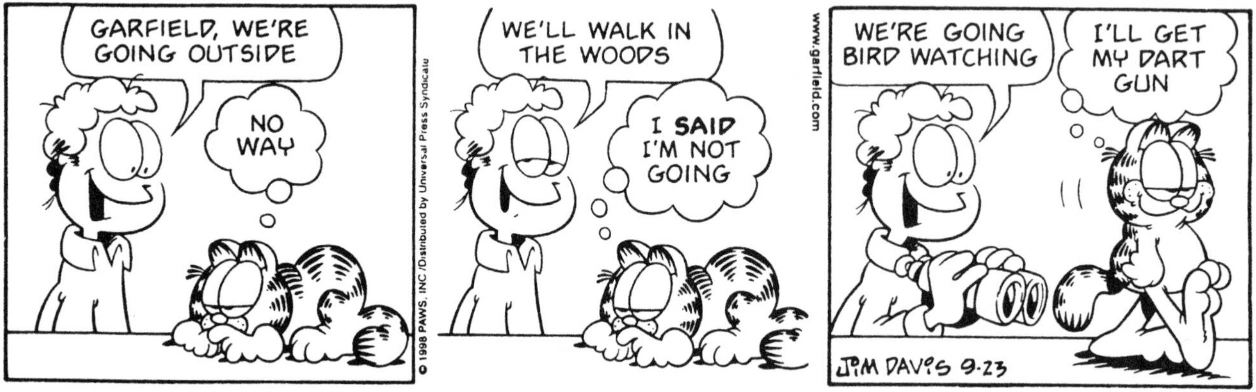
GARFIELD, WE'RE GOING OUTSIDE
NO WAY
WE'LL WALK IN THE WOODS
I **SAID** I'M NOT GOING
WE'RE GOING BIRD WATCHING
I'LL GET MY DART GUN
© 1998 PAWS, INC./Distributed by Universal Press Syndicate
www.garfield.com
JIM DAVIS 9-23

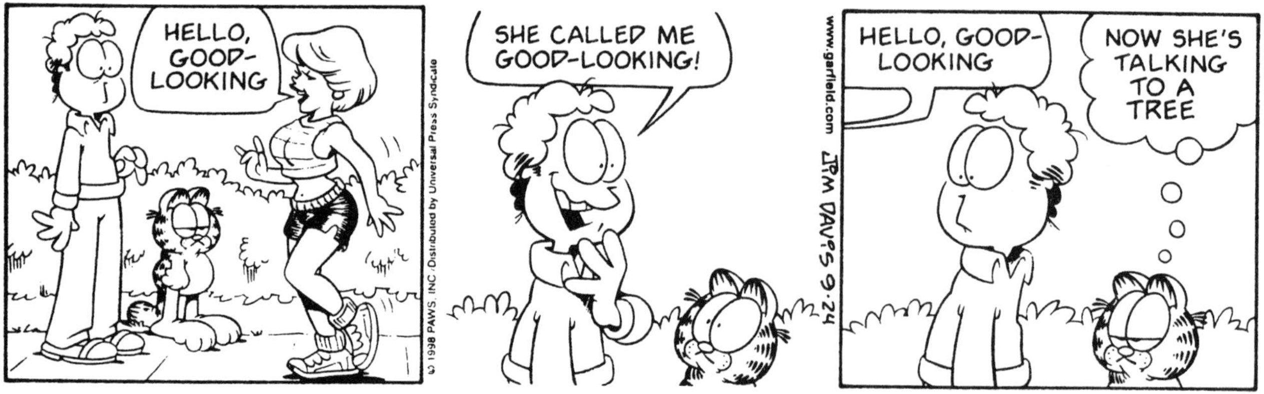
HELLO, GOOD-LOOKING
SHE CALLED ME GOOD-LOOKING!
HELLO, GOOD-LOOKING
NOW SHE'S TALKING TO A TREE
© 1998 PAWS, INC./Distributed by Universal Press Syndicate
www.garfield.com
JIM DAVIS 9-24

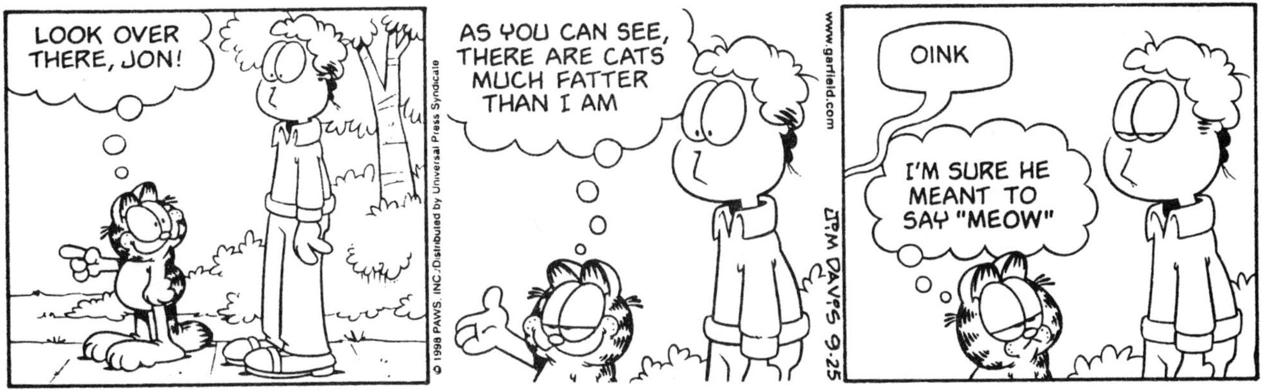
LOOK OVER THERE, JON!
© 1998 PAWS, INC./Distributed by Universal Press Syndicate
AS YOU CAN SEE, THERE ARE CATS MUCH FATTER THAN I AM
www.garfield.com
JPM DAVPS 9.25
OINK
I'M SURE HE MEANT TO SAY "MEOW"

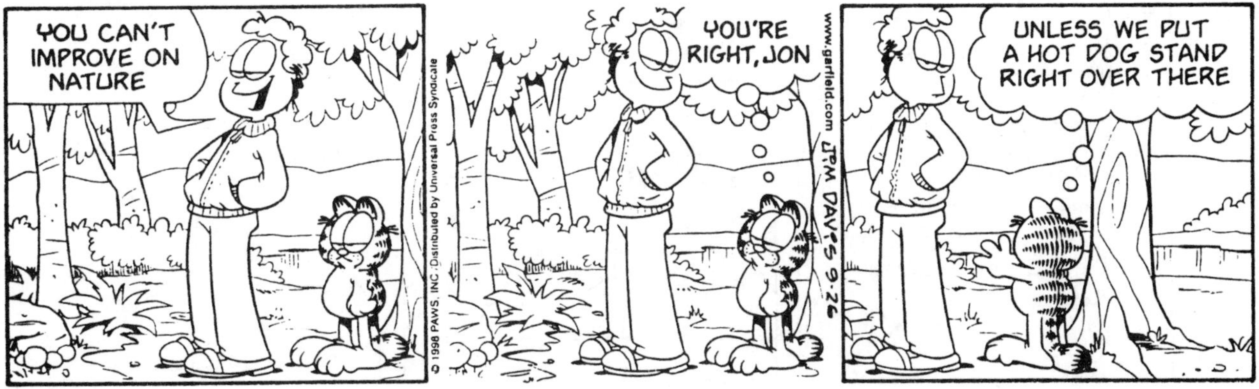
YOU CAN'T IMPROVE ON NATURE
© 1998 PAWS, INC./Distributed by Universal Press Syndicate
YOU'RE RIGHT, JON
www.garfield.com
JPM DAVPS 9.26
UNLESS WE PUT A HOT DOG STAND RIGHT OVER THERE

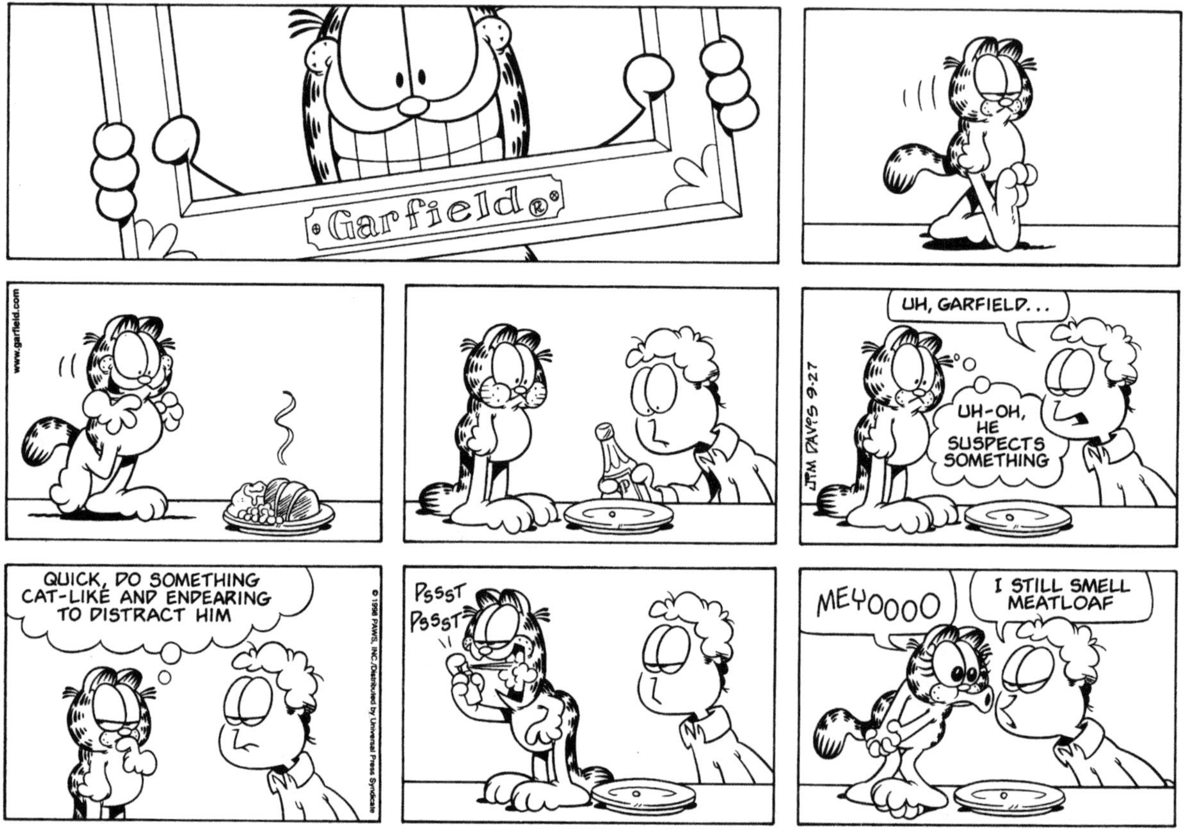
Garfield®
www.garfield.com
UH, GARFIELD...
UH-OH, HE SUSPECTS SOMETHING
JIM DAVIS 9-27
QUICK, DO SOMETHING CAT-LIKE AND ENDEARING TO DISTRACT HIM
© 1998 PAWS, INC./Distributed by Universal Press Syndicate
PSSST PSSST
MEYOOOO
I STILL SMELL MEATLOAF

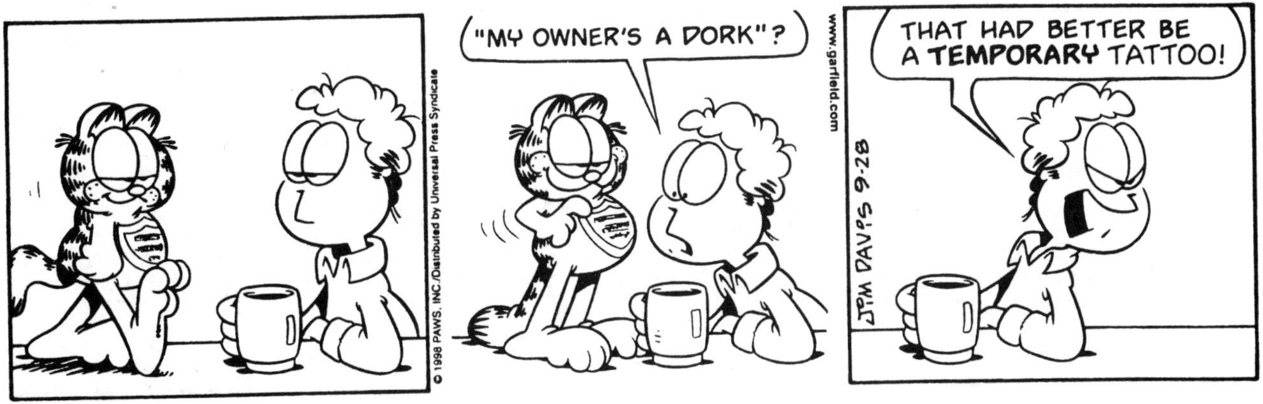
"MY OWNER'S A DORK"?
THAT HAD BETTER BE A TEMPORARY TATTOO!
JIM DAVIS 9-28
© 1998 PAWS, INC./Distributed by Universal Press Syndicate
www.garfield.com

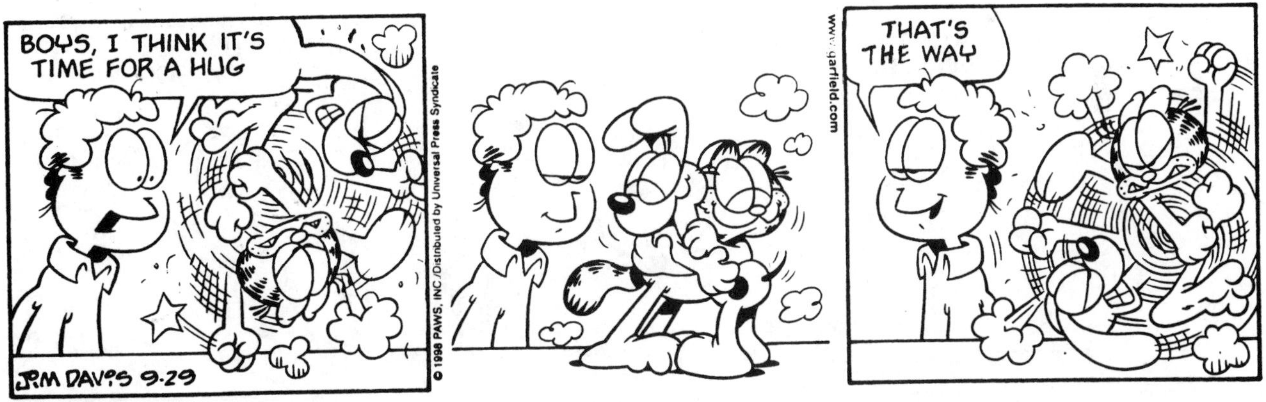
BOYS, I THINK IT'S TIME FOR A HUG
THAT'S THE WAY
JIM DAVIS 9-29
© 1998 PAWS, INC./Distributed by Universal Press Syndicate
www.garfield.com

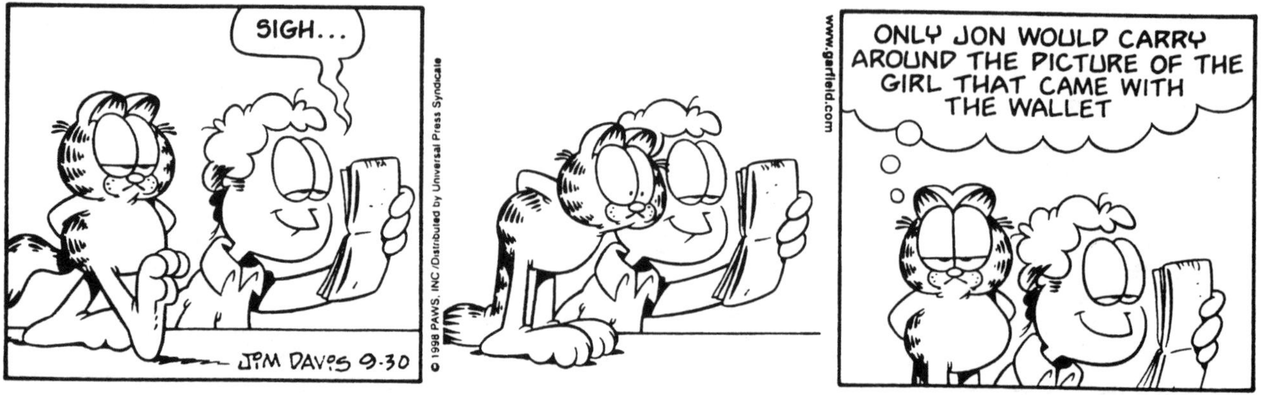
SIGH...
ONLY JON WOULD CARRY AROUND THE PICTURE OF THE GIRL THAT CAME WITH THE WALLET
JIM DAVIS 9-30
© 1998 PAWS, INC./Distributed by Universal Press Syndicate
www.garfield.com

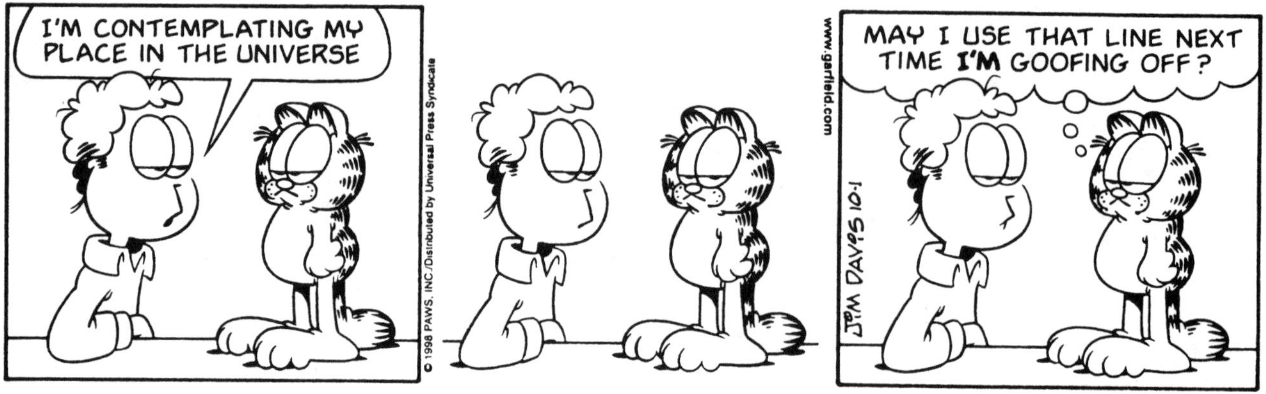
I'M CONTEMPLATING MY PLACE IN THE UNIVERSE
MAY I USE THAT LINE NEXT TIME **I'M** GOOFING OFF?
JIM DAVIS 10-1
© 1998 PAWS, INC./Distributed by Universal Press Syndicate
www.garfield.com

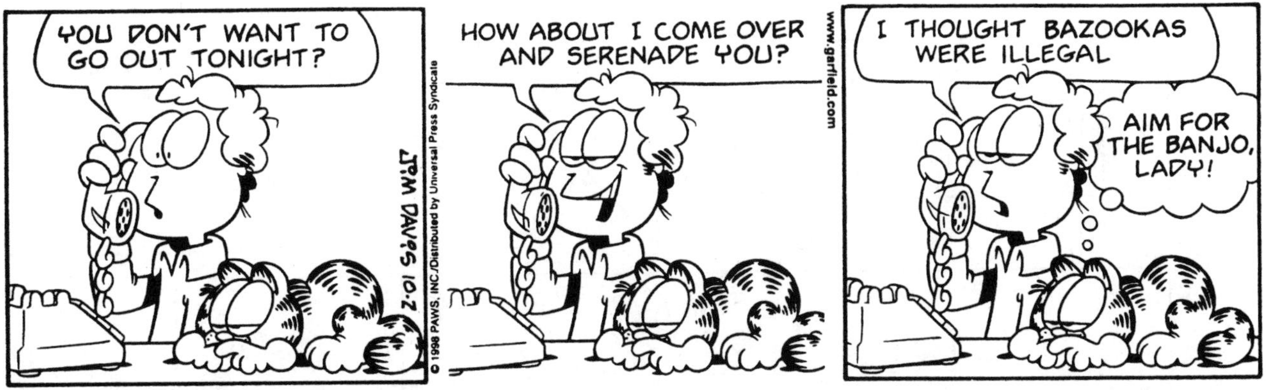
YOU DON'T WANT TO GO OUT TONIGHT?
JIM DAVIS 10-2
© 1998 PAWS, INC./Distributed by Universal Press Syndicate
HOW ABOUT I COME OVER AND SERENADE YOU?
www.garfield.com
I THOUGHT BAZOOKAS WERE ILLEGAL
AIM FOR THE BANJO, LADY!

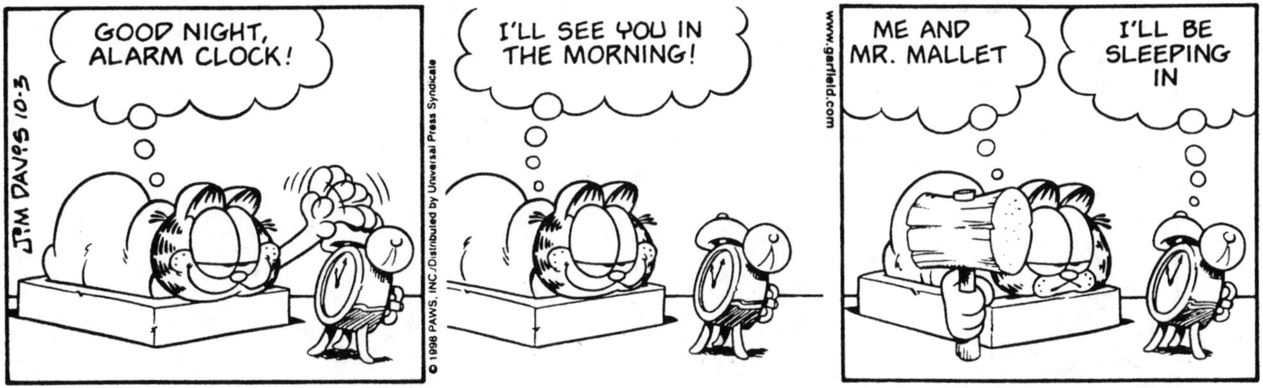
GOOD NIGHT, ALARM CLOCK!
JIM DAVIS 10-3
© 1998 PAWS, INC./Distributed by Universal Press Syndicate
I'LL SEE YOU IN THE MORNING!
www.garfield.com
ME AND MR. MALLET
I'LL BE SLEEPING IN

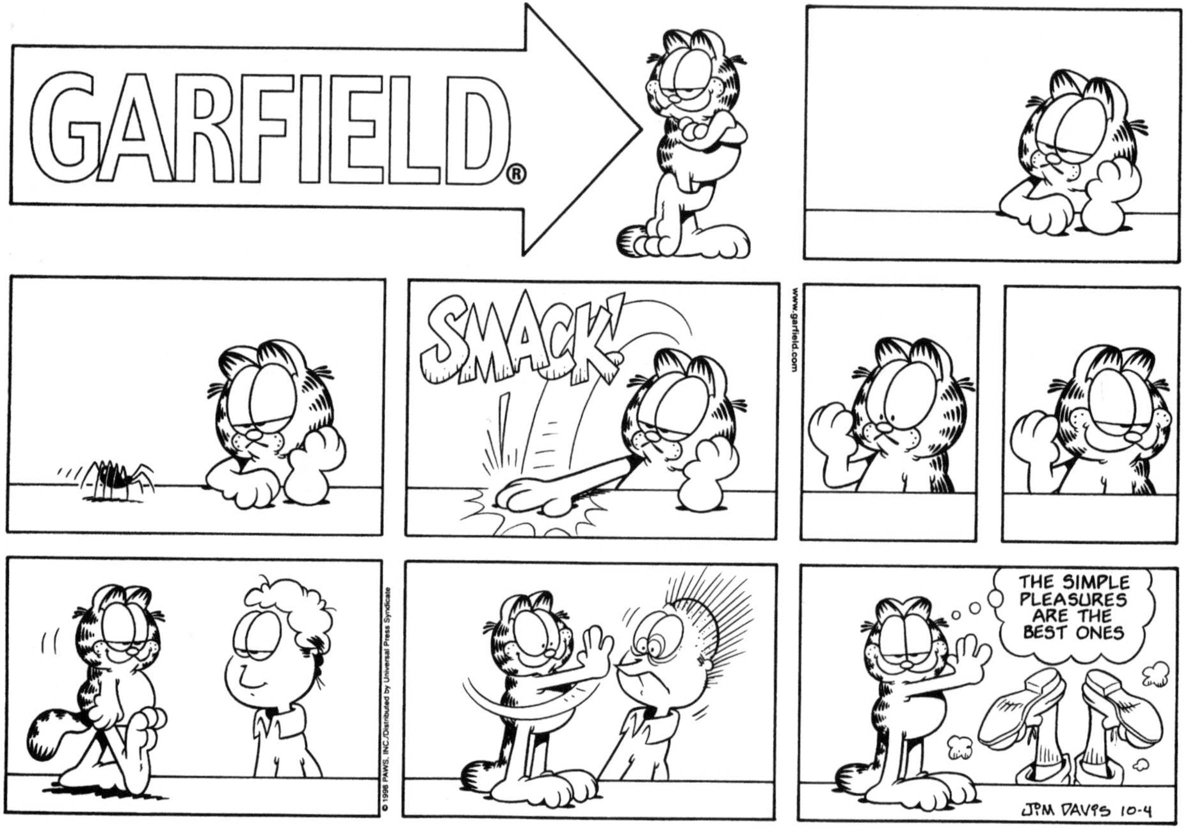

GARFIELD®
SMACK!
www.garfield.com
© 1998 PAWS, INC./Distributed by Universal Press Syndicate
THE SIMPLE PLEASURES ARE THE BEST ONES
JIM DAVIS 10-4

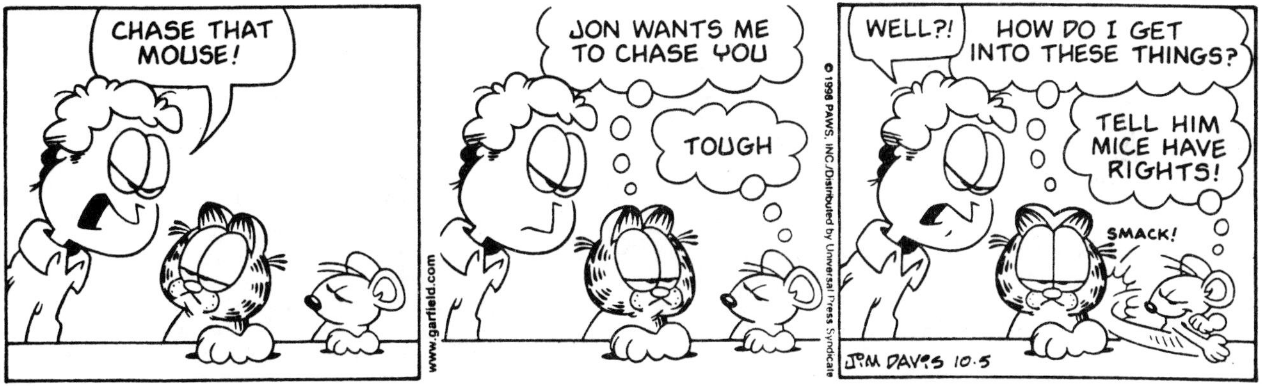
CHASE THAT MOUSE!
www.garfield.com
JON WANTS ME TO CHASE YOU
TOUGH
© 1998 PAWS, INC./Distributed by Universal Press Syndicate
WELL?!
HOW DO I GET INTO THESE THINGS?
TELL HIM MICE HAVE RIGHTS!
SMACK!
JIM DAVIS 10-5

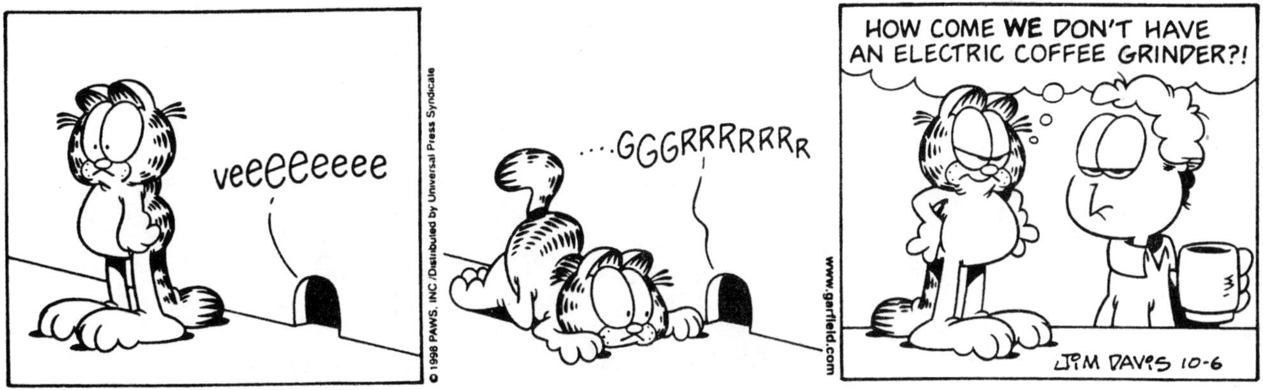
veeeeeeee
© 1998 PAWS, INC./Distributed by Universal Press Syndicate
....GGGRRRRRRR
www.garfield.com
HOW COME WE DON'T HAVE AN ELECTRIC COFFEE GRINDER?!
JIM DAVIS 10-6

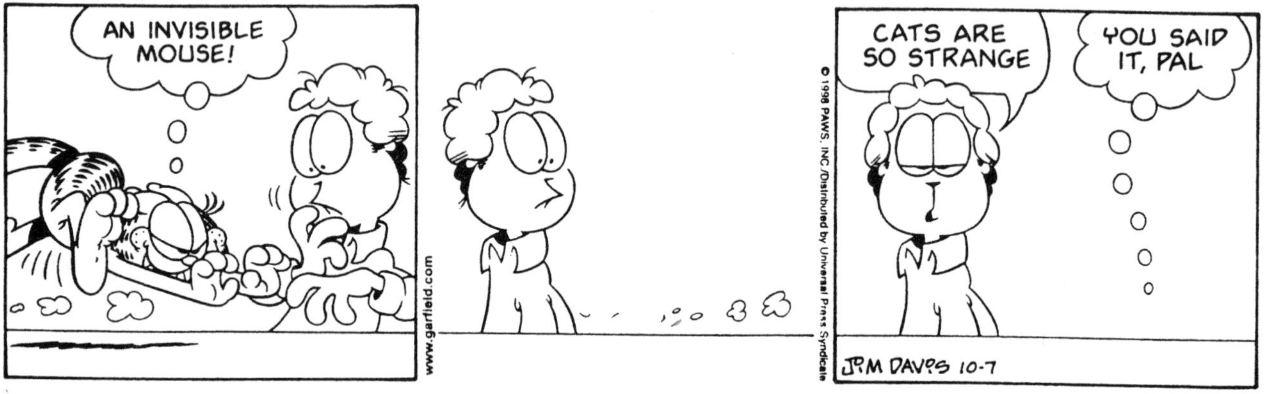
AN INVISIBLE MOUSE!
CATS ARE SO STRANGE
YOU SAID IT, PAL
www.garfield.com
© 1998 PAWS, INC./Distributed by Universal Press Syndicate
JIM DAVIS 10-7

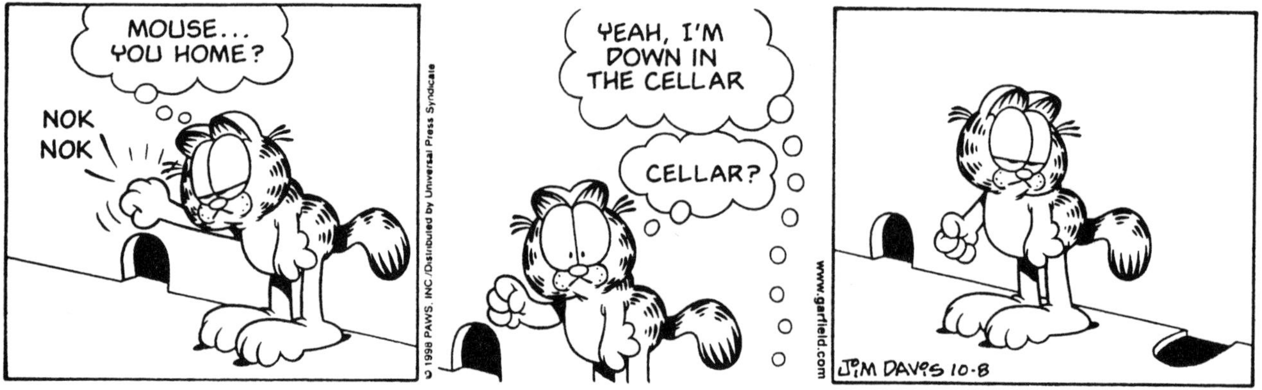
MOUSE... YOU HOME?
NOK NOK
YEAH, I'M DOWN IN THE CELLAR
CELLAR?
© 1998 PAWS, INC./Distributed by Universal Press Syndicate
www.garfield.com
JIM DAVIS 10-8

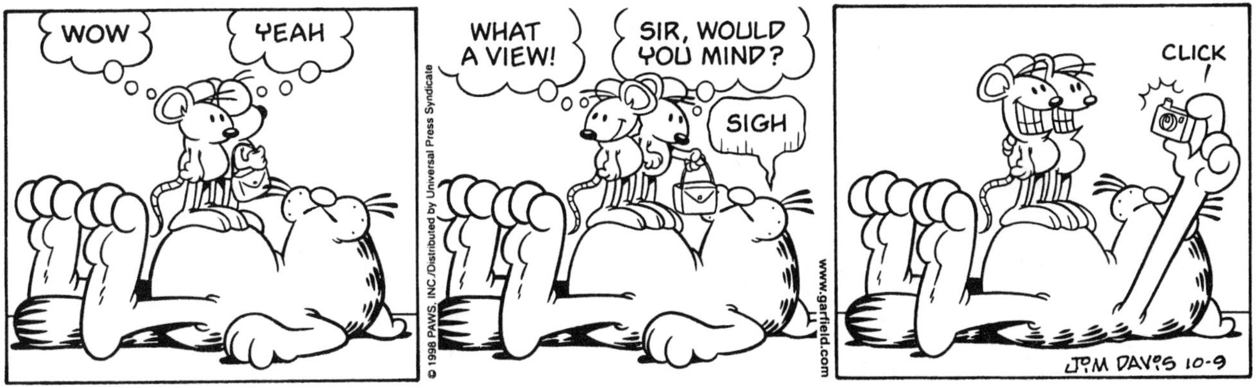
WOW
YEAH
WHAT A VIEW!
SIR, WOULD YOU MIND?
SIGH
CLICK
JIM DAVIS 10-9
© 1998 PAWS, INC./Distributed by Universal Press Syndicate
www.garfield.com

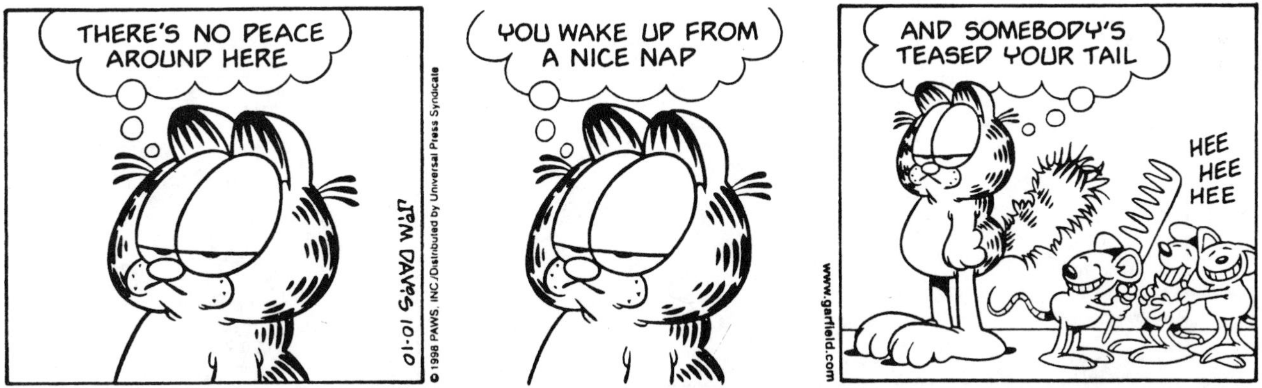
THERE'S NO PEACE AROUND HERE
JIM DAVIS 10-10
© 1998 PAWS, INC./Distributed by Universal Press Syndicate
YOU WAKE UP FROM A NICE NAP
www.garfield.com
AND SOMEBODY'S TEASED YOUR TAIL
HEE HEE HEE

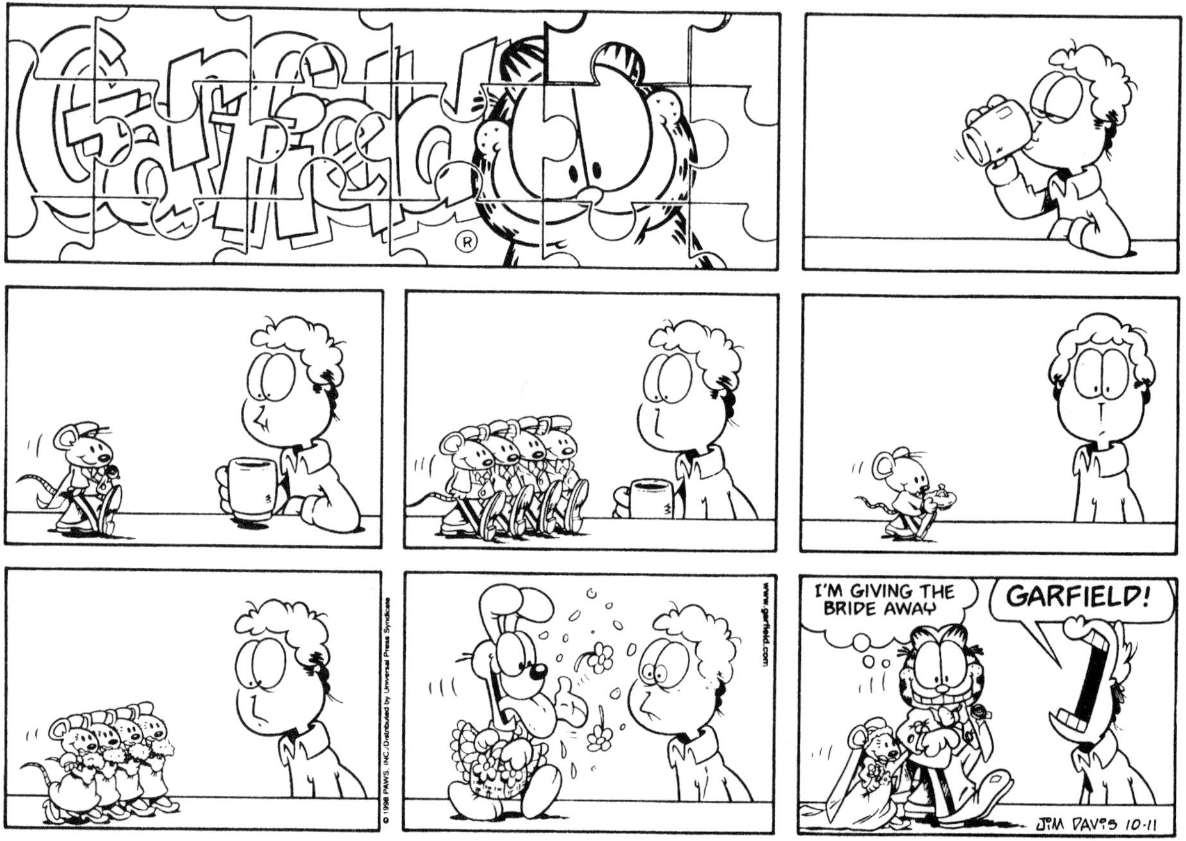
Garfield ®
© 1998 PAWS, INC./Distributed by Universal Press Syndicate
www.garfield.com
I'M GIVING THE BRIDE AWAY
GARFIELD!
JIM DAVIS 10-11

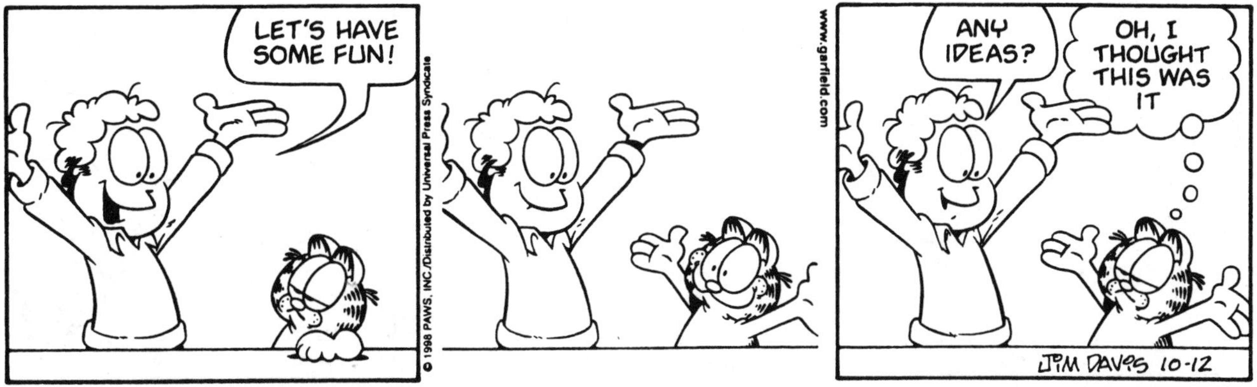
LET'S HAVE SOME FUN!
© 1998 PAWS, INC./Distributed by Universal Press Syndicate
www.garfield.com
ANY IDEAS?
OH, I THOUGHT THIS WAS IT
JIM DAVIS 10-12

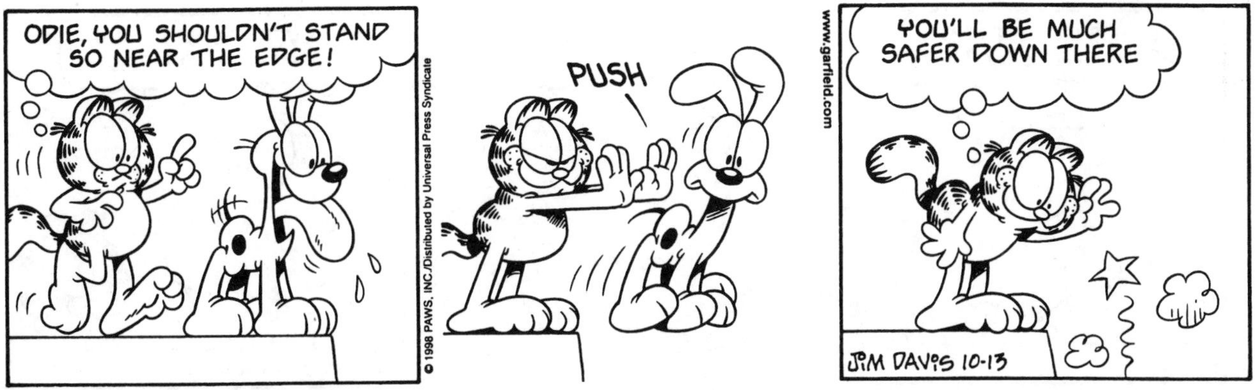
ODIE, YOU SHOULDN'T STAND SO NEAR THE EDGE!
© 1998 PAWS, INC./Distributed by Universal Press Syndicate
PUSH
www.garfield.com
YOU'LL BE MUCH SAFER DOWN THERE
JIM DAVIS 10-13

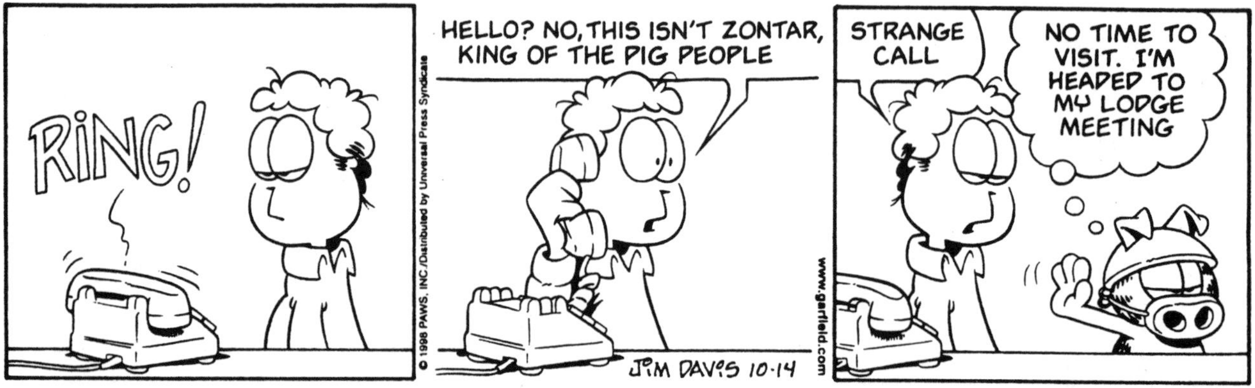
RING!
HELLO? NO, THIS ISN'T ZONTAR, KING OF THE PIG PEOPLE
© 1998 PAWS, INC./Distributed by Universal Press Syndicate
JIM DAVIS 10-14
www.garfield.com
STRANGE CALL
NO TIME TO VISIT. I'M HEADED TO MY LODGE MEETING

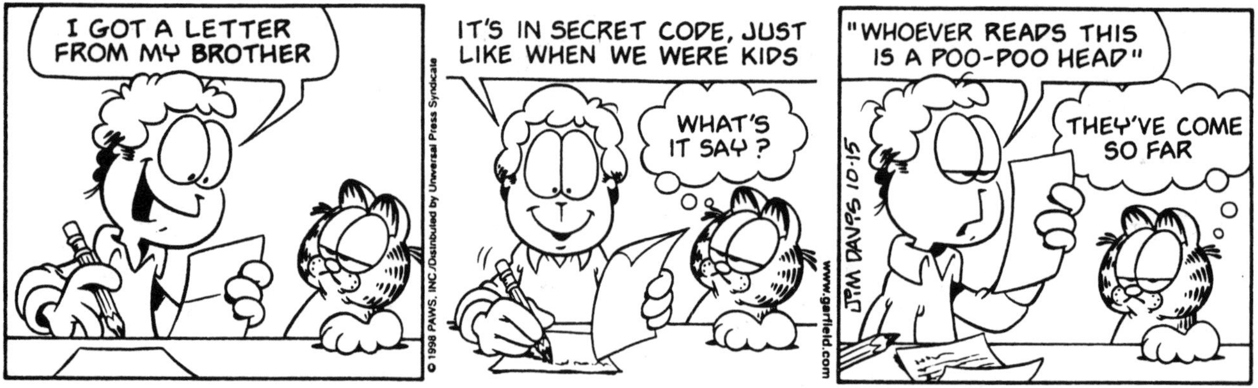
I GOT A LETTER FROM MY BROTHER
© 1998 PAWS, INC./Distributed by Universal Press Syndicate
IT'S IN SECRET CODE, JUST LIKE WHEN WE WERE KIDS
WHAT'S IT SAY ?
www.garfield.com
JIM DAVIS 10-15
"WHOEVER READS THIS IS A POO-POO HEAD"
THEY'VE COME SO FAR

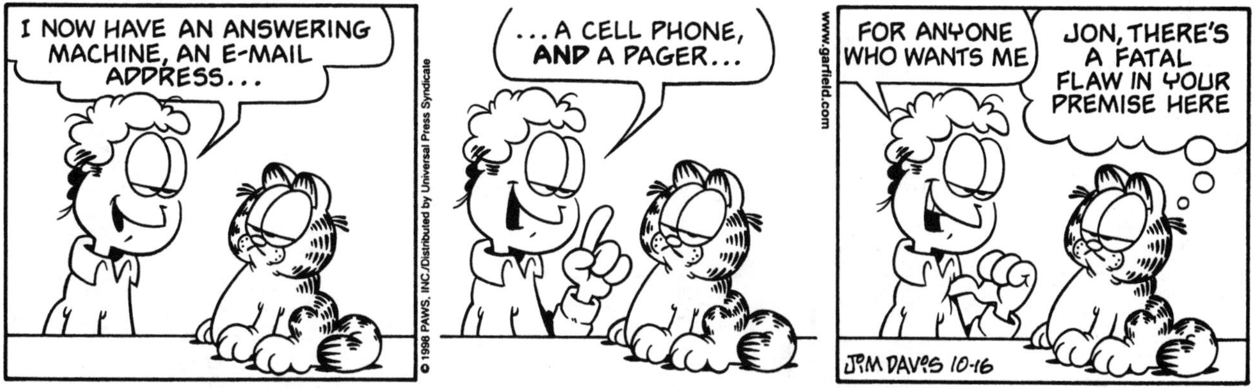
I NOW HAVE AN ANSWERING MACHINE, AN E-MAIL ADDRESS...
...A CELL PHONE, **AND** A PAGER...
FOR ANYONE WHO WANTS ME
JON, THERE'S A FATAL FLAW IN YOUR PREMISE HERE
© 1998 PAWS, INC./Distributed by Universal Press Syndicate
www.garfield.com
JIM DAVIS 10-16

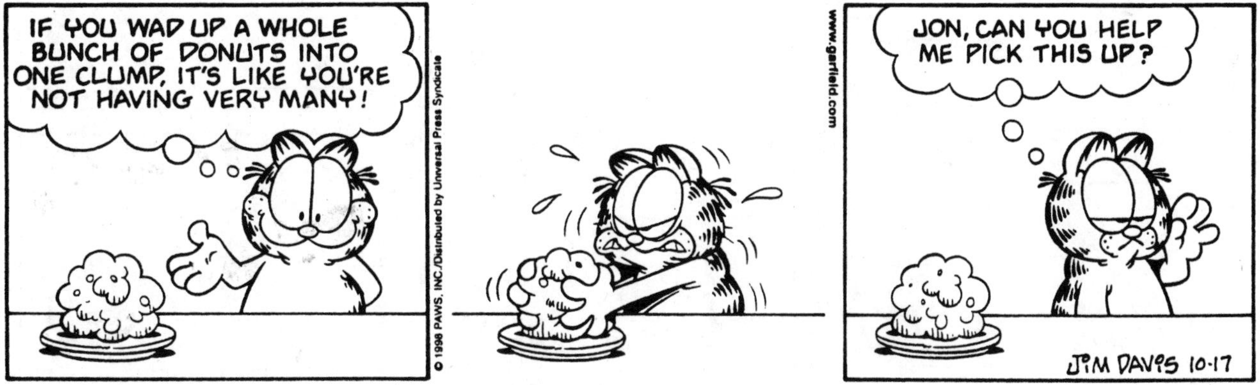
IF YOU WAD UP A WHOLE BUNCH OF DONUTS INTO ONE CLUMP, IT'S LIKE YOU'RE NOT HAVING VERY MANY!
JON, CAN YOU HELP ME PICK THIS UP?
© 1998 PAWS, INC./Distributed by Universal Press Syndicate
www.garfield.com
JIM DAVIS 10-17

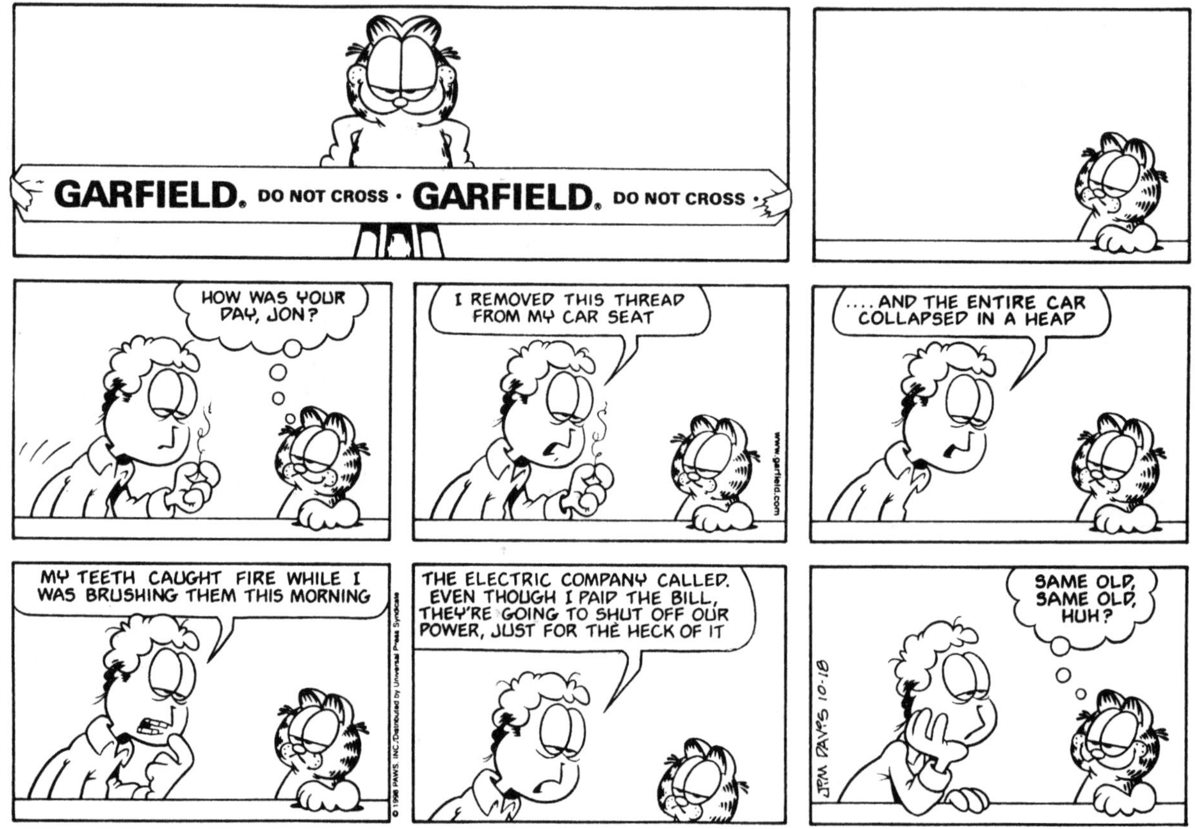

GARFIELD. DO NOT CROSS • GARFIELD. DO NOT CROSS •
HOW WAS YOUR DAY, JON?
I REMOVED THIS THREAD FROM MY CAR SEAT
www.garfield.com
....AND THE ENTIRE CAR COLLAPSED IN A HEAP
MY TEETH CAUGHT FIRE WHILE I WAS BRUSHING THEM THIS MORNING
© 1998 PAWS, INC./Distributed by Universal Press Syndicate
THE ELECTRIC COMPANY CALLED. EVEN THOUGH I PAID THE BILL, THEY'RE GOING TO SHUT OFF OUR POWER, JUST FOR THE HECK OF IT
JPM DAVPS 10-18
SAME OLD, SAME OLD, HUH?

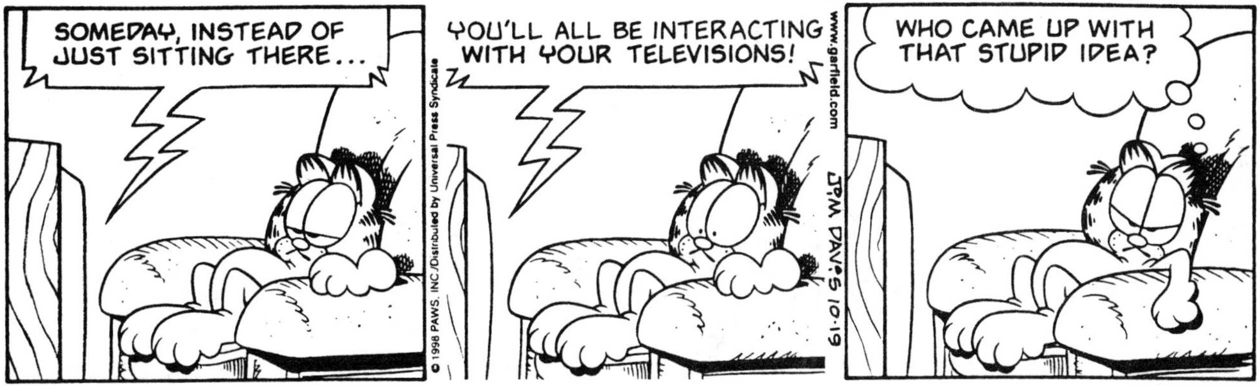
SOMEDAY, INSTEAD OF JUST SITTING THERE...
YOU'LL ALL BE INTERACTING WITH YOUR TELEVISIONS!
WHO CAME UP WITH THAT STUPID IDEA?
© 1998 PAWS, INC./Distributed by Universal Press Syndicate
www.garfield.com
JIM DAVIS 10·19

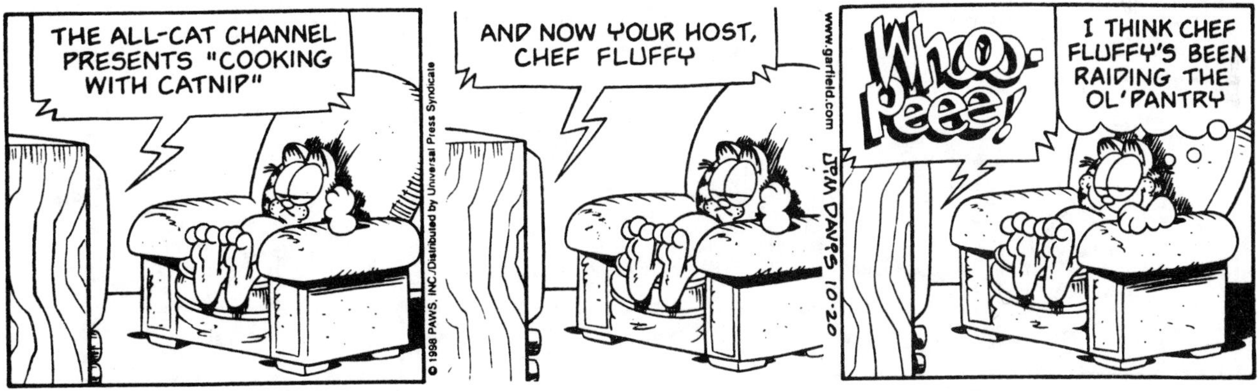
THE ALL-CAT CHANNEL PRESENTS "COOKING WITH CATNIP"
AND NOW YOUR HOST, CHEF FLUFFY
Whoo-peee!
I THINK CHEF FLUFFY'S BEEN RAIDING THE OL' PANTRY
© 1998 PAWS, INC./Distributed by Universal Press Syndicate
www.garfield.com
JIM DAVIS 10·20

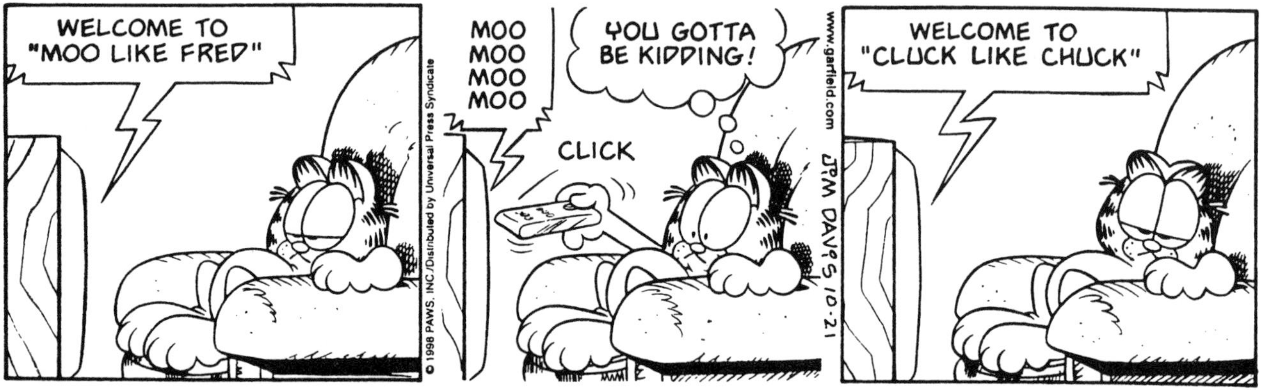
WELCOME TO "MOO LIKE FRED"
© 1998 PAWS, INC./Distributed by Universal Press Syndicate
MOO MOO MOO MOO
YOU GOTTA BE KIDDING!
CLICK
www.garfield.com
JIM DAVIS 10-21
WELCOME TO "CLUCK LIKE CHUCK"

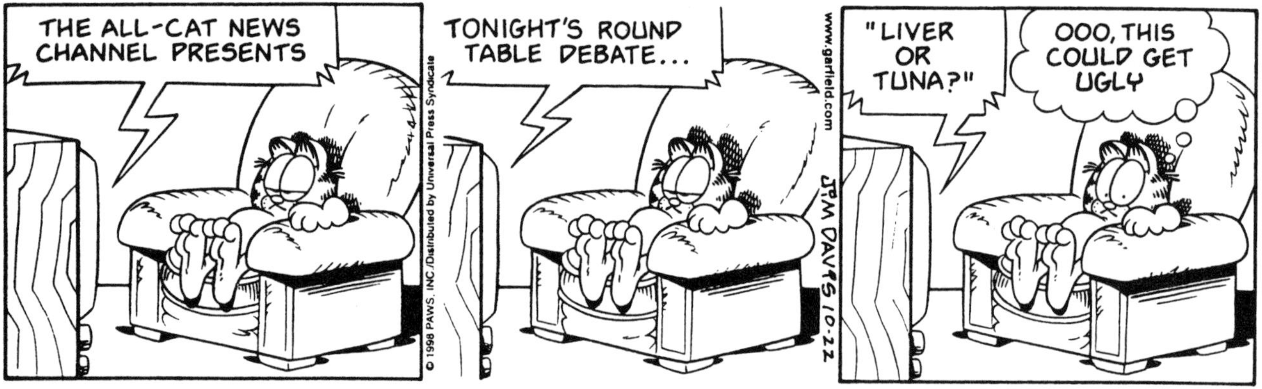
THE ALL-CAT NEWS CHANNEL PRESENTS
© 1998 PAWS, INC./Distributed by Universal Press Syndicate
TONIGHT'S ROUND TABLE DEBATE...
www.garfield.com
JIM DAVIS 10-22
"LIVER OR TUNA?"
OOO, THIS COULD GET UGLY

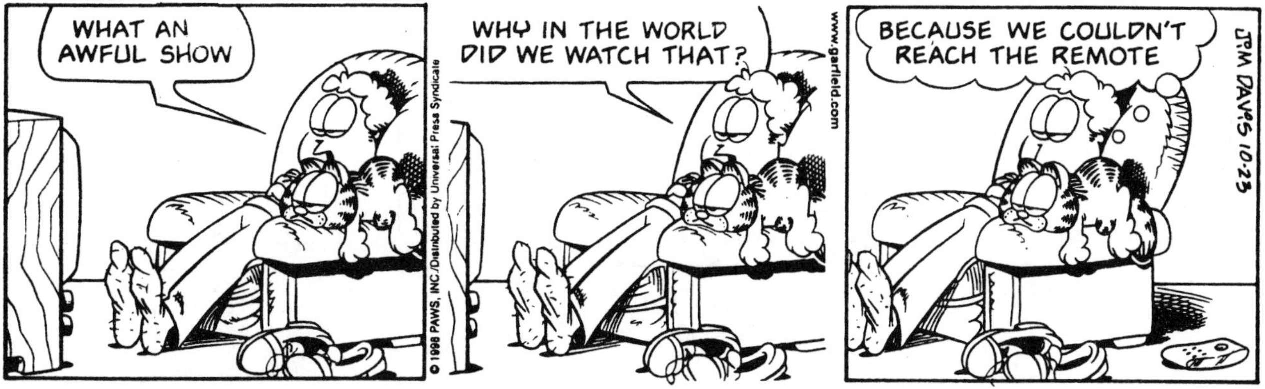
WHAT AN AWFUL SHOW
WHY IN THE WORLD DID WE WATCH THAT?
BECAUSE WE COULDN'T REACH THE REMOTE
© 1998 PAWS, INC./Distributed by Universal Press Syndicate
www.garfield.com
JIM DAVIS 10-23

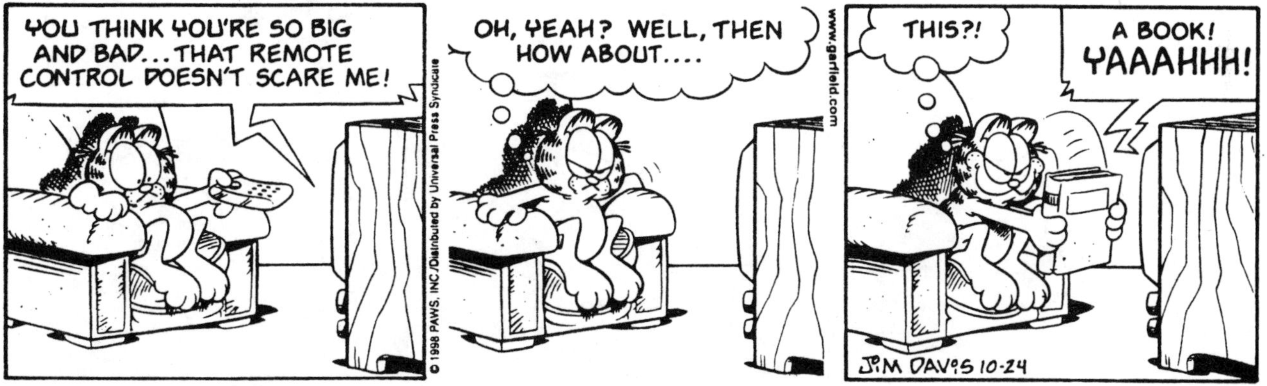
YOU THINK YOU'RE SO BIG AND BAD...THAT REMOTE CONTROL DOESN'T SCARE ME!
OH, YEAH? WELL, THEN HOW ABOUT....
THIS?!
A BOOK! YAAAHHH!
© 1998 PAWS, INC./Distributed by Universal Press Syndicate
www.garfield.com
JIM DAVIS 10-24

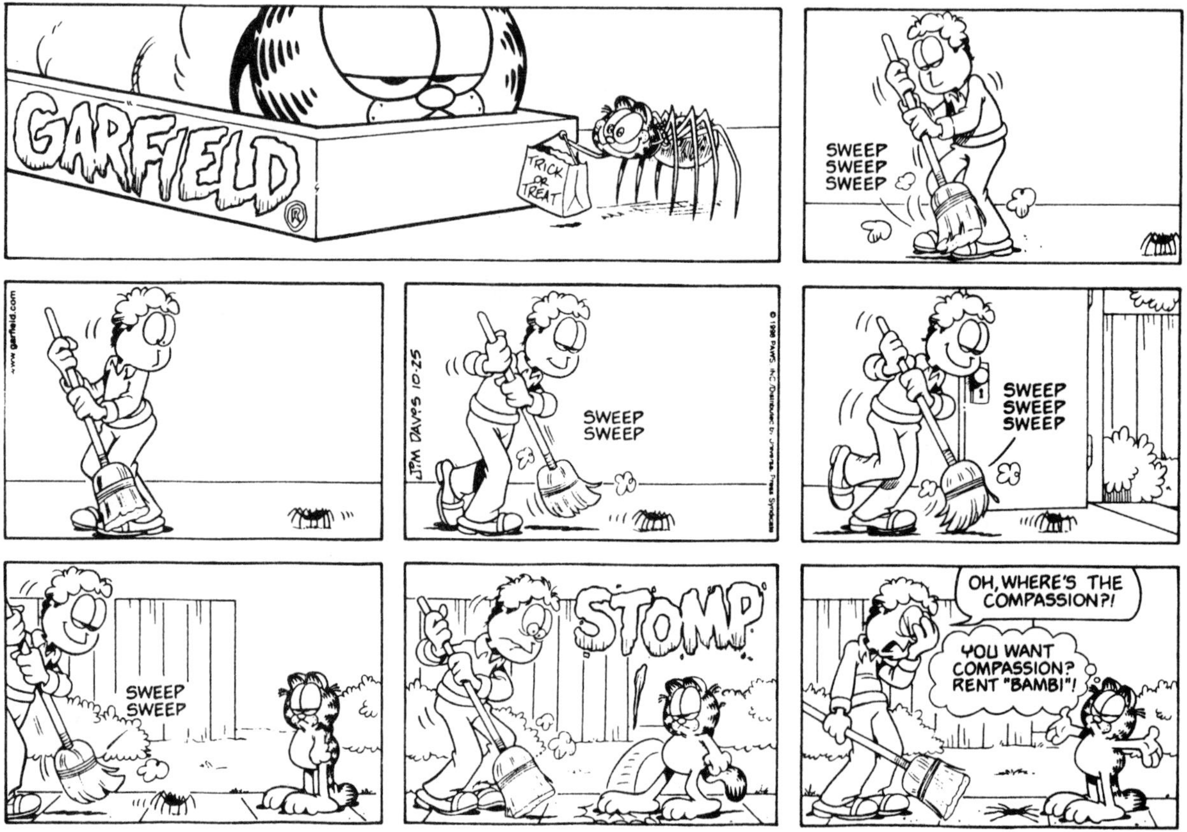
GARFIELD®
TRICK OR TREAT
SWEEP SWEEP SWEEP
www.garfield.com
JIM DAVIS 10-25
SWEEP SWEEP
SWEEP SWEEP SWEEP
SWEEP SWEEP
STOMP
OH, WHERE'S THE COMPASSION?!
YOU WANT COMPASSION? RENT "BAMBI"!

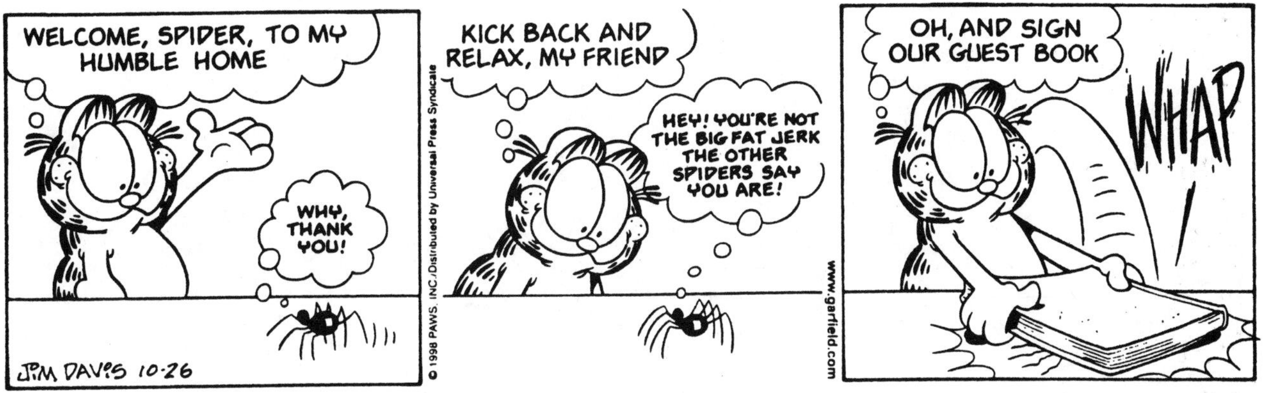
WELCOME, SPIDER, TO MY HUMBLE HOME
WHY, THANK YOU!
JIM DAVIS 10-26
© 1998 PAWS, INC./Distributed by Universal Press Syndicate
KICK BACK AND RELAX, MY FRIEND
HEY! YOU'RE NOT THE BIG FAT JERK THE OTHER SPIDERS SAY YOU ARE!
www.garfield.com
OH, AND SIGN OUR GUEST BOOK
WHAP

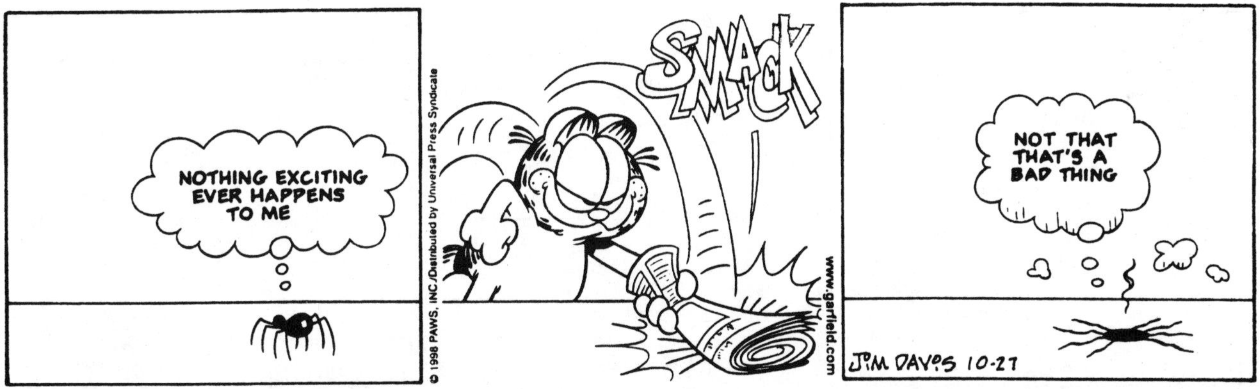
NOTHING EXCITING EVER HAPPENS TO ME
© 1998 PAWS, INC./Distributed by Universal Press Syndicate
SMACK
www.garfield.com
NOT THAT THAT'S A BAD THING
JIM DAVIS 10-27

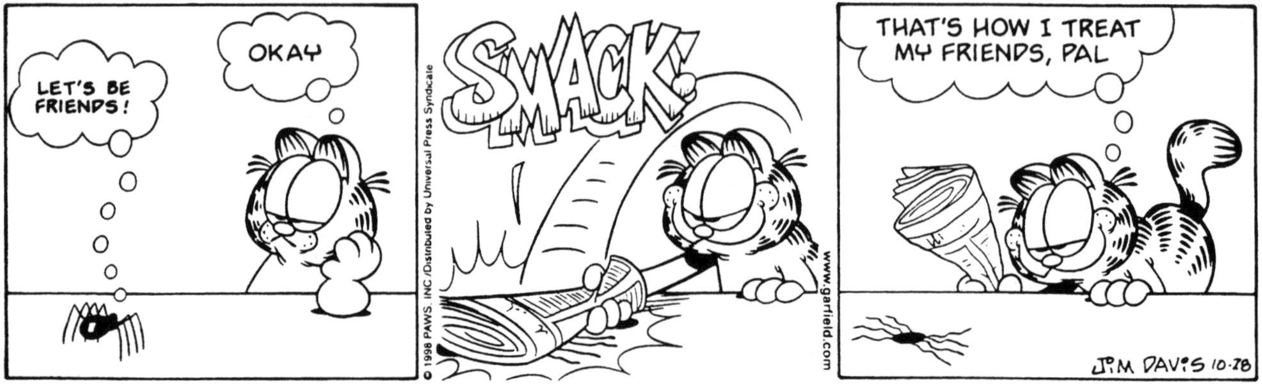
LET'S BE FRIENDS!
OKAY
© 1998 PAWS, INC./Distributed by Universal Press Syndicate
SMACK!
www.garfield.com
THAT'S HOW I TREAT MY FRIENDS, PAL
JIM DAVIS 10-28

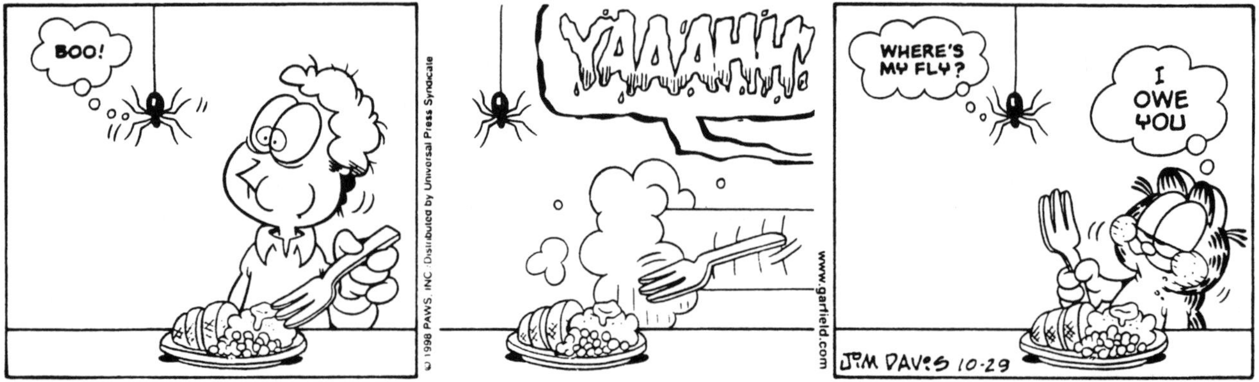
BOO!
© 1998 PAWS, INC./Distributed by Universal Press Syndicate
YAAAHH!
www.garfield.com
WHERE'S MY FLY?
I OWE YOU
JIM DAVIS 10-29

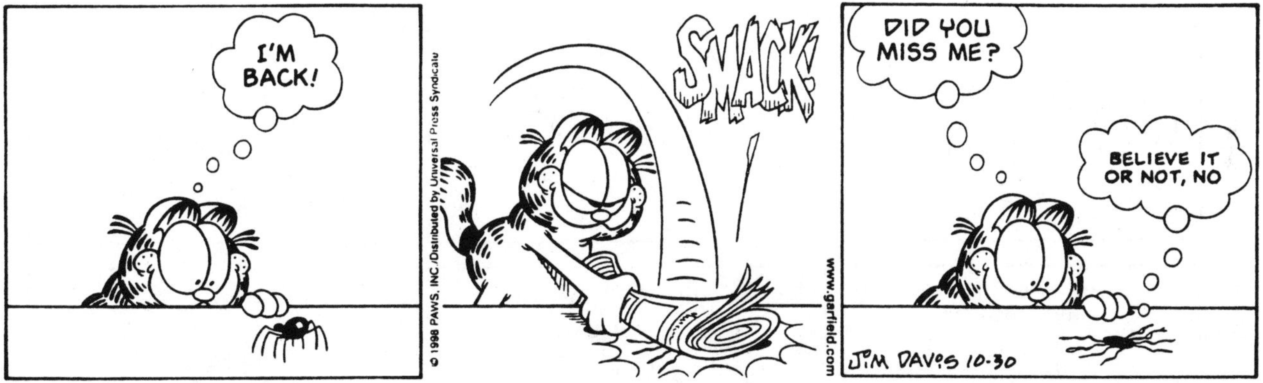
I'M BACK!
SMACK!
DID YOU MISS ME?
BELIEVE IT OR NOT, NO
© 1998 PAWS, INC./Distributed by Universal Press Syndicate
www.garfield.com
JIM DAVIS 10-30

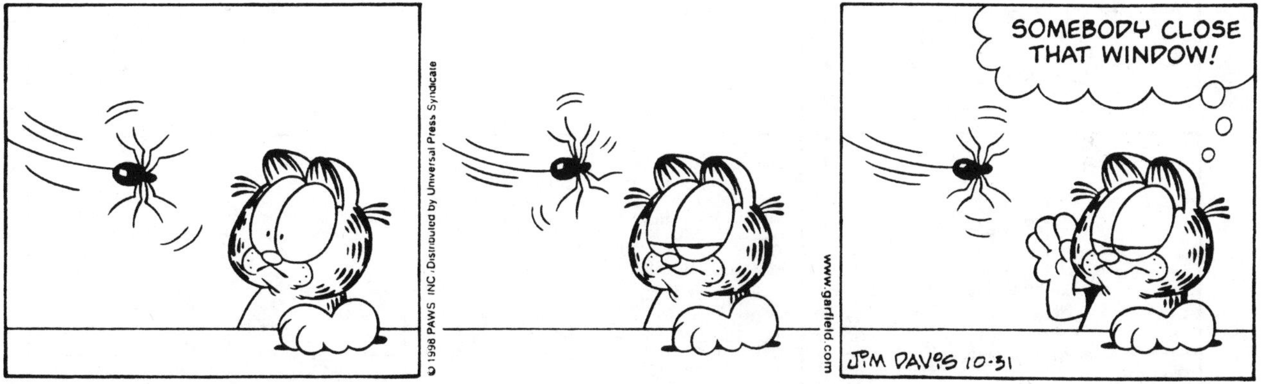
SOMEBODY CLOSE THAT WINDOW!
© 1998 PAWS, INC./Distributed by Universal Press Syndicate
www.garfield.com
JIM DAVIS 10-31

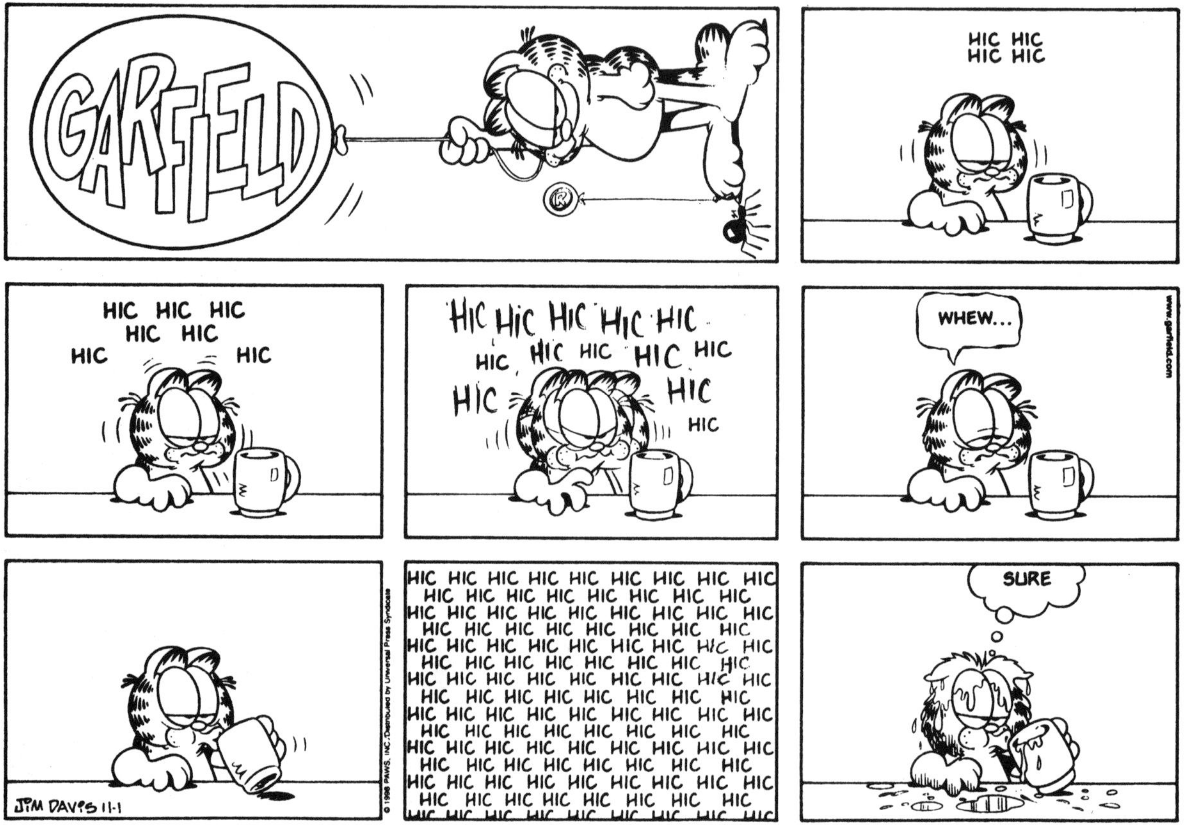
GARFIELD
HIC HIC
HIC HIC
HIC HIC HIC
HIC HIC
HIC
HIC
HIC HIC HIC HIC HIC
HIC HIC HIC HIC HIC
HIC
HIC
HIC
WHEW...
www.garfield.com
JIM DAVIS 11-1
© 1998 PAWS, INC. Distributed by Universal Press Syndicate
HIC HIC HIC HIC HIC HIC HIC HIC HIC
HIC HIC HIC HIC HIC HIC HIC HIC
HIC HIC HIC HIC HIC HIC HIC HIC HIC
HIC HIC HIC HIC HIC HIC HIC HIC
HIC HIC HIC HIC HIC HIC HIC HIC HIC
HIC HIC HIC HIC HIC HIC HIC HIC
HIC HIC HIC HIC HIC HIC HIC HIC HIC
HIC HIC HIC HIC HIC HIC HIC HIC
HIC HIC HIC HIC HIC HIC HIC HIC HIC
HIC HIC HIC HIC HIC HIC HIC HIC
HIC HIC HIC HIC HIC HIC HIC HIC HIC
HIC HIC HIC HIC HIC HIC HIC HIC
HIC HIC HIC HIC HIC HIC HIC HIC HIC
HIC HIC HIC HIC HIC HIC HIC HIC
SURE

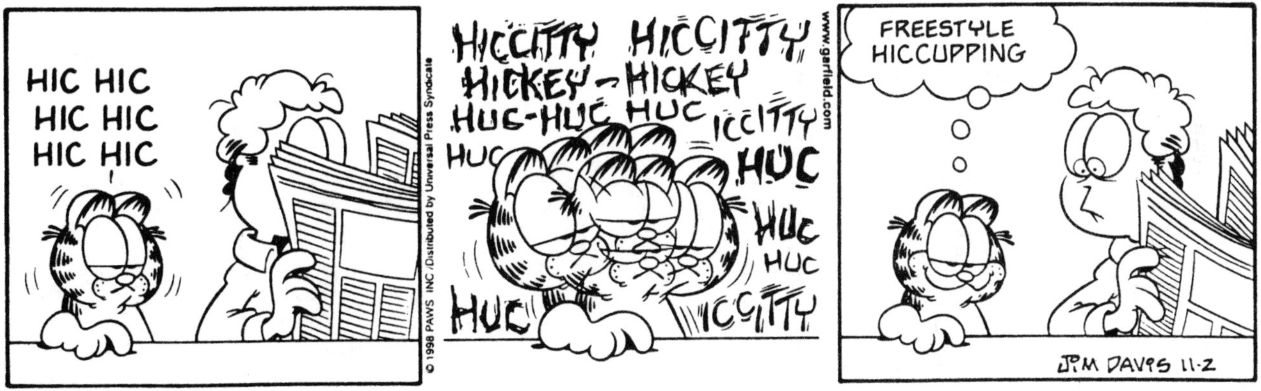
HIC HIC
HIC HIC
HIC HIC
© 1998 PAWS INC./Distributed by Universal Press Syndicate
HICCITTY HICCITTY
HICKEY-HICKEY
HUC-HUC HUC
ICCITTY
HUC
HUC
HUC
HUC
HUC
ICCITTY
www.garfield.com
FREESTYLE
HICCUPPING
JIM DAVIS 11-2

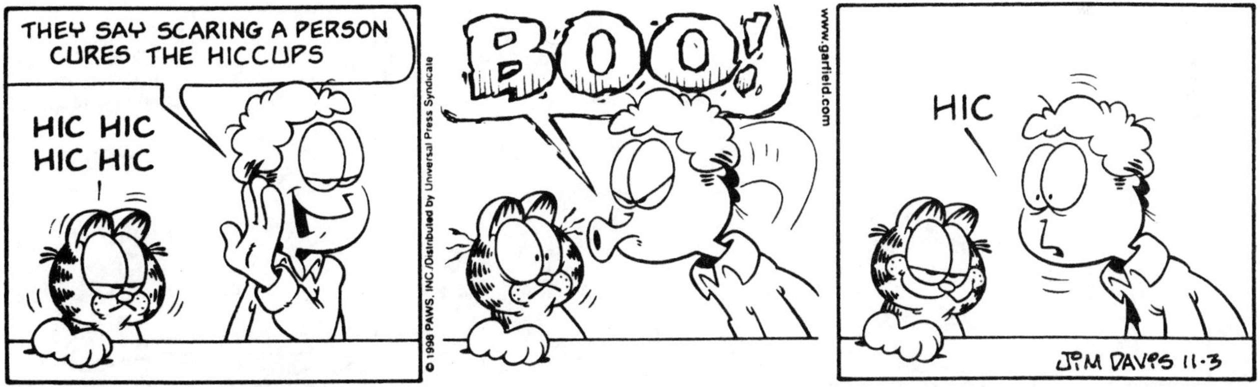
THEY SAY SCARING A PERSON
CURES THE HICCUPS
HIC HIC
HIC HIC
© 1998 PAWS, INC./Distributed by Universal Press Syndicate
BOO!
www.garfield.com
HIC
JIM DAVIS 11-3

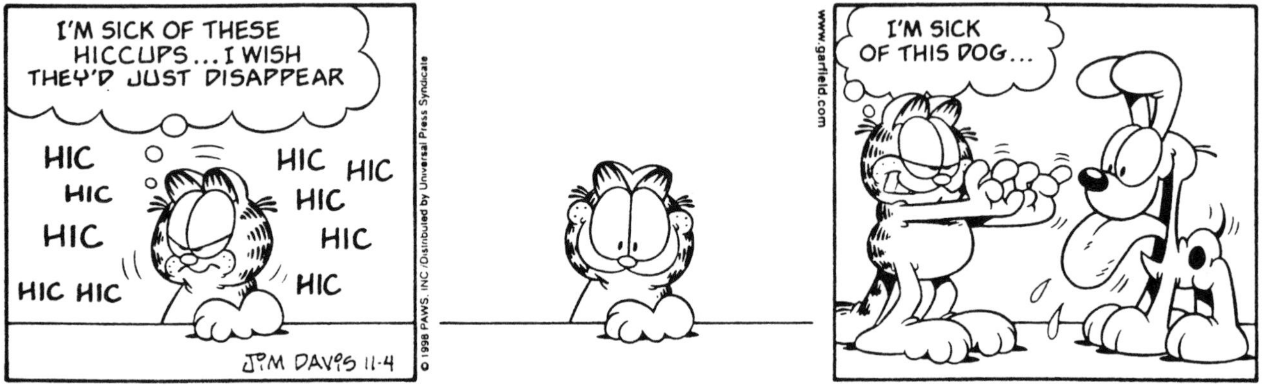
I'M SICK OF THESE HICCUPS... I WISH THEY'D JUST DISAPPEAR
HIC
HIC
HIC
HIC HIC
HIC
HIC
HIC
HIC
HIC
JIM DAVIS 11-4
© 1998 PAWS, INC./Distributed by Universal Press Syndicate
www.garfield.com
I'M SICK OF THIS DOG...

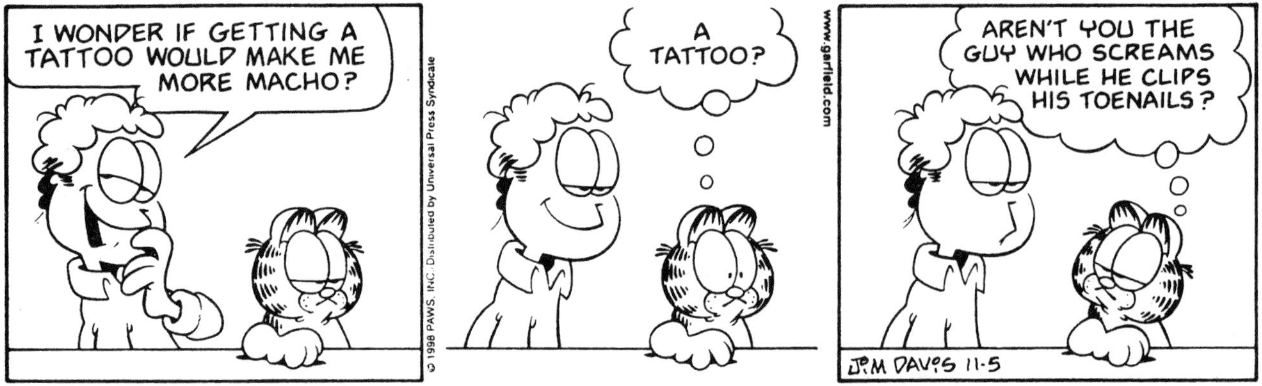
I WONDER IF GETTING A TATTOO WOULD MAKE ME MORE MACHO?
© 1998 PAWS, INC./Distributed by Universal Press Syndicate
A TATTOO?
www.garfield.com
AREN'T YOU THE GUY WHO SCREAMS WHILE HE CLIPS HIS TOENAILS?
JIM DAVIS 11-5

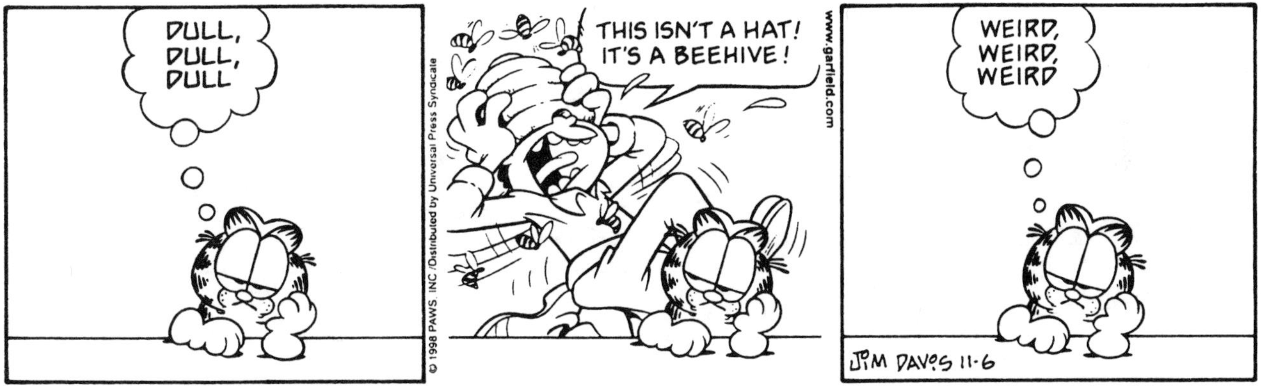
DULL, DULL, DULL
THIS ISN'T A HAT! IT'S A BEEHIVE!
WEIRD, WEIRD, WEIRD
JIM DAVIS 11-6
© 1998 PAWS, INC./Distributed by Universal Press Syndicate
www.garfield.com

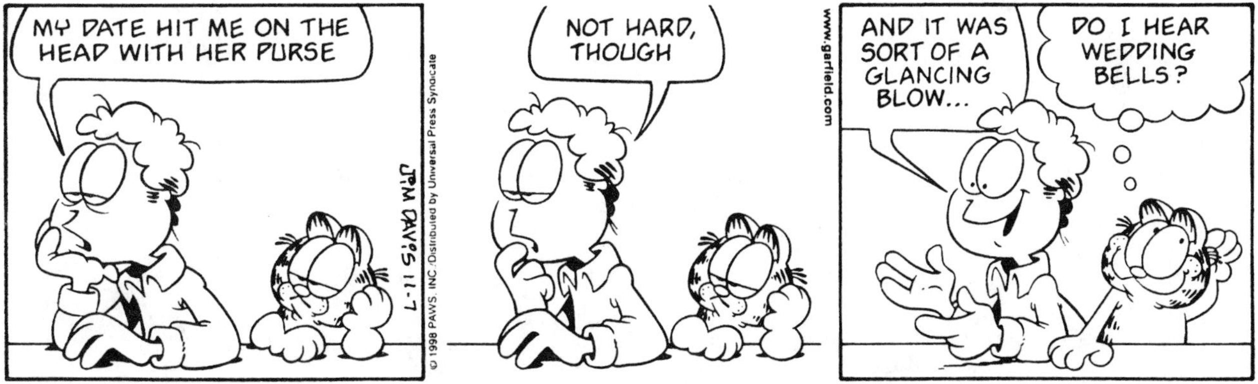
MY DATE HIT ME ON THE HEAD WITH HER PURSE
JIM DAVIS 11-7
© 1998 PAWS, INC./Distributed by Universal Press Syndicate
NOT HARD, THOUGH
www.garfield.com
AND IT WAS SORT OF A GLANCING BLOW...
DO I HEAR WEDDING BELLS?

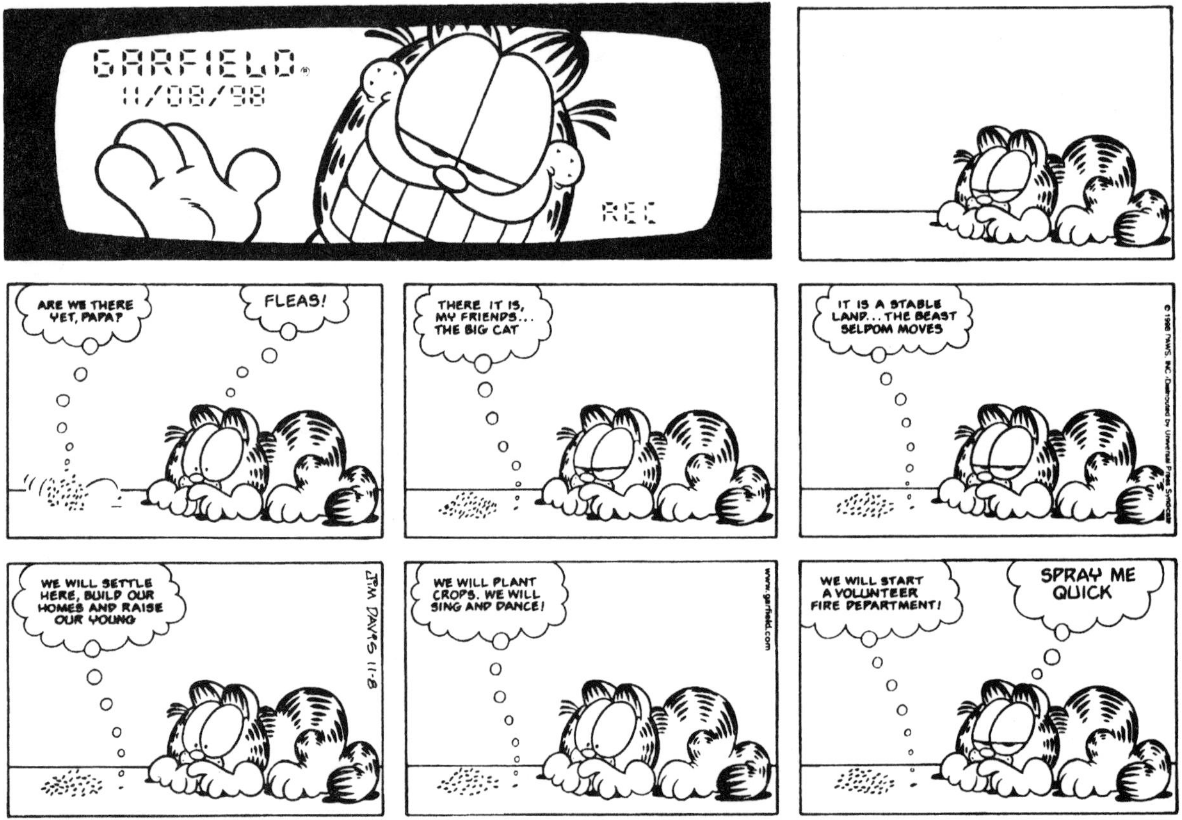
GARFIELD®
11/08/98
REC
ARE WE THERE YET, PAPA?
FLEAS!
THERE IT IS, MY FRIENDS... THE BIG CAT
IT IS A STABLE LAND... THE BEAST SELDOM MOVES
© 1998 PAWS, INC./Distributed by Universal Press Syndicate
WE WILL SETTLE HERE, BUILD OUR HOMES AND RAISE OUR YOUNG
JIM DAVIS 11-8
WE WILL PLANT CROPS. WE WILL SING AND DANCE!
www.garfield.com
WE WILL START A VOLUNTEER FIRE DEPARTMENT!
SPRAY ME QUICK

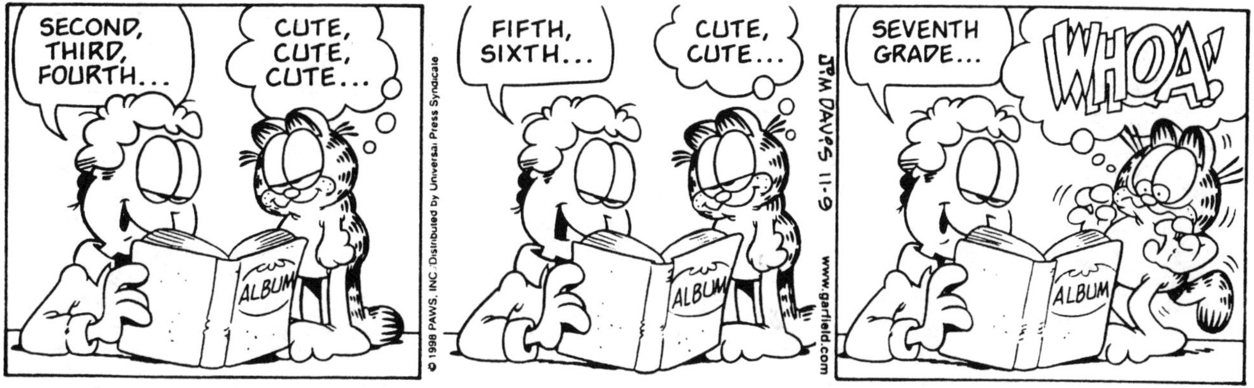
SECOND, THIRD, FOURTH...
CUTE, CUTE, CUTE...
© 1998 PAWS, INC./Distributed by Universal Press Syndicate
FIFTH, SIXTH...
CUTE, CUTE...
JIM DAVIS 11-9
www.garfield.com
SEVENTH GRADE...
WHOA!
ALBUM

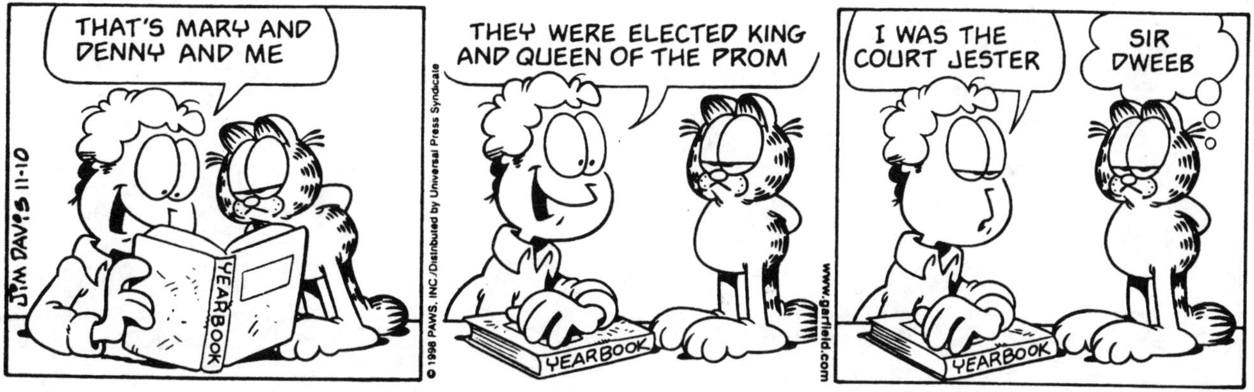
JIM DAVIS 11-10
THAT'S MARY AND DENNY AND ME
YEARBOOK
© 1998 PAWS, INC./Distributed by Universal Press Syndicate
THEY WERE ELECTED KING AND QUEEN OF THE PROM
YEARBOOK
www.garfield.com
I WAS THE COURT JESTER
SIR DWEEB
YEARBOOK

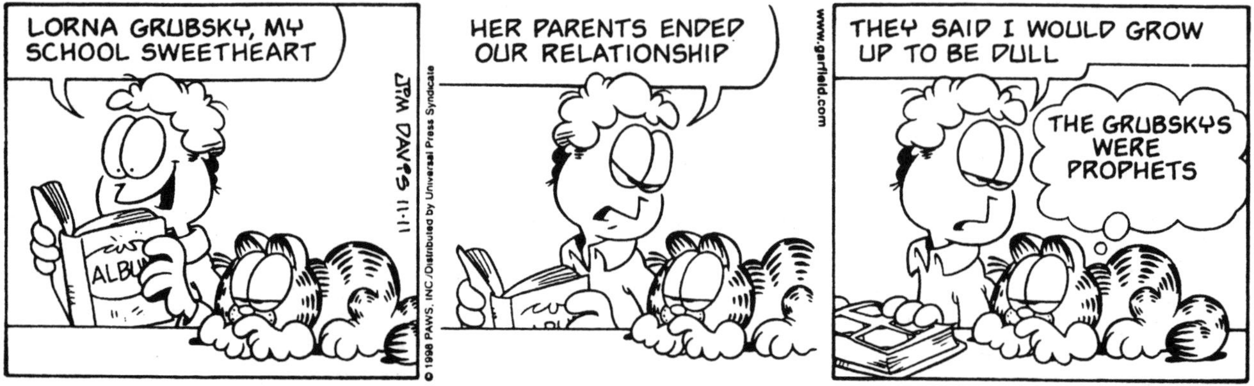
LORNA GRUBSKY, MY SCHOOL SWEETHEART
ALBUM
JIM DAVIS 11-11
© 1998 PAWS, INC./Distributed by Universal Press Syndicate
HER PARENTS ENDED OUR RELATIONSHIP
www.garfield.com
THEY SAID I WOULD GROW UP TO BE DULL
THE GRUBSKYS WERE PROPHETS

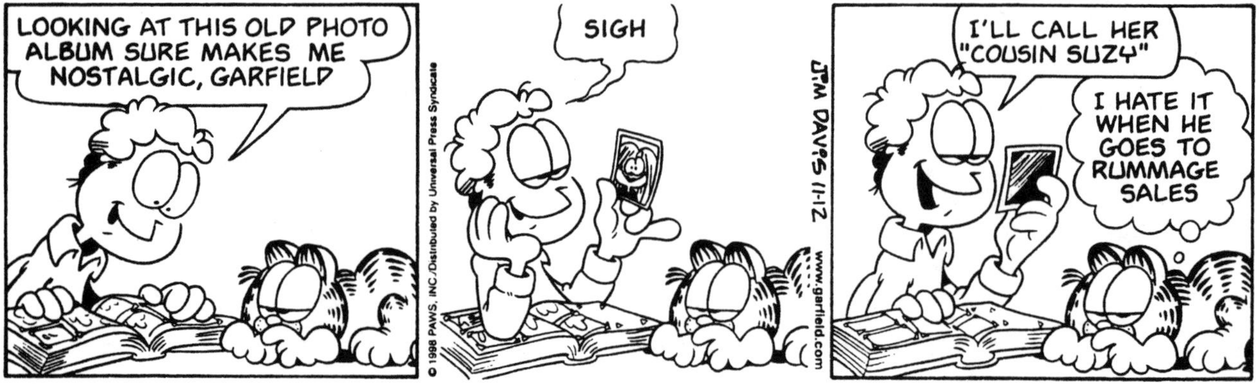
LOOKING AT THIS OLD PHOTO ALBUM SURE MAKES ME NOSTALGIC, GARFIELD
© 1998 PAWS, INC./Distributed by Universal Press Syndicate
SIGH
JIM DAVIS 11-12
www.garfield.com
I'LL CALL HER "COUSIN SUZY"
I HATE IT WHEN HE GOES TO RUMMAGE SALES

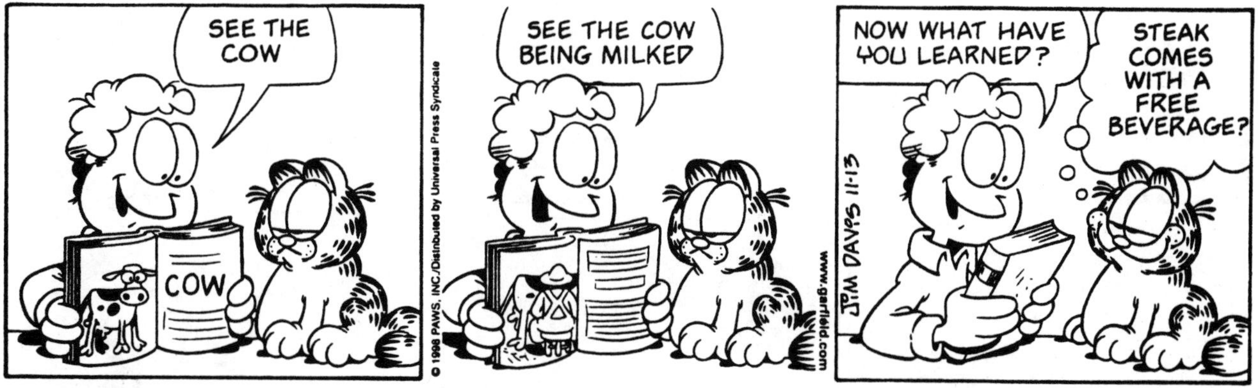
SEE THE COW
COW
SEE THE COW BEING MILKED
NOW WHAT HAVE YOU LEARNED?
STEAK COMES WITH A FREE BEVERAGE?
© 1998 PAWS, INC./Distributed by Universal Press Syndicate
www.garfield.com
JPM DAVPS 11-13

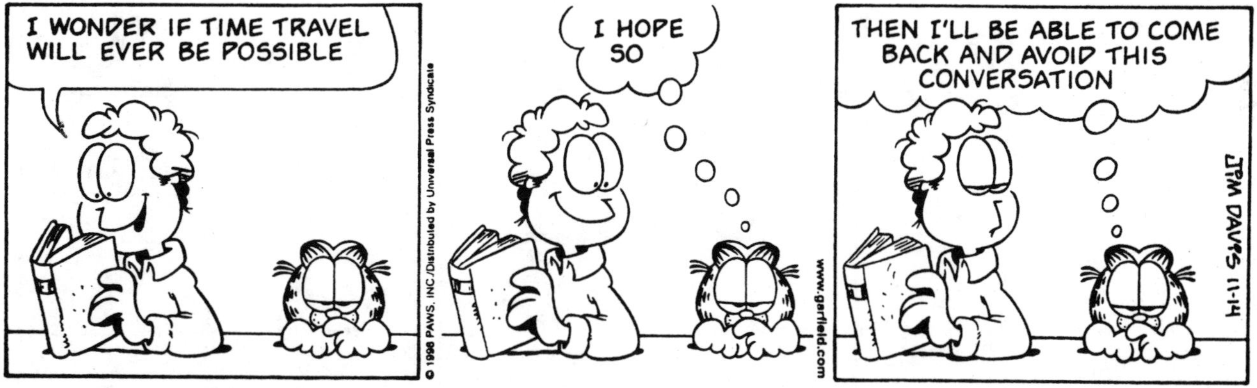
I WONDER IF TIME TRAVEL WILL EVER BE POSSIBLE
I HOPE SO
THEN I'LL BE ABLE TO COME BACK AND AVOID THIS CONVERSATION
© 1998 PAWS, INC./Distributed by Universal Press Syndicate
www.garfield.com
JPM DAVPS 11-14

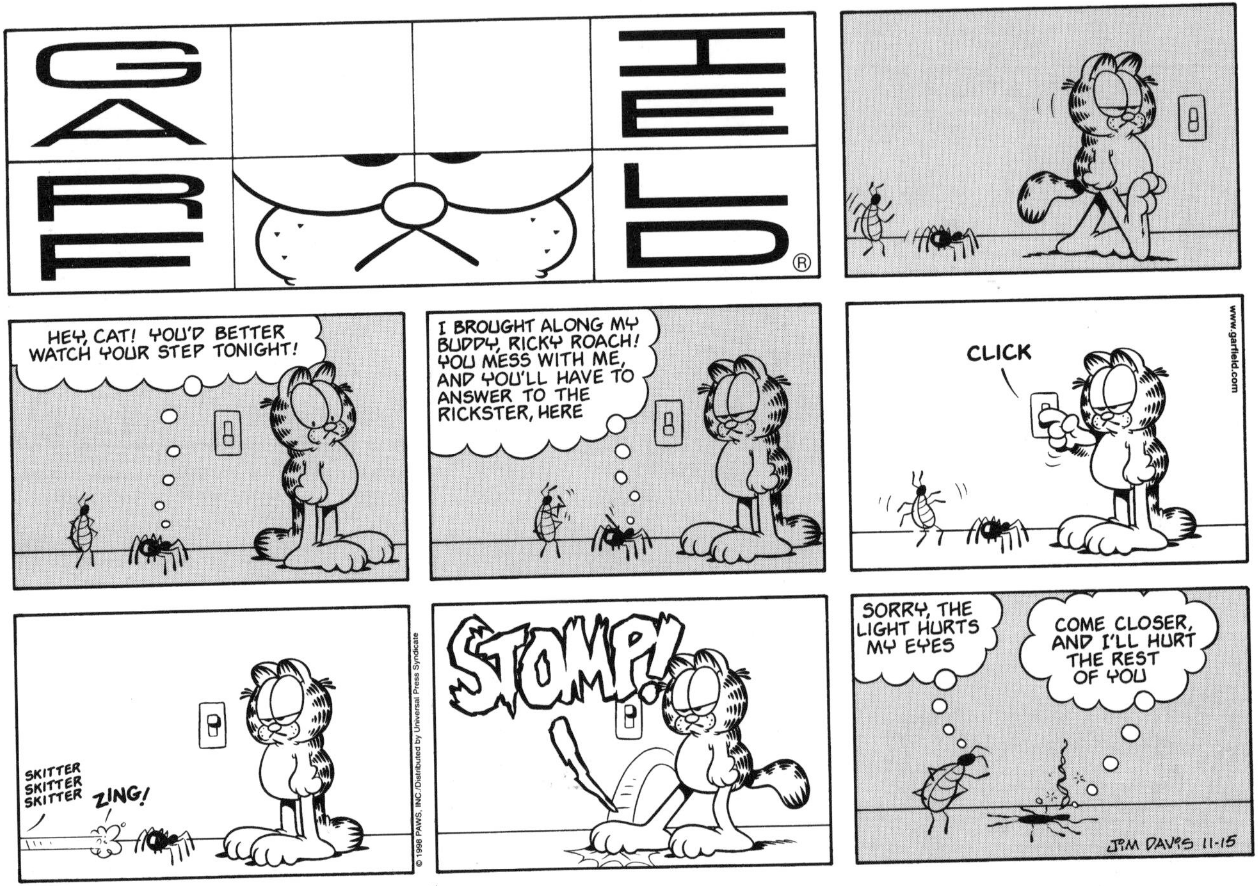
GARFIELD®
HEY, CAT! YOU'D BETTER WATCH YOUR STEP TONIGHT!
I BROUGHT ALONG MY BUDDY, RICKY ROACH! YOU MESS WITH ME, AND YOU'LL HAVE TO ANSWER TO THE RICKSTER, HERE
CLICK
www.garfield.com
SKITTER SKITTER SKITTER
ZING!
© 1998 PAWS, INC./Distributed by Universal Press Syndicate
STOMP!
SORRY, THE LIGHT HURTS MY EYES
COME CLOSER, AND I'LL HURT THE REST OF YOU
JIM DAVIS 11-15

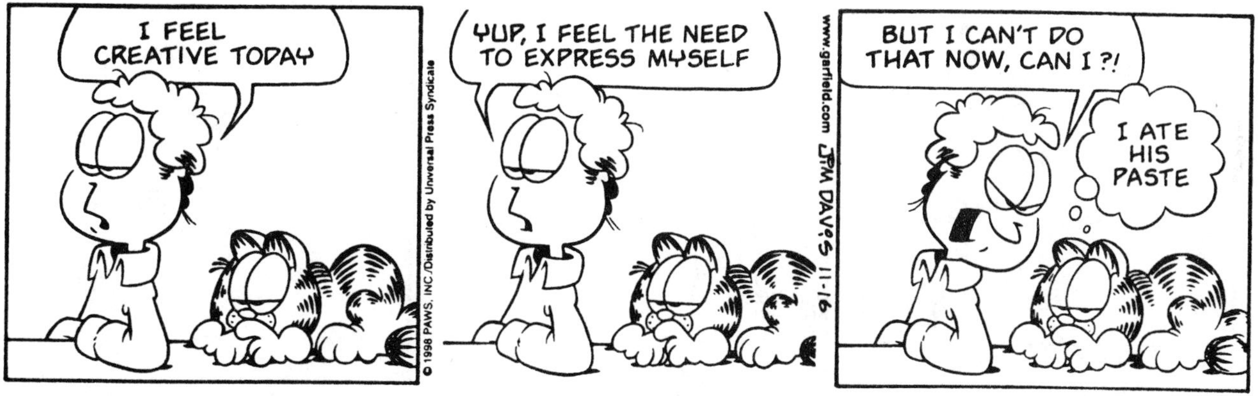
I FEEL CREATIVE TODAY
YUP, I FEEL THE NEED TO EXPRESS MYSELF
BUT I CAN'T DO THAT NOW, CAN I ?!
I ATE HIS PASTE
© 1998 PAWS, INC./Distributed by Universal Press Syndicate
www.garfield.com
JIM DAVIS 11-16

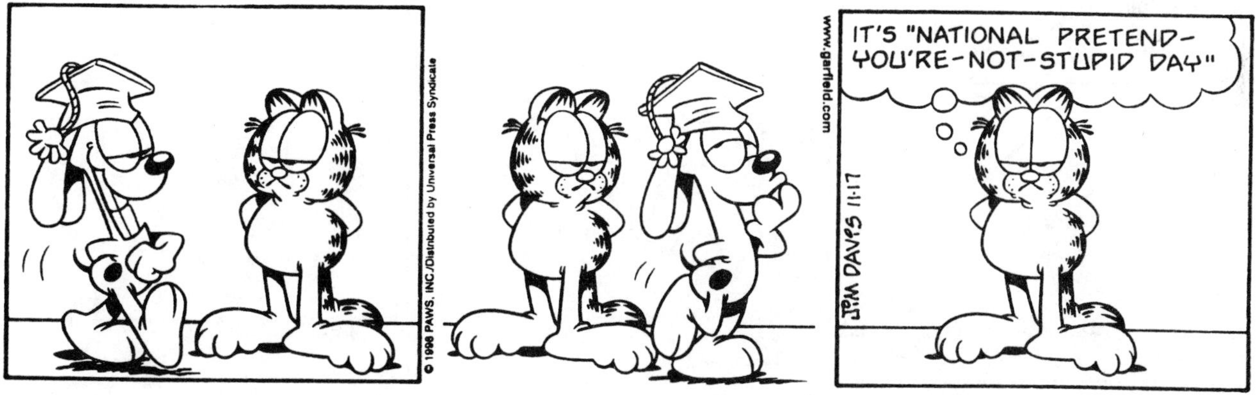
IT'S "NATIONAL PRETEND-YOU'RE-NOT-STUPID DAY"
© 1998 PAWS, INC./Distributed by Universal Press Syndicate
www.garfield.com
JIM DAVIS 11-17

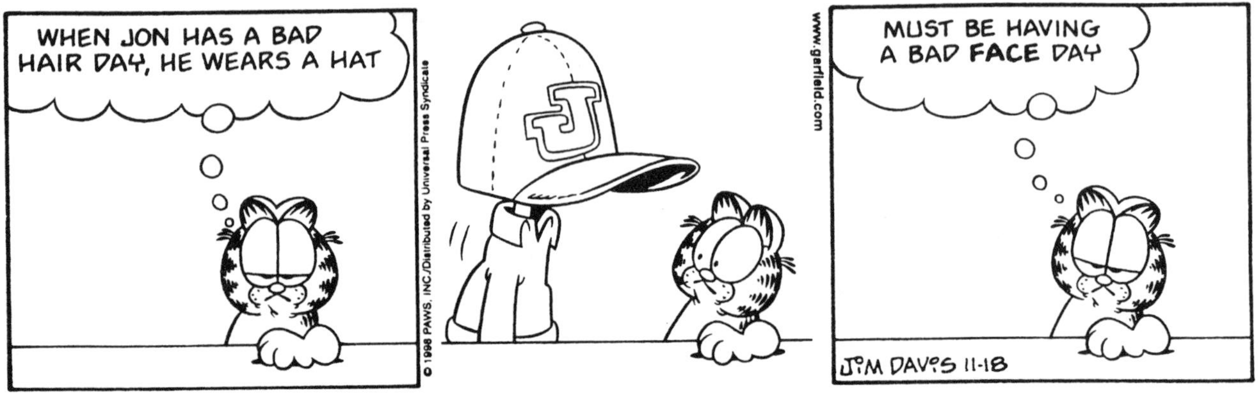
WHEN JON HAS A BAD HAIR DAY, HE WEARS A HAT
© 1998 PAWS, INC./Distributed by Universal Press Syndicate
www.garfield.com
MUST BE HAVING A BAD FACE DAY
JIM DAVIS 11-18

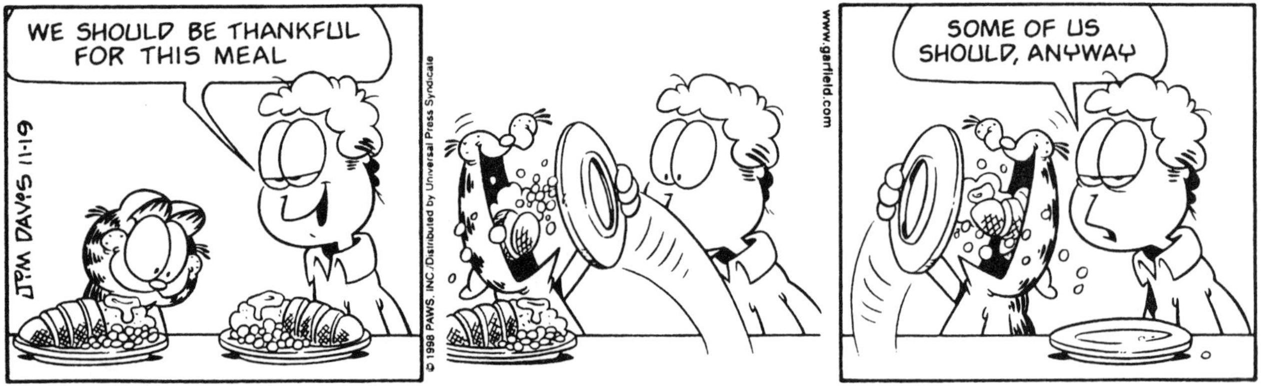
WE SHOULD BE THANKFUL FOR THIS MEAL
JIM DAVIS 11-19
© 1998 PAWS, INC./Distributed by Universal Press Syndicate
www.garfield.com
SOME OF US SHOULD, ANYWAY

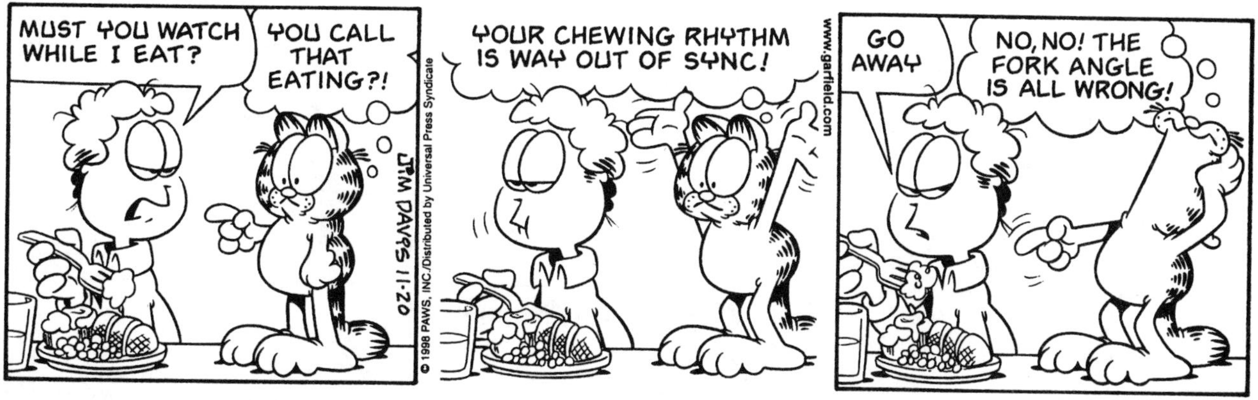
MUST YOU WATCH WHILE I EAT?
YOU CALL THAT EATING?!
JIM DAVIS 11-20
© 1998 PAWS, INC./Distributed by Universal Press Syndicate
YOUR CHEWING RHYTHM IS WAY OUT OF SYNC!
www.garfield.com
GO AWAY
NO, NO! THE FORK ANGLE IS ALL WRONG!

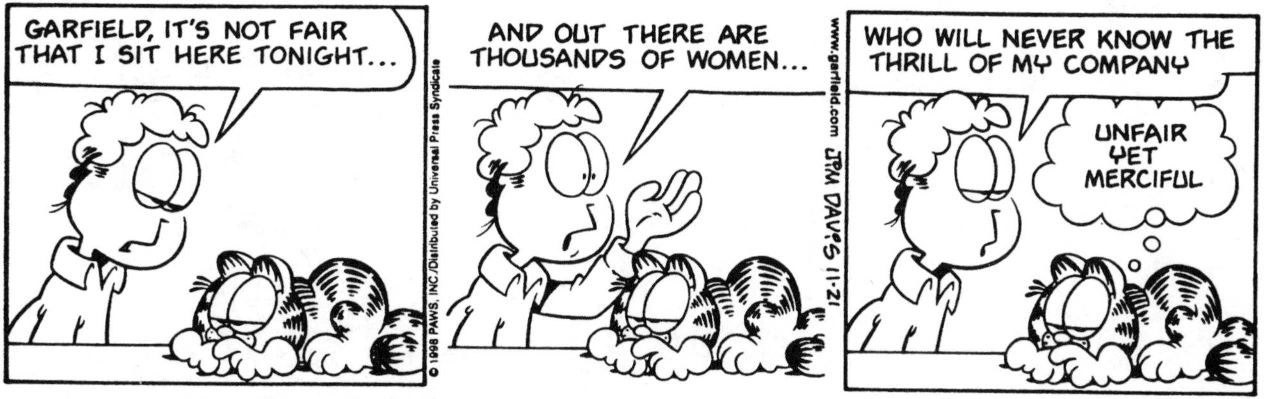
GARFIELD, IT'S NOT FAIR THAT I SIT HERE TONIGHT...
© 1998 PAWS, INC./Distributed by Universal Press Syndicate
AND OUT THERE ARE THOUSANDS OF WOMEN...
www.garfield.com
JIM DAVIS 11-21
WHO WILL NEVER KNOW THE THRILL OF MY COMPANY
UNFAIR YET MERCIFUL

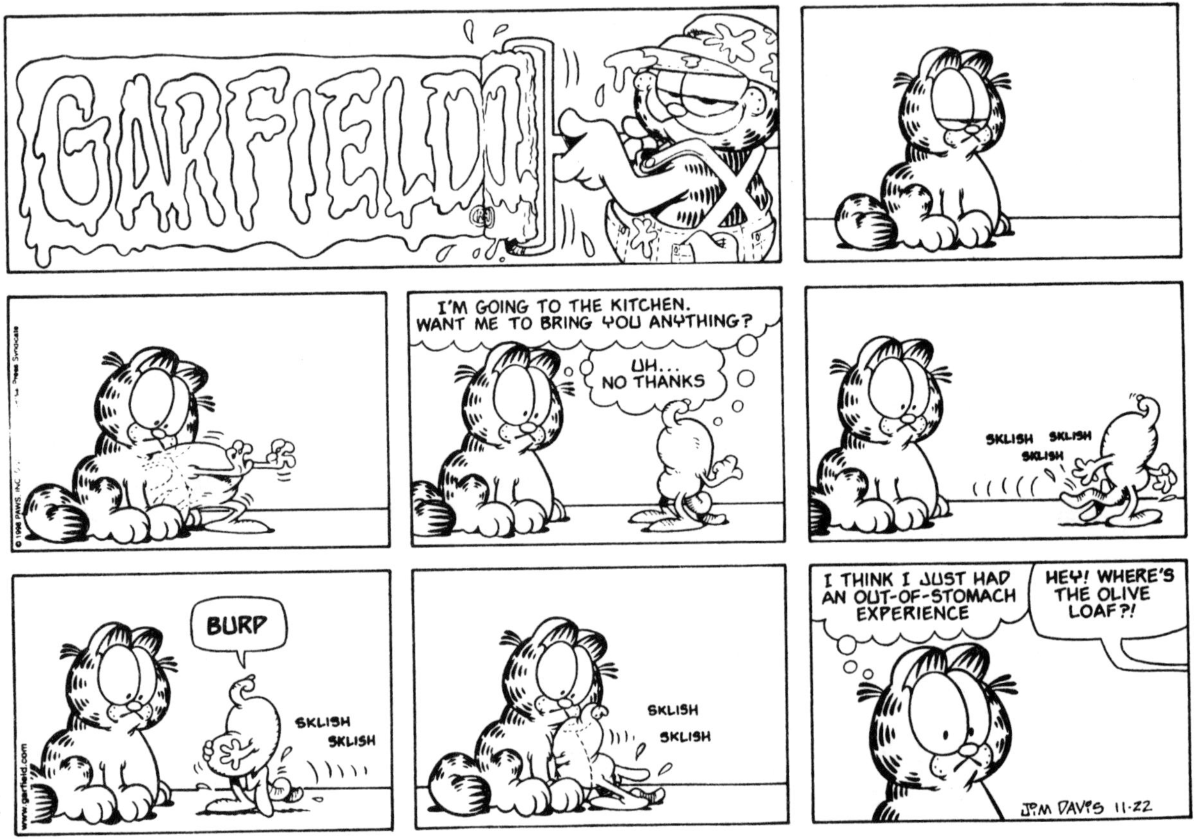
GARFIELD
I'M GOING TO THE KITCHEN. WANT ME TO BRING YOU ANYTHING?
UH... NO THANKS
SKLISH SKLISH SKLISH
BURP
SKLISH SKLISH
www.garfield.com
SKLISH SKLISH
I THINK I JUST HAD AN OUT-OF-STOMACH EXPERIENCE
HEY! WHERE'S THE OLIVE LOAF?!
JIM DAVIS 11-22

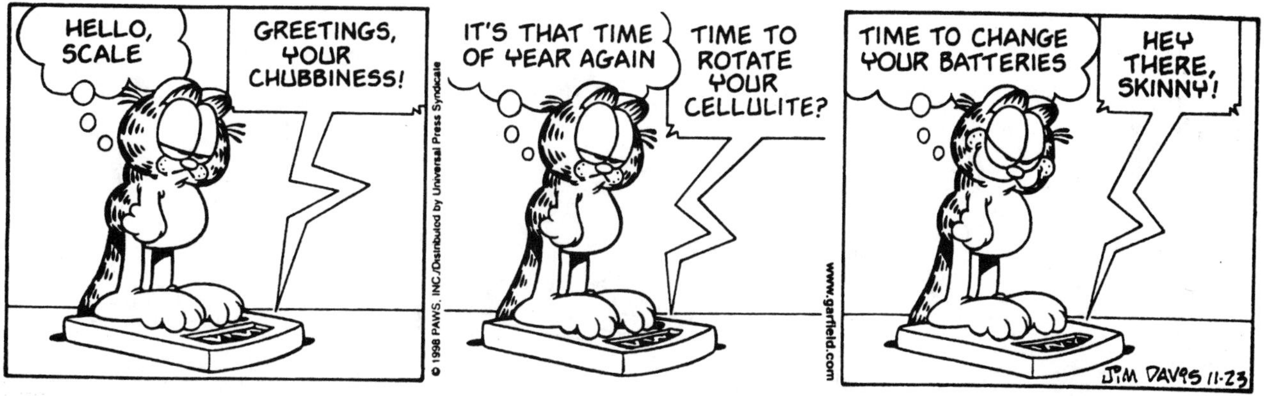
HELLO, SCALE
GREETINGS, YOUR CHUBBINESS!
IT'S THAT TIME OF YEAR AGAIN
TIME TO ROTATE YOUR CELLULITE?
TIME TO CHANGE YOUR BATTERIES
HEY THERE, SKINNY!
© 1998 PAWS, INC./Distributed by Universal Press Syndicate
www.garfield.com
JIM DAVIS 11-23

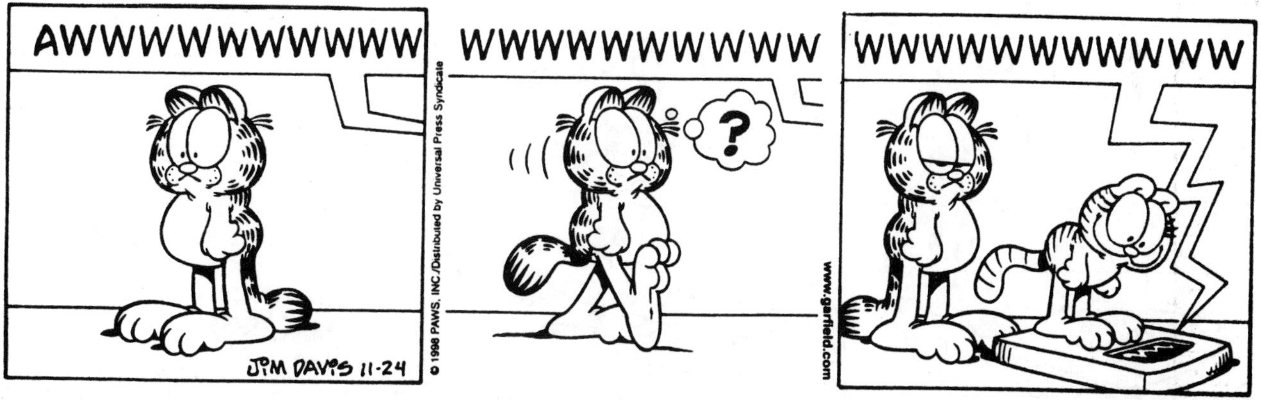
AWWWWWWWWWWW
WWWWWWWWWWWWW
?
WWWWWWWWWWWWWW
© 1998 PAWS, INC./Distributed by Universal Press Syndicate
www.garfield.com
JIM DAVIS 11-24

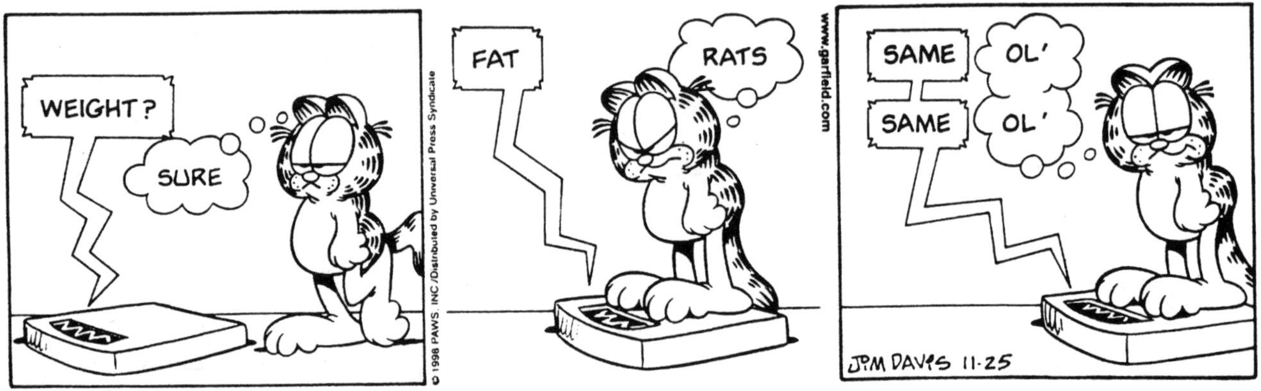
WEIGHT?
SURE
FAT
RATS
SAME
SAME
OL'
OL'
© 1998 PAWS, INC./Distributed by Universal Press Syndicate
www.garfield.com
JIM DAVIS 11-25

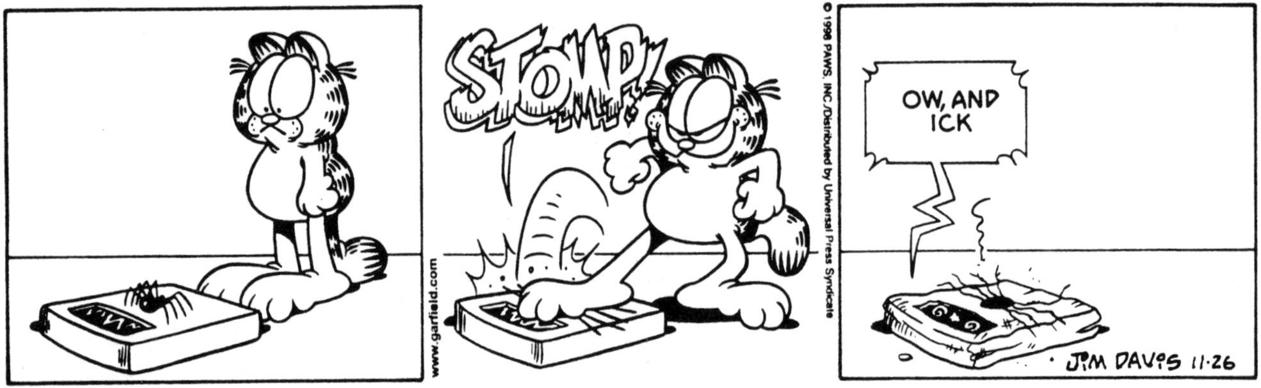
www.garfield.com
STOMP!
© 1998 PAWS, INC./Distributed by Universal Press Syndicate
OW, AND ICK
JIM DAVIS 11-26

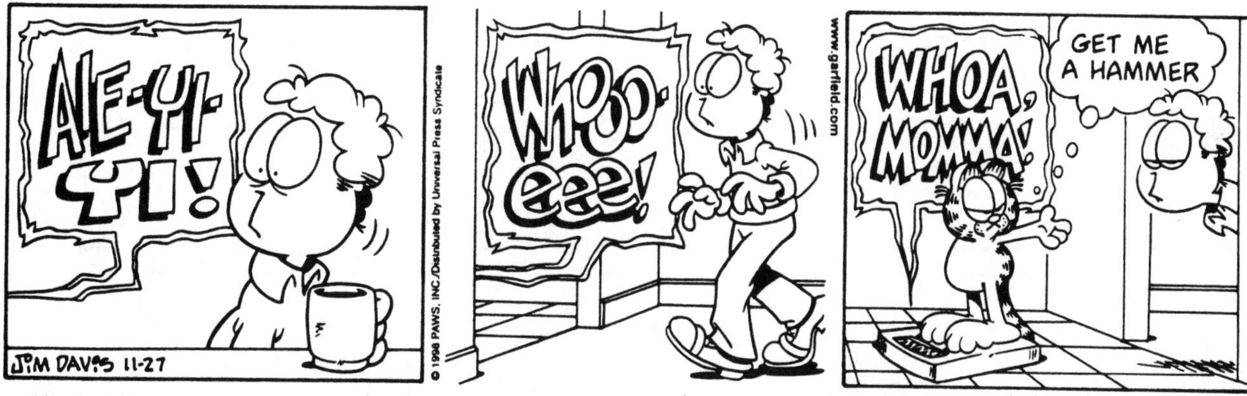
AIE-YI-YI!
JIM DAVIS 11-27
© 1998 PAWS, INC./Distributed by Universal Press Syndicate
WHOOO-EEE!
www.garfield.com
WHOA, MOMMA!
GET ME A HAMMER

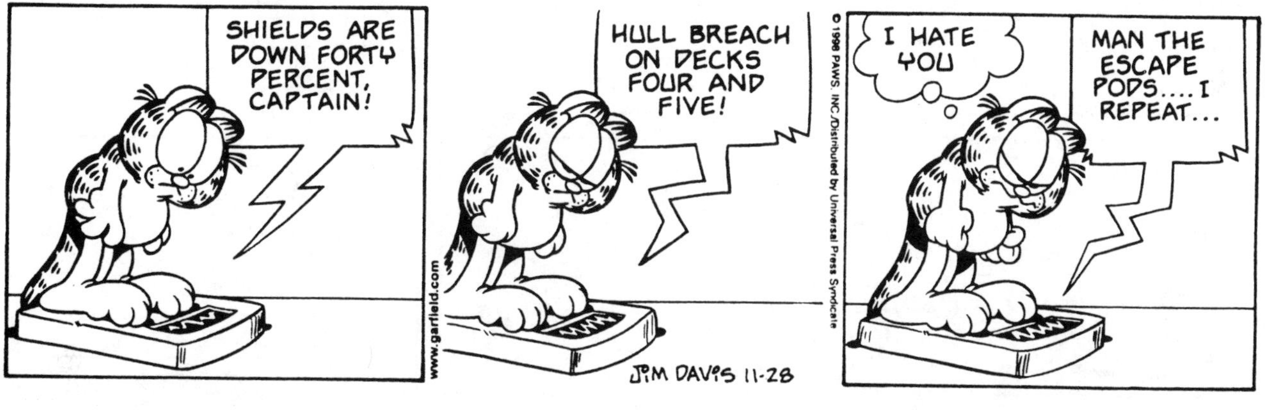
SHIELDS ARE DOWN FORTY PERCENT, CAPTAIN!
www.garfield.com
HULL BREACH ON DECKS FOUR AND FIVE!
JIM DAVIS 11-28
© 1998 PAWS, INC./Distributed by Universal Press Syndicate
I HATE YOU
MAN THE ESCAPE PODS.... I REPEAT...

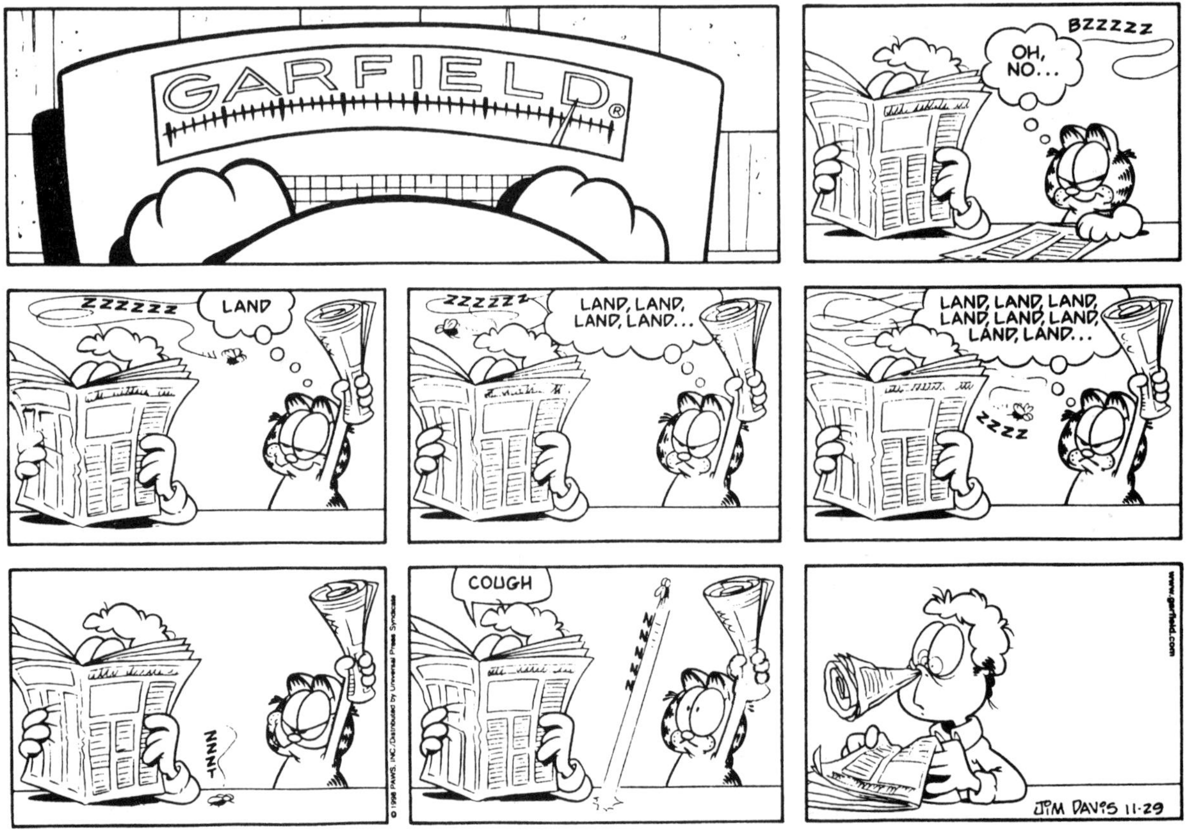

GARFIELD®
BZZZZZ
OH, NO...
ZZZZZZ
LAND
ZZZZZZ
LAND, LAND, LAND, LAND...
LAND, LAND, LAND, LAND, LAND, LAND, LAND, LAND...
ZZZZ
© 1998 PAWS, INC./Distributed by Universal Press Syndicate
COUGH
www.garfield.com
JIM DAVIS 11-29

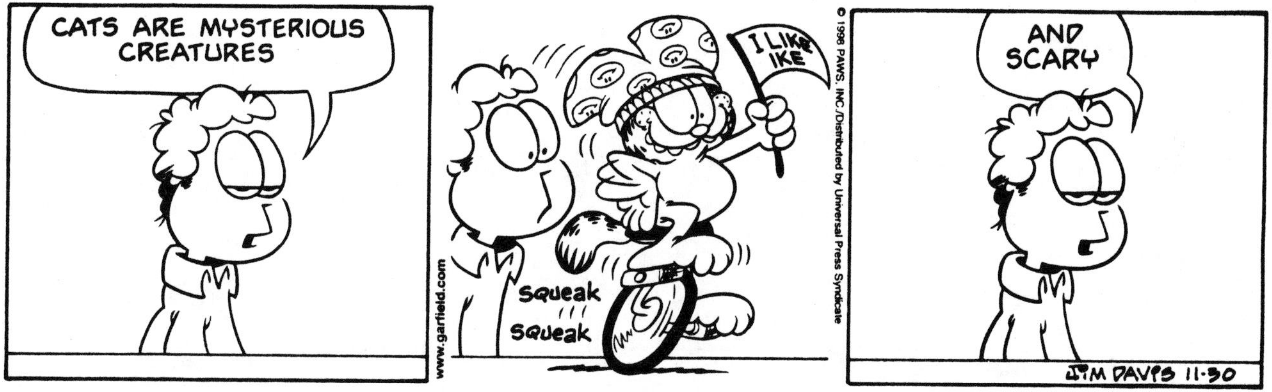
CATS ARE MYSTERIOUS CREATURES
I LIKE IKE
Squeak
Squeak
AND SCARY
www.garfield.com
© 1998 PAWS, INC./Distributed by Universal Press Syndicate
JIM DAVIS 11-30

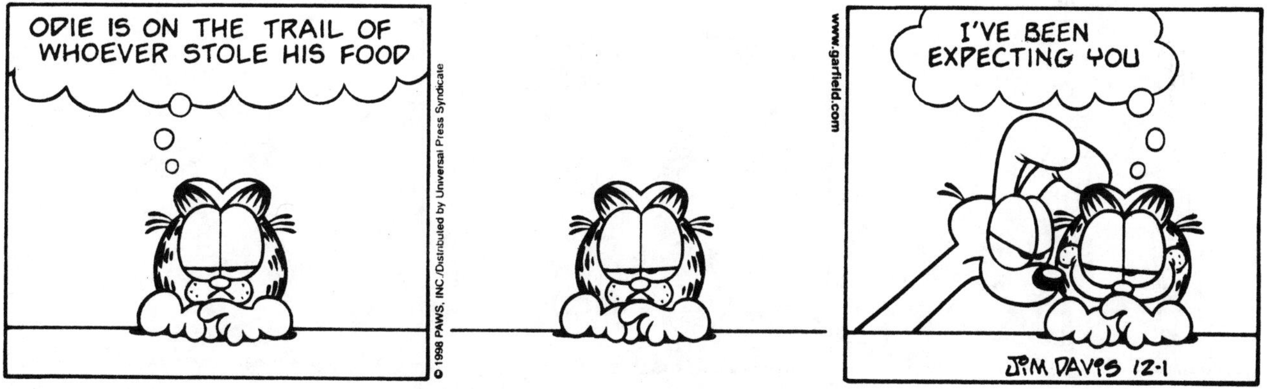
ODIE IS ON THE TRAIL OF WHOEVER STOLE HIS FOOD
I'VE BEEN EXPECTING YOU
© 1998 PAWS, INC./Distributed by Universal Press Syndicate
www.garfield.com
JIM DAVIS 12-1

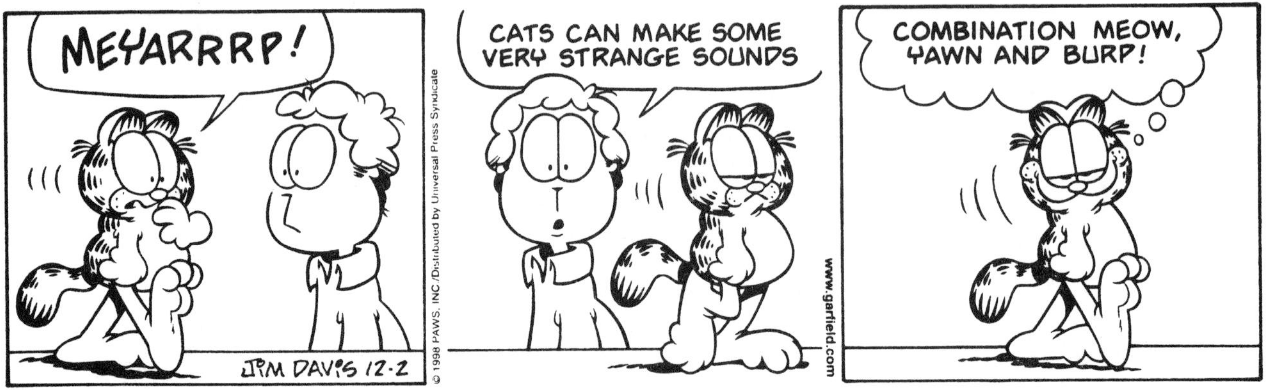
MEYARRRP!
JIM DAVIS 12-2
© 1998 PAWS, INC./Distributed by Universal Press Syndicate
CATS CAN MAKE SOME VERY STRANGE SOUNDS
www.garfield.com
COMBINATION MEOW, YAWN AND BURP!

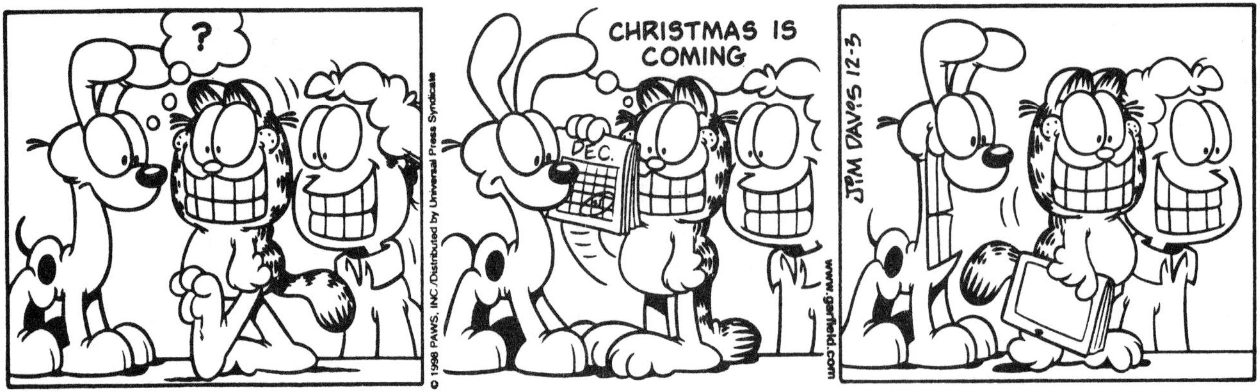
?
© 1998 PAWS, INC./Distributed by Universal Press Syndicate
CHRISTMAS IS COMING
DEC.
www.garfield.com
JIM DAVIS 12-3

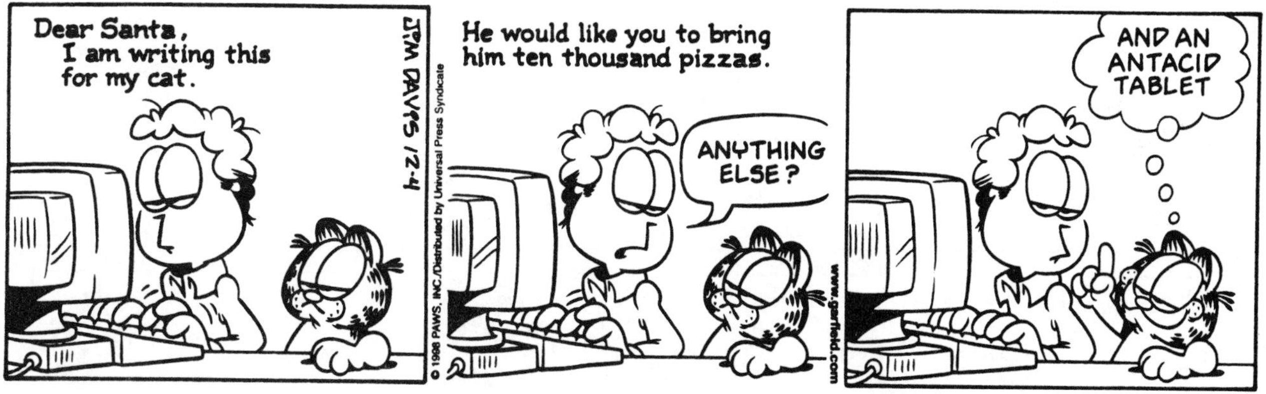
Dear Santa,
I am writing this for my cat.
JIM DAVIS 12-4
© 1998 PAWS, INC./Distributed by Universal Press Syndicate
He would like you to bring him ten thousand pizzas.
ANYTHING ELSE?
www.garfield.com
AND AN ANTACID TABLET

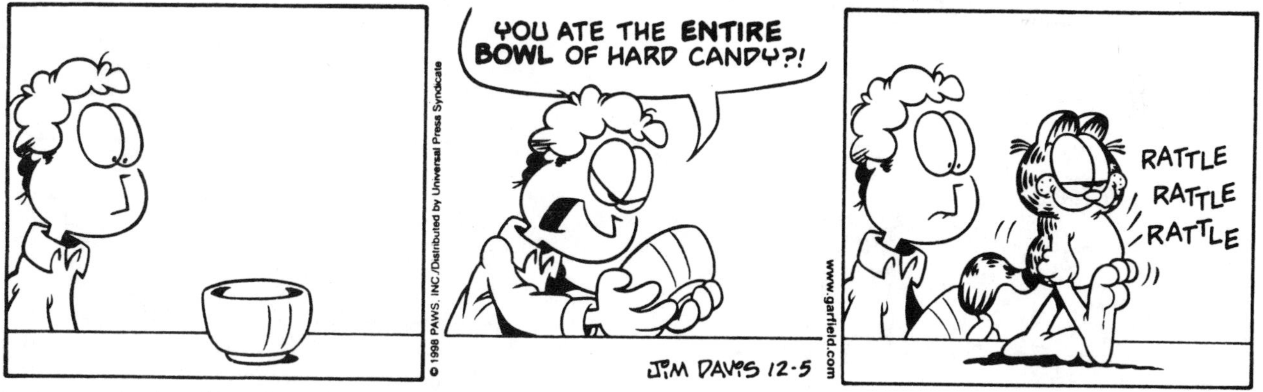
© 1998 PAWS, INC./Distributed by Universal Press Syndicate
YOU ATE THE ENTIRE BOWL OF HARD CANDY?!
JIM DAVIS 12-5
www.garfield.com
RATTLE
RATTLE
RATTLE

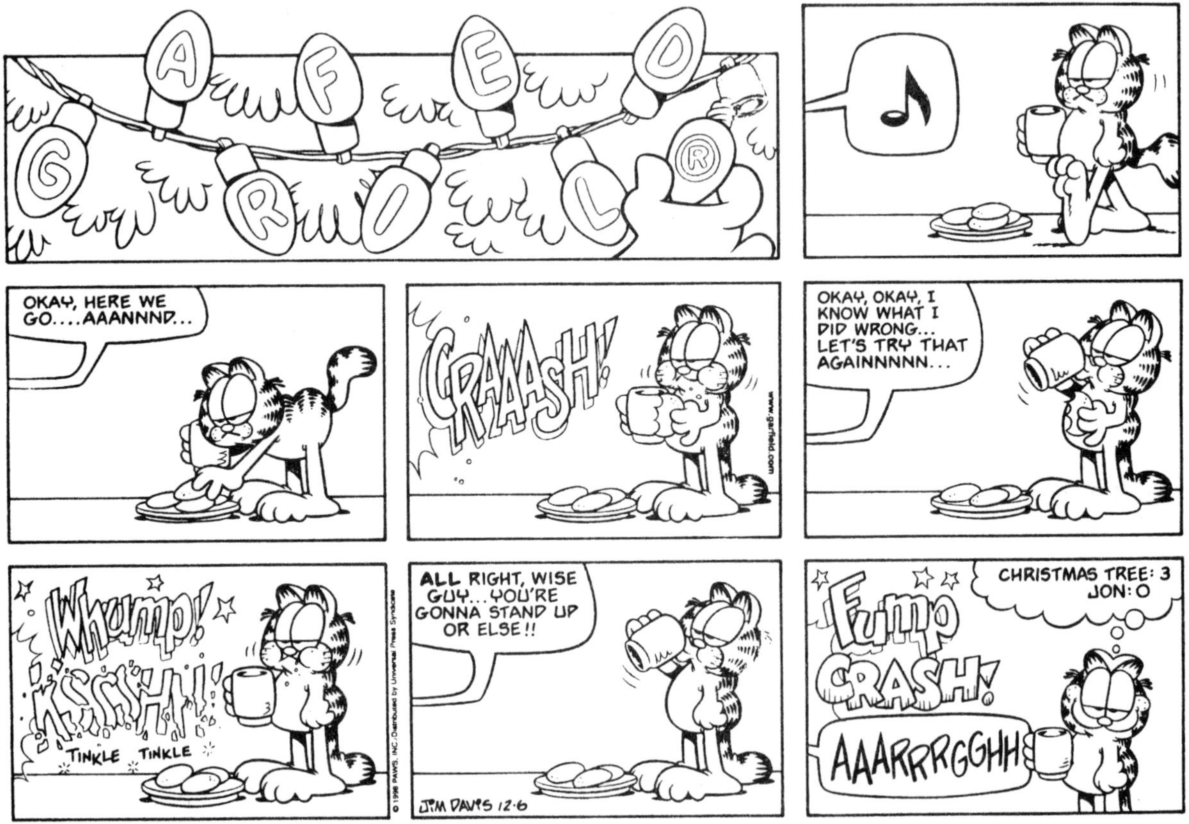
GARFIELD®
♪
OKAY, HERE WE GO....AAANNND...
CRAAASH!
www.garfield.com
OKAY, OKAY, I KNOW WHAT I DID WRONG... LET'S TRY THAT AGAINNNNN...
Whump!
KSSSHH!!
TINKLE TINKLE
© 1998 PAWS, INC./Distributed by Universal Press Syndicate
ALL RIGHT, WISE GUY... YOU'RE GONNA STAND UP OR ELSE!!
JIM DAVIS 12·6
Fump
CRASH!
AAARRRGGHH
CHRISTMAS TREE: 3
JON: 0

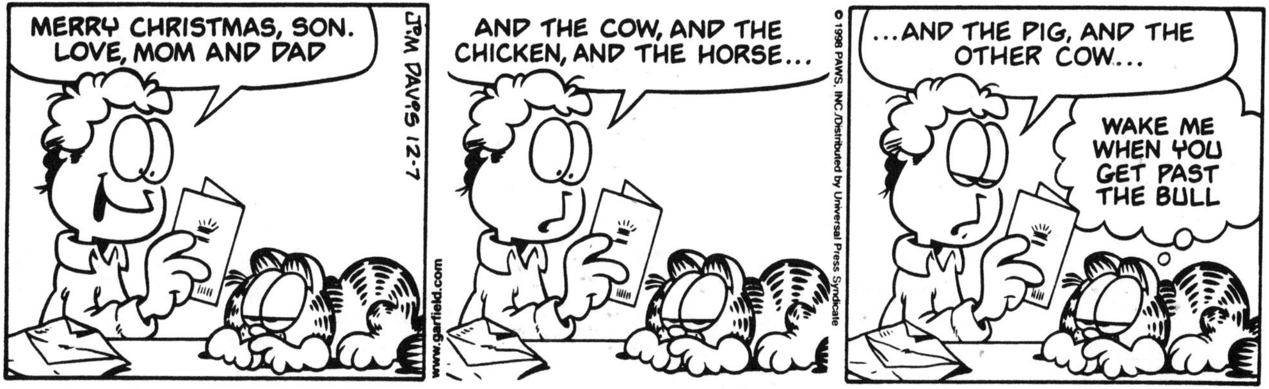
MERRY CHRISTMAS, SON. LOVE, MOM AND DAD
JIM DAVIS 12-7
www.garfield.com
AND THE COW, AND THE CHICKEN, AND THE HORSE...
© 1998 PAWS, INC./Distributed by Universal Press Syndicate
...AND THE PIG, AND THE OTHER COW...
WAKE ME WHEN YOU GET PAST THE BULL

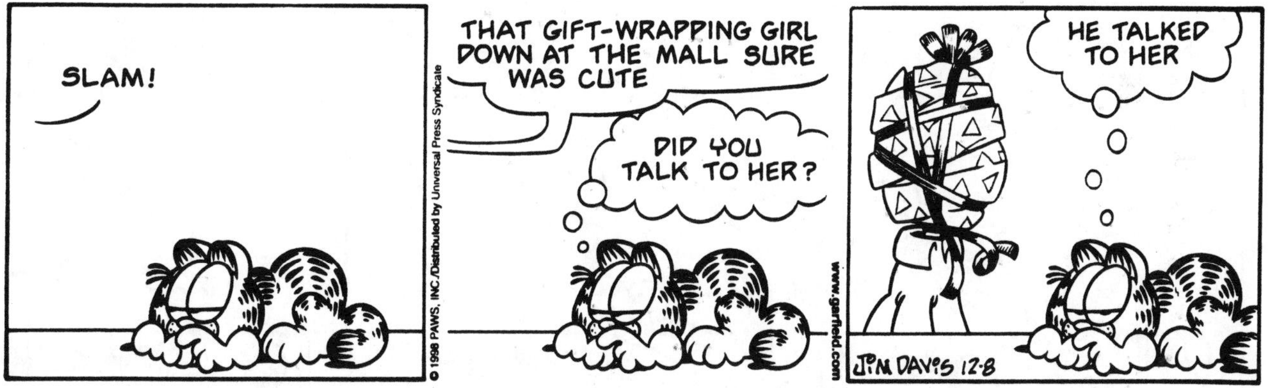
SLAM!
© 1998 PAWS, INC./Distributed by Universal Press Syndicate
THAT GIFT-WRAPPING GIRL DOWN AT THE MALL SURE WAS CUTE
DID YOU TALK TO HER?
www.garfield.com
HE TALKED TO HER
JIM DAVIS 12-8

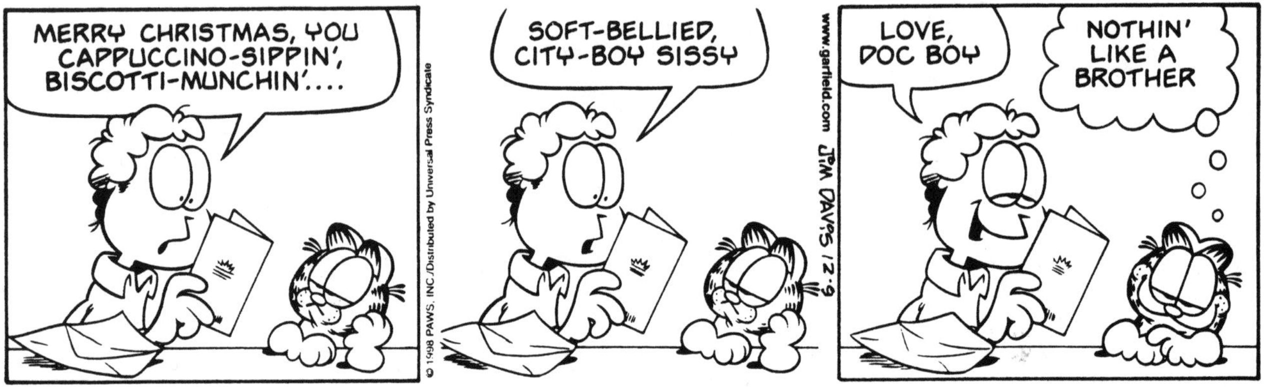
MERRY CHRISTMAS, YOU CAPPUCCINO-SIPPIN', BISCOTTI-MUNCHIN'....
SOFT-BELLIED, CITY-BOY SISSY
LOVE, DOC BOY
NOTHIN' LIKE A BROTHER
© 1998 PAWS, INC./Distributed by Universal Press Syndicate
www.garfield.com
JIM DAVIS 12-9

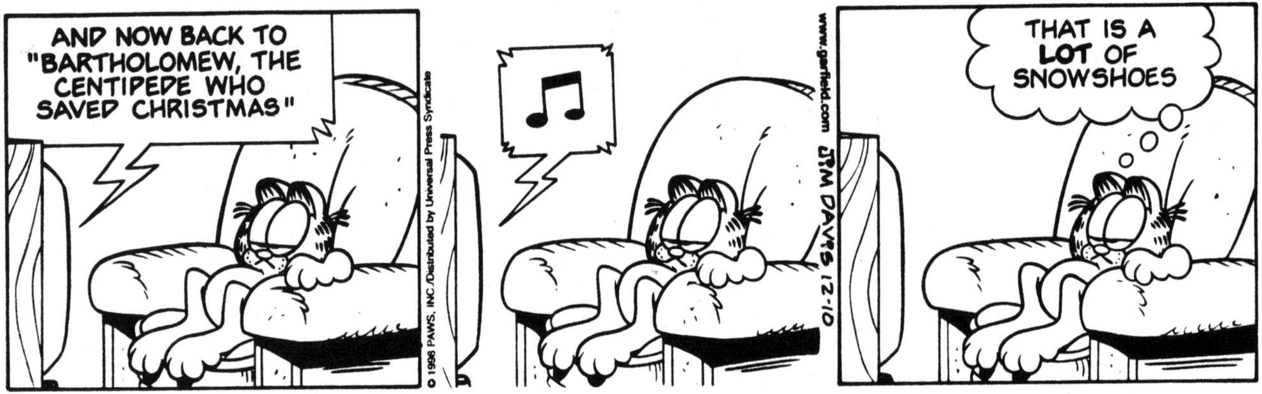
AND NOW BACK TO "BARTHOLOMEW, THE CENTIPEDE WHO SAVED CHRISTMAS"
THAT IS A LOT OF SNOWSHOES
© 1998 PAWS, INC./Distributed by Universal Press Syndicate
www.garfield.com
JIM DAVIS 12-10

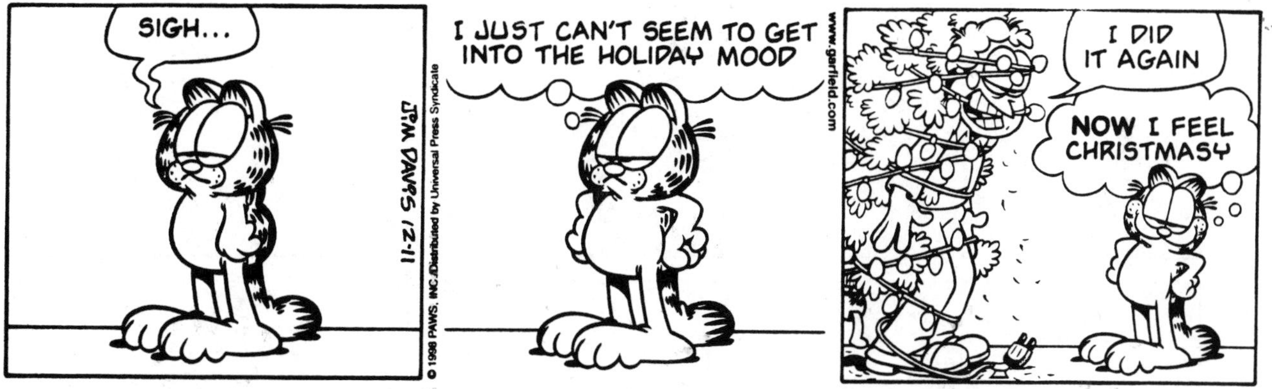
SIGH...
I JUST CAN'T SEEM TO GET INTO THE HOLIDAY MOOD
I DID IT AGAIN
NOW I FEEL CHRISTMASY
JIM DAVIS 12-11
© 1998 PAWS, INC./Distributed by Universal Press Syndicate
www.garfield.com

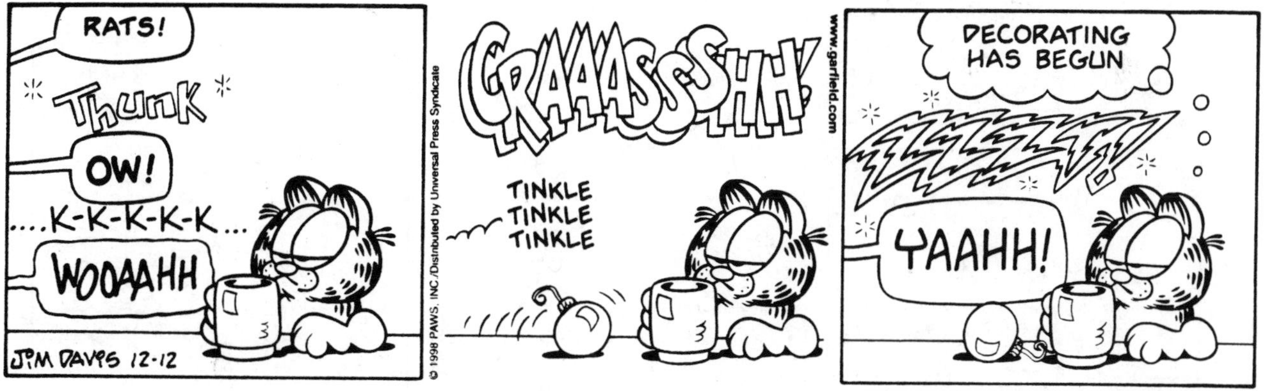
RATS!
Thunk
OW!
....K-K-K-K-K...
WOOAAHH
CRAAASSSHH
TINKLE
TINKLE
TINKLE
DECORATING HAS BEGUN
YAAHH!
JIM DAVIS 12-12
© 1998 PAWS, INC./Distributed by Universal Press Syndicate
www.garfield.com

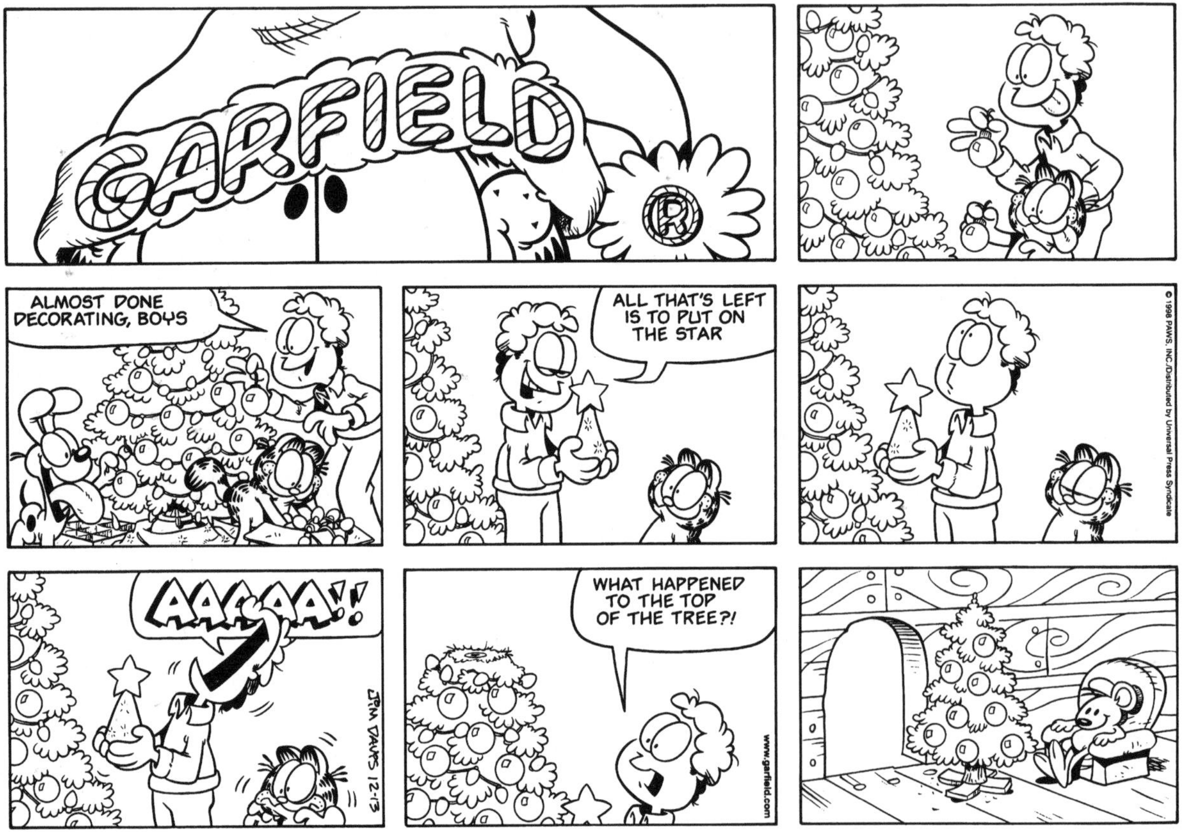
GARFIELD®
ALMOST DONE DECORATING, BOYS
ALL THAT'S LEFT IS TO PUT ON THE STAR
© 1998 PAWS, INC./Distributed by Universal Press Syndicate
AAGAA!!
JIM DAVIS 12-13
WHAT HAPPENED TO THE TOP OF THE TREE?!
www.garfield.com

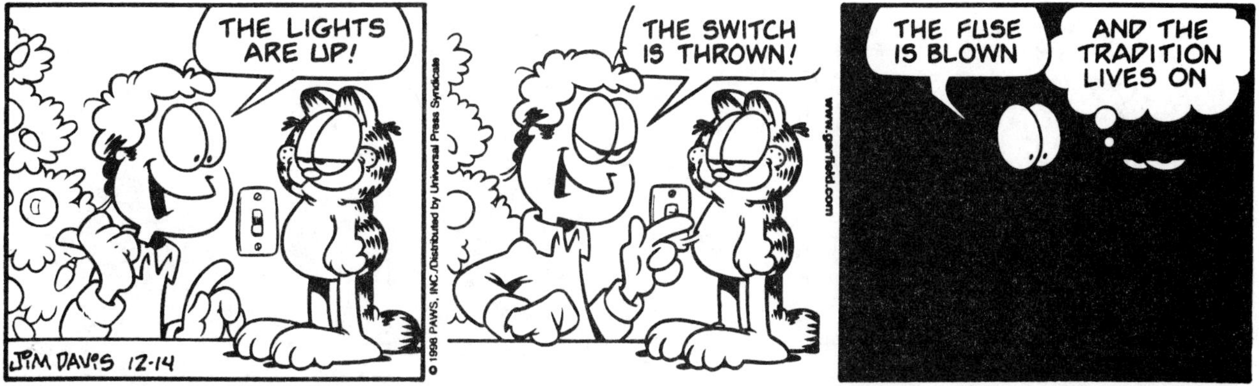
THE LIGHTS ARE UP!
THE SWITCH IS THROWN!
THE FUSE IS BLOWN
AND THE TRADITION LIVES ON
JIM DAVIS 12-14
© 1998 PAWS, INC./Distributed by Universal Press Syndicate
www.garfield.com

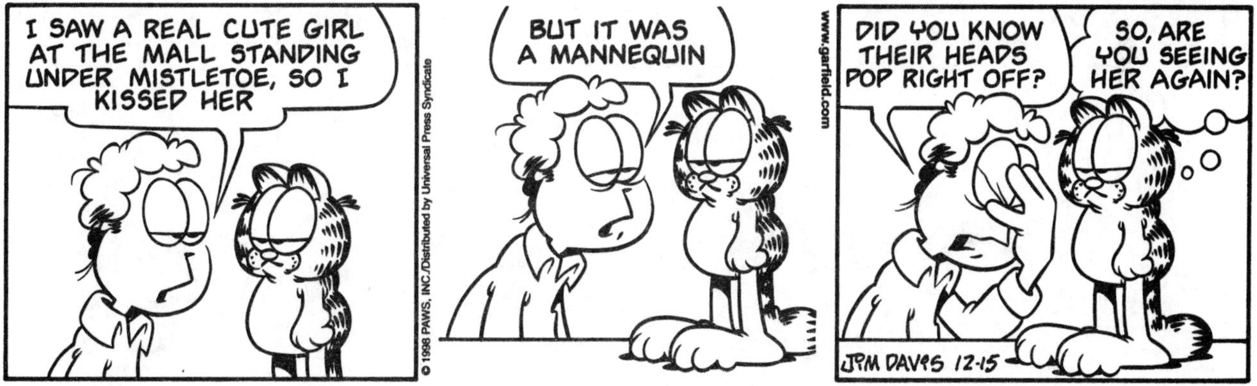
I SAW A REAL CUTE GIRL AT THE MALL STANDING UNDER MISTLETOE, SO I KISSED HER
BUT IT WAS A MANNEQUIN
DID YOU KNOW THEIR HEADS POP RIGHT OFF?
SO, ARE YOU SEEING HER AGAIN?
JIM DAVIS 12-15
© 1998 PAWS, INC./Distributed by Universal Press Syndicate
www.garfield.com

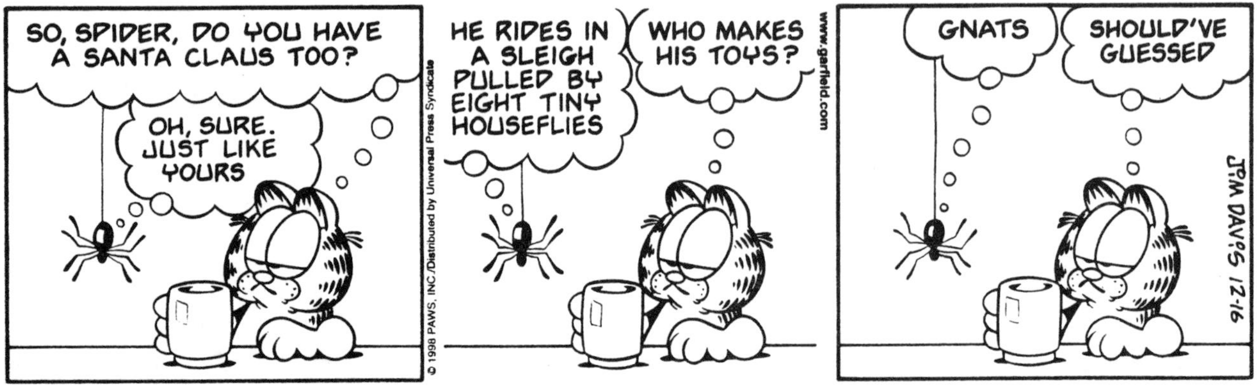
SO, SPIDER, DO YOU HAVE A SANTA CLAUS TOO?
OH, SURE. JUST LIKE YOURS
HE RIDES IN A SLEIGH PULLED BY EIGHT TINY HOUSEFLIES
WHO MAKES HIS TOYS?
GNATS
SHOULD'VE GUESSED
© 1998 PAWS, INC./Distributed by Universal Press Syndicate
www.garfield.com
JIM DAVIS 12-16

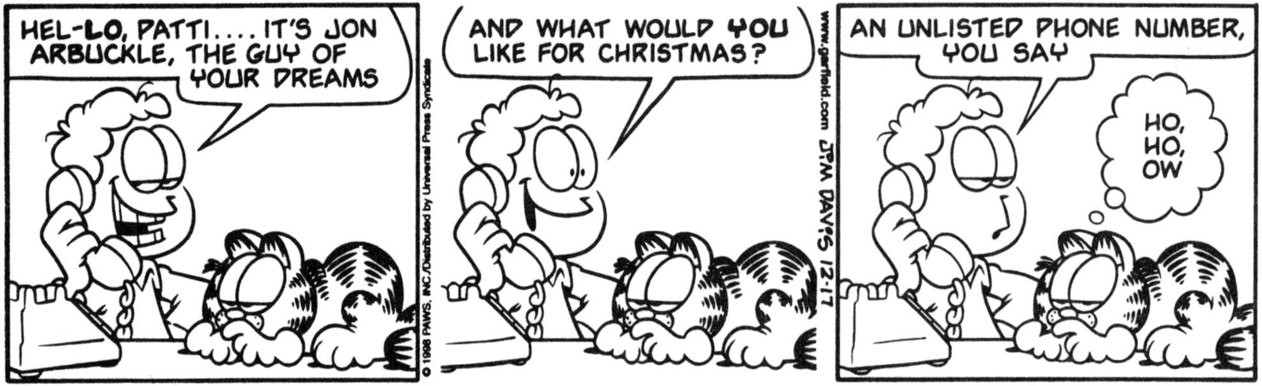
HEL-**LO**, PATTI.... IT'S JON ARBUCKLE, THE GUY OF YOUR DREAMS
AND WHAT WOULD **YOU** LIKE FOR CHRISTMAS?
AN UNLISTED PHONE NUMBER, YOU SAY
HO, HO, OW
© 1998 PAWS, INC./Distributed by Universal Press Syndicate
www.garfield.com
JIM DAVIS 12-17

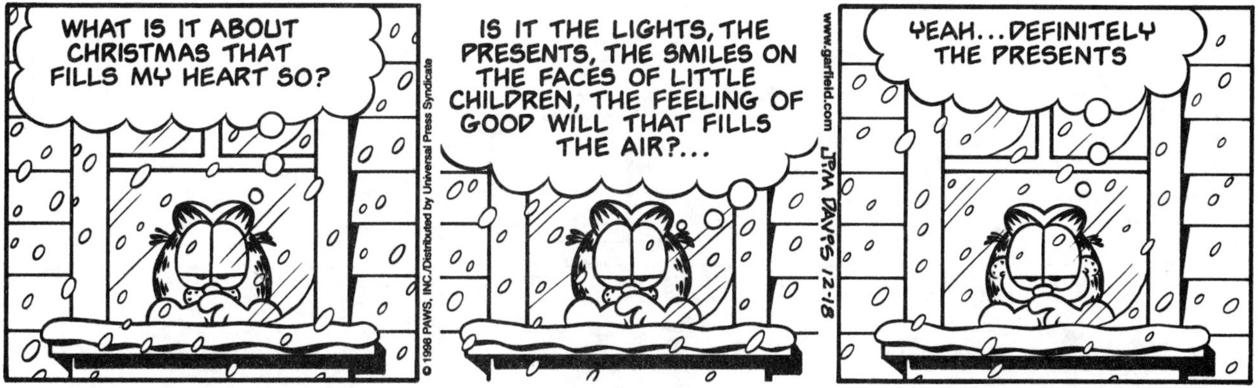
WHAT IS IT ABOUT CHRISTMAS THAT FILLS MY HEART SO?
© 1998 PAWS, INC./Distributed by Universal Press Syndicate
IS IT THE LIGHTS, THE PRESENTS, THE SMILES ON THE FACES OF LITTLE CHILDREN, THE FEELING OF GOOD WILL THAT FILLS THE AIR?...
www.garfield.com
JIM DAVIS 12-18
YEAH...DEFINITELY THE PRESENTS

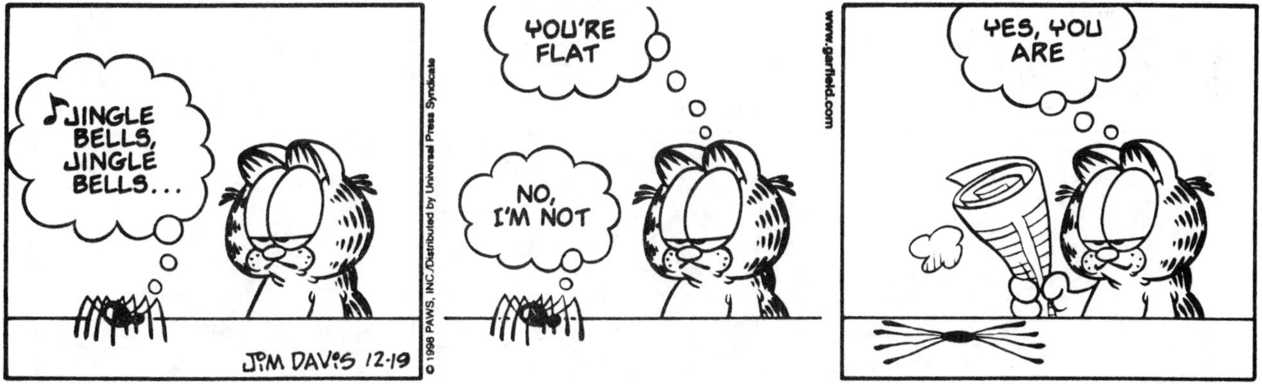
♪JINGLE BELLS, JINGLE BELLS...
JIM DAVIS 12-19
© 1998 PAWS, INC./Distributed by Universal Press Syndicate
YOU'RE FLAT
NO, I'M NOT
www.garfield.com
YES, YOU ARE

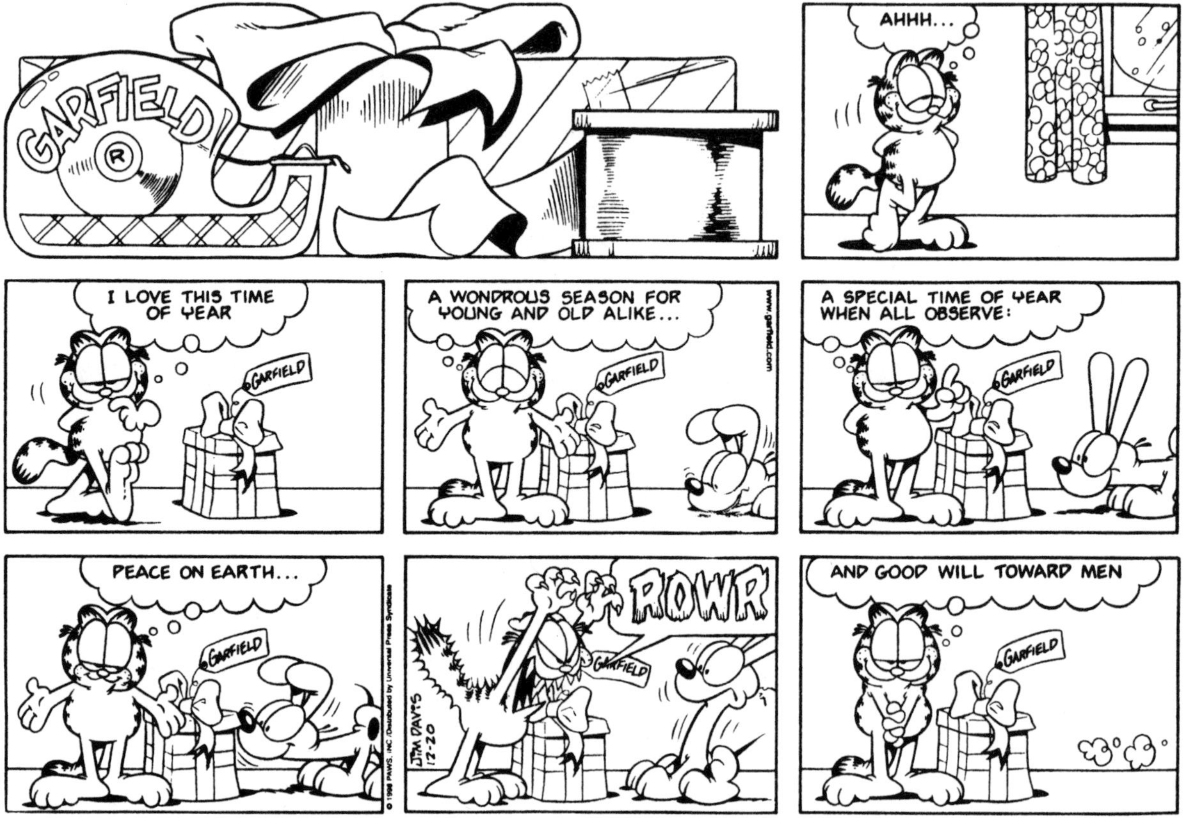
GARFIELD ®
AHHH...
I LOVE THIS TIME OF YEAR
GARFIELD
A WONDROUS SEASON FOR YOUNG AND OLD ALIKE...
GARFIELD
www.garfield.com
A SPECIAL TIME OF YEAR WHEN ALL OBSERVE:
GARFIELD
PEACE ON EARTH...
GARFIELD
© 1998 PAWS, INC./Distributed by Universal Press Syndicate
JIM DAVIS 12-20
ROWR
GARFIELD
AND GOOD WILL TOWARD MEN
GARFIELD

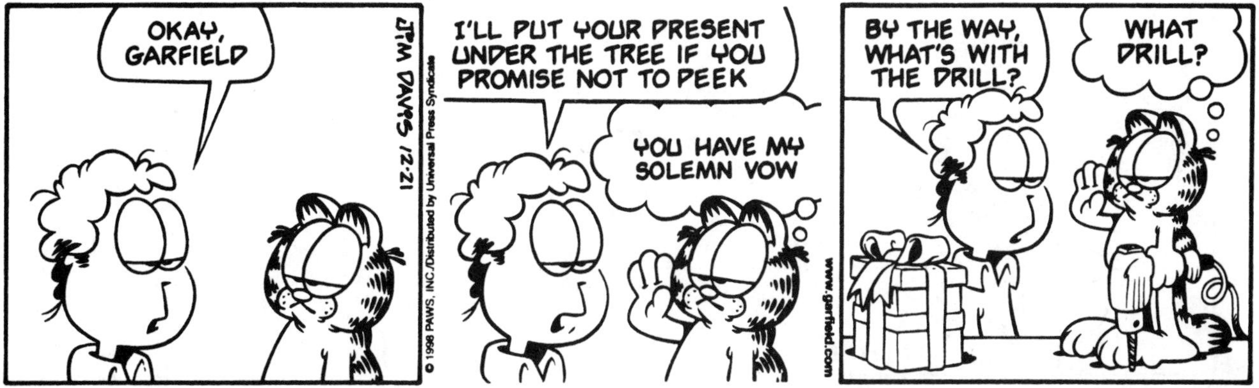
OKAY, GARFIELD
JIM DAVIS 12-21
© 1998 PAWS, INC./Distributed by Universal Press Syndicate
I'LL PUT YOUR PRESENT UNDER THE TREE IF YOU PROMISE NOT TO PEEK
YOU HAVE MY SOLEMN VOW
www.garfield.com
BY THE WAY, WHAT'S WITH THE DRILL?
WHAT DRILL?

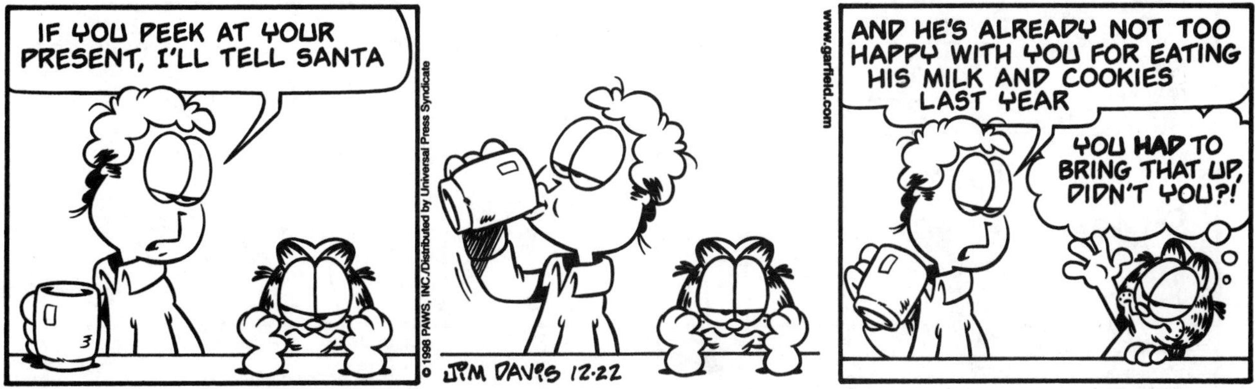
IF YOU PEEK AT YOUR PRESENT, I'LL TELL SANTA
© 1998 PAWS, INC./Distributed by Universal Press Syndicate
JIM DAVIS 12-22
www.garfield.com
AND HE'S ALREADY NOT TOO HAPPY WITH YOU FOR EATING HIS MILK AND COOKIES LAST YEAR
YOU HAD TO BRING THAT UP, DIDN'T YOU?!

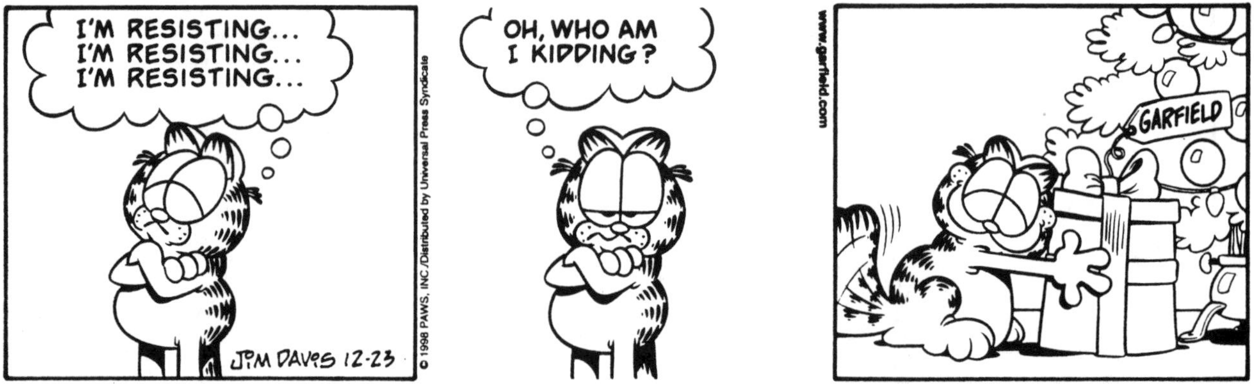
I'M RESISTING... I'M RESISTING... I'M RESISTING...
JIM DAVIS 12-23
© 1998 PAWS, INC./Distributed by Universal Press Syndicate
OH, WHO AM I KIDDING?
www.garfield.com
GARFIELD

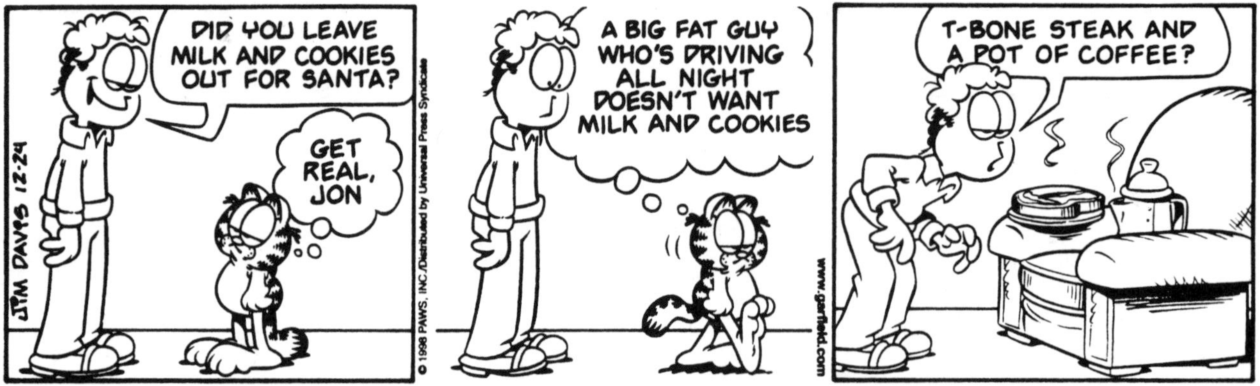
JIM DAVIS 12-24
DID YOU LEAVE MILK AND COOKIES OUT FOR SANTA?
GET REAL, JON
© 1998 PAWS, INC./Distributed by Universal Press Syndicate
A BIG FAT GUY WHO'S DRIVING ALL NIGHT DOESN'T WANT MILK AND COOKIES
www.garfield.com
T-BONE STEAK AND A POT OF COFFEE?

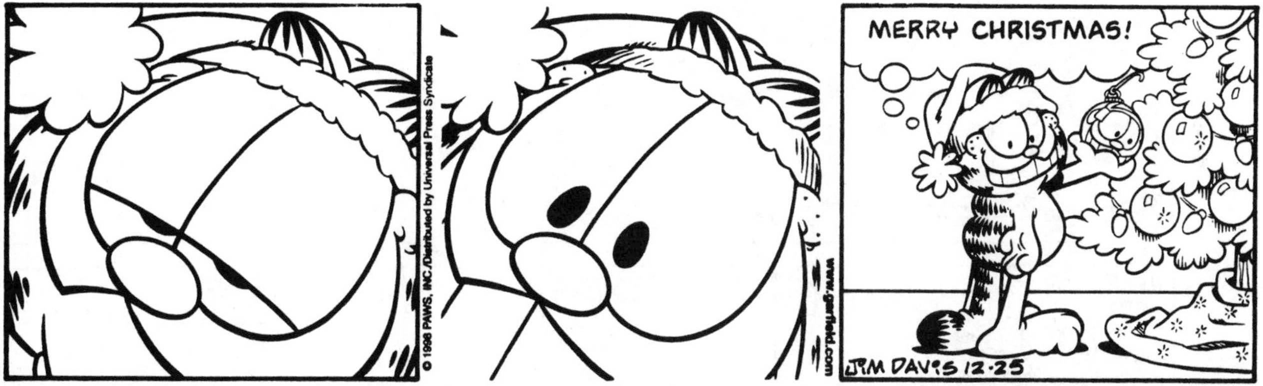

© 1998 PAWS, INC./Distributed by Universal Press Syndicate
www.garfield.com
MERRY CHRISTMAS!
JIM DAVIS 12-25

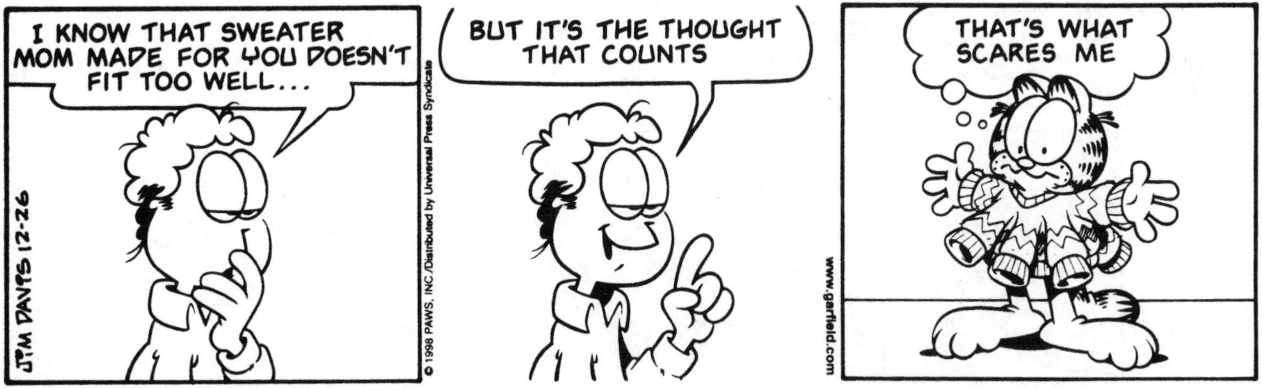

I KNOW THAT SWEATER MOM MADE FOR YOU DOESN'T FIT TOO WELL...
JIM DAVIS 12-26
© 1998 PAWS, INC./Distributed by Universal Press Syndicate
BUT IT'S THE THOUGHT THAT COUNTS
www.garfield.com
THAT'S WHAT SCARES ME

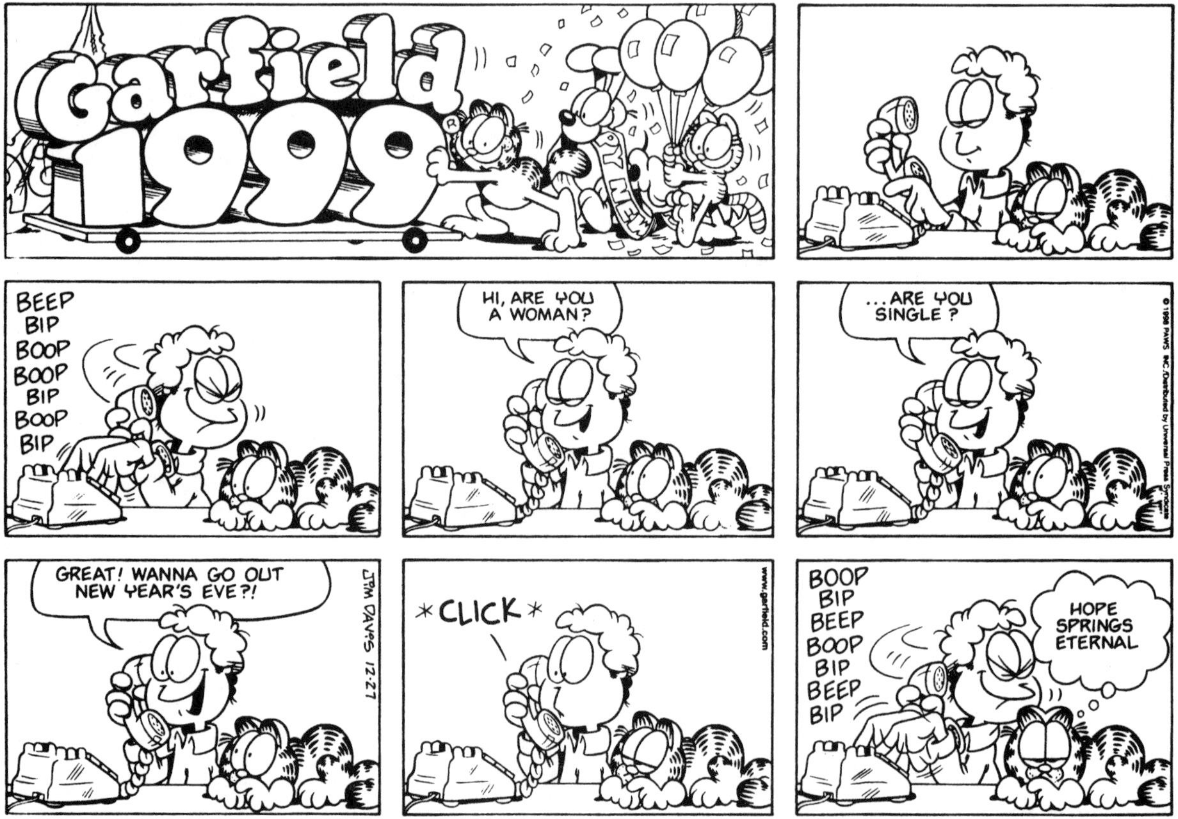

Garfield 1999
BEEP BIP BOOP BOOP BIP BOOP BIP
HI, ARE YOU A WOMAN?
...ARE YOU SINGLE?
© 1998 PAWS INC./Distributed by Universal Press Syndicate
GREAT! WANNA GO OUT NEW YEAR'S EVE?!
JPM DAVIS 12-27
CLICK
www.garfield.com
BOOP BIP BEEP BOOP BIP BEEP BIP
HOPE SPRINGS ETERNAL

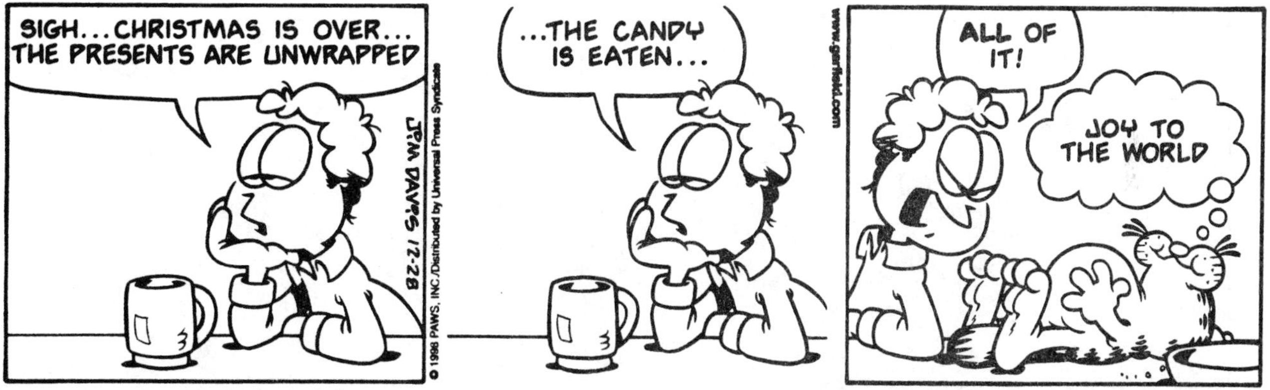
SIGH...CHRISTMAS IS OVER... THE PRESENTS ARE UNWRAPPED
JIM DAVIS 12-28
© 1998 PAWS, INC./Distributed by Universal Press Syndicate
...THE CANDY IS EATEN...
www.garfield.com
ALL OF IT!
JOY TO THE WORLD

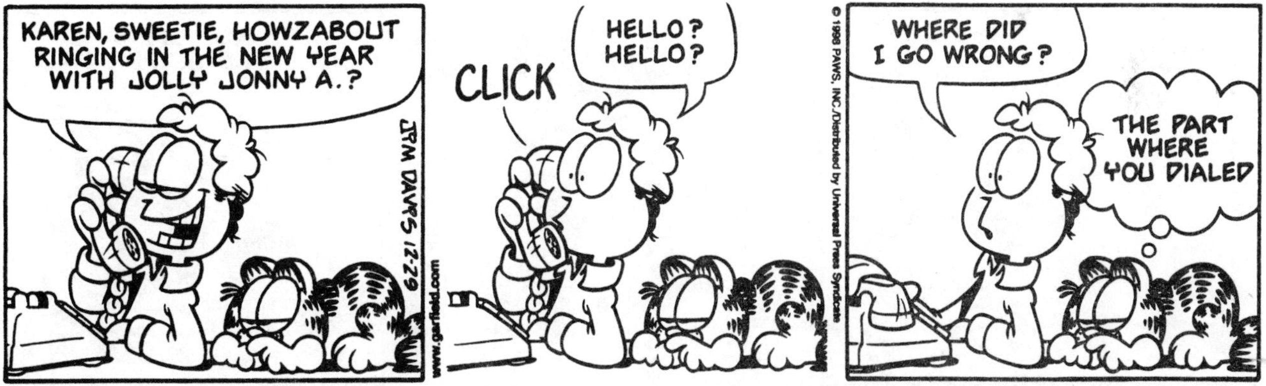
KAREN, SWEETIE, HOWZABOUT RINGING IN THE NEW YEAR WITH JOLLY JONNY A.?
JIM DAVIS 12-29
www.garfield.com
CLICK
HELLO? HELLO?
© 1998 PAWS, INC./Distributed by Universal Press Syndicate
WHERE DID I GO WRONG?
THE PART WHERE YOU DIALED

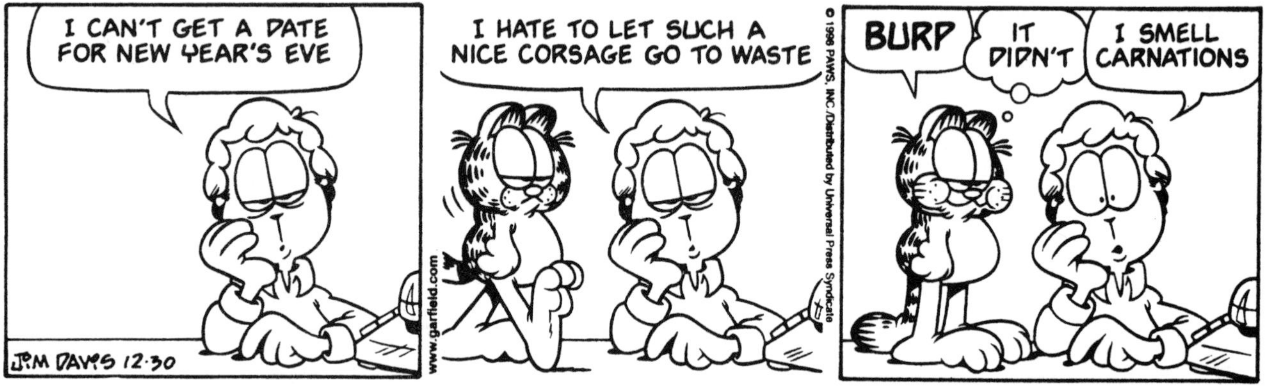
I CAN'T GET A DATE FOR NEW YEAR'S EVE
JIM DAVIS 12-30
www.garfield.com
I HATE TO LET SUCH A NICE CORSAGE GO TO WASTE
© 1998 PAWS, INC./Distributed by Universal Press Syndicate
BURP
IT DIDN'T
I SMELL CARNATIONS

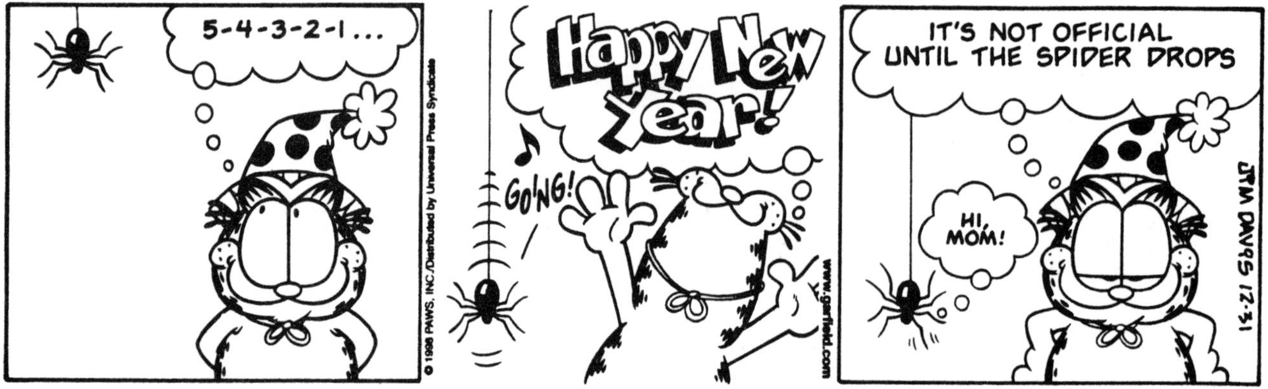
5-4-3-2-1...
© 1998 PAWS, INC./Distributed by Universal Press Syndicate
Happy New Year!
GONG!
www.garfield.com
IT'S NOT OFFICIAL UNTIL THE SPIDER DROPS
HI, MOM!
JIM DAVIS 12-31

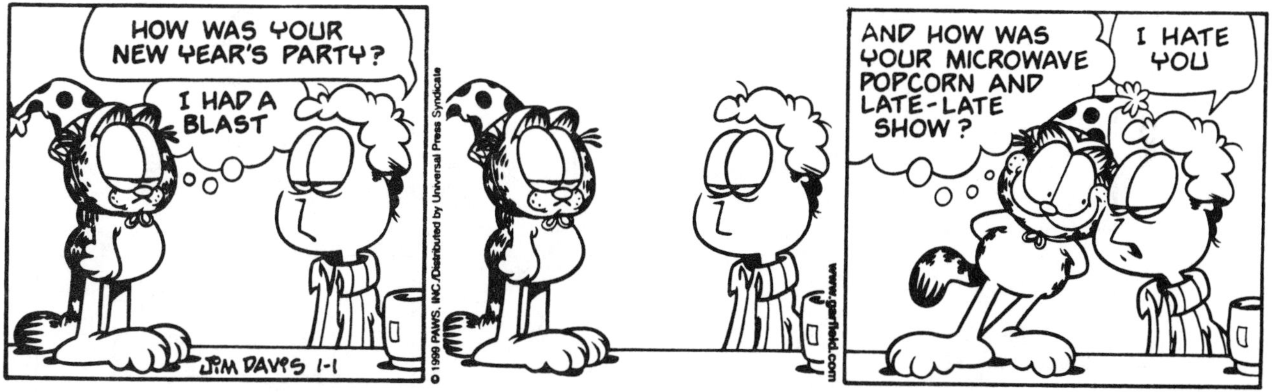
HOW WAS YOUR NEW YEAR'S PARTY?
I HAD A BLAST
JIM DAVIS 1-1
© 1999 PAWS, INC./Distributed by Universal Press Syndicate
www.garfield.com
AND HOW WAS YOUR MICROWAVE POPCORN AND LATE-LATE SHOW?
I HATE YOU

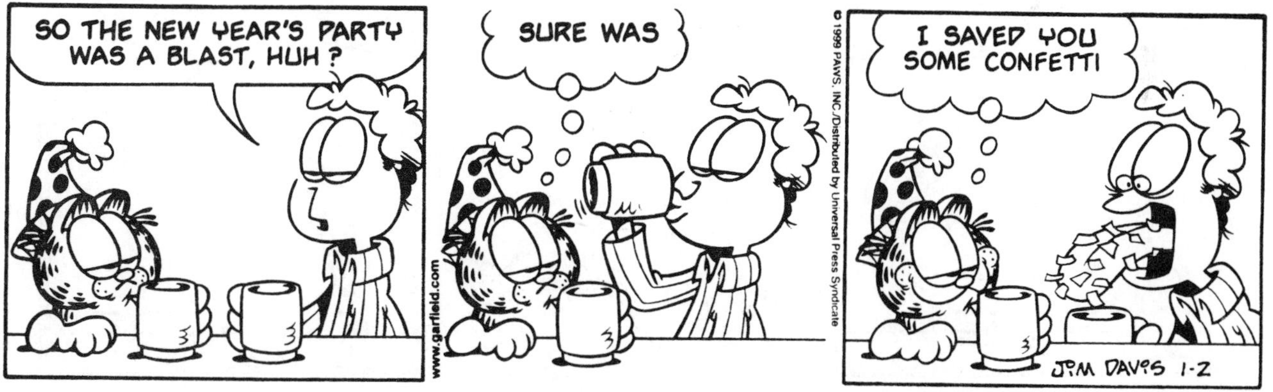
SO THE NEW YEAR'S PARTY WAS A BLAST, HUH?
www.garfield.com
SURE WAS
© 1999 PAWS, INC./Distributed by Universal Press Syndicate
I SAVED YOU SOME CONFETTI
JIM DAVIS 1-2

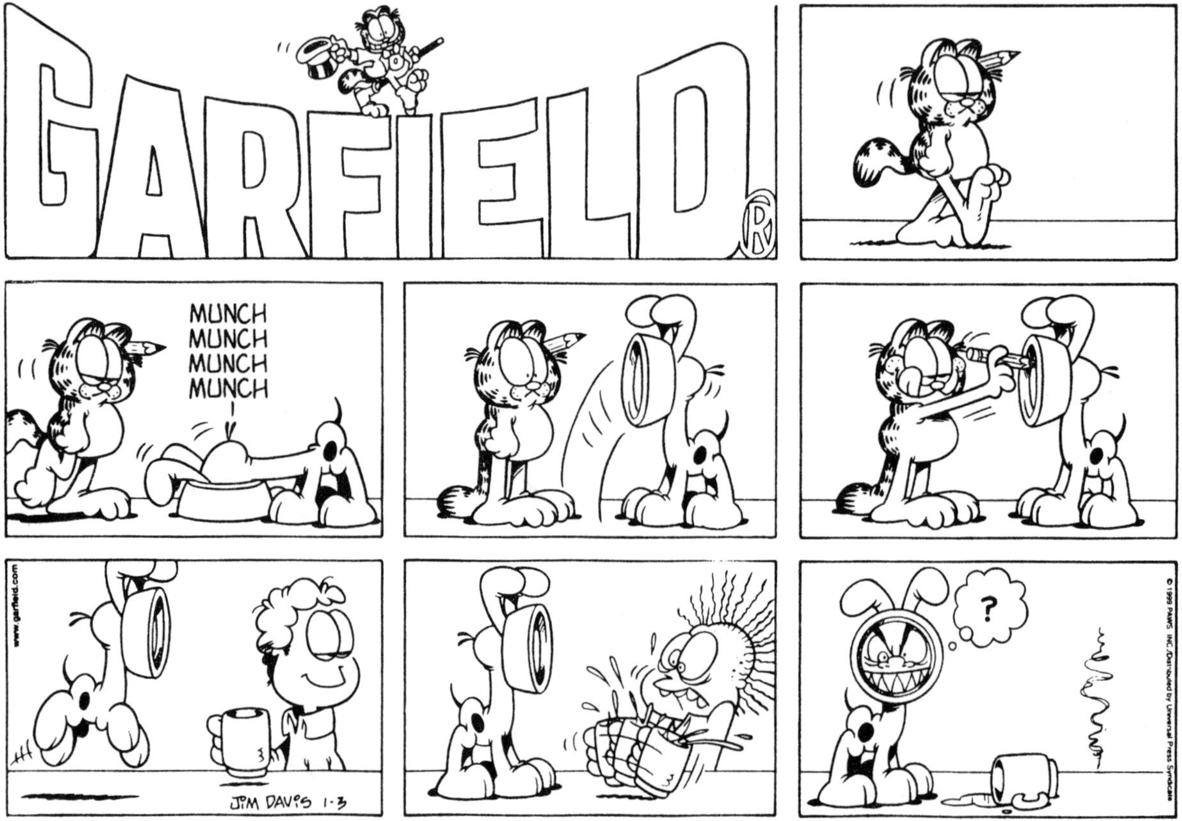
GARFIELD
MUNCH
MUNCH
MUNCH
MUNCH
www.garfield.com
JIM DAVIS 1-3
?
© 1999 PAWS INC./Distributed by Universal Press Syndicate

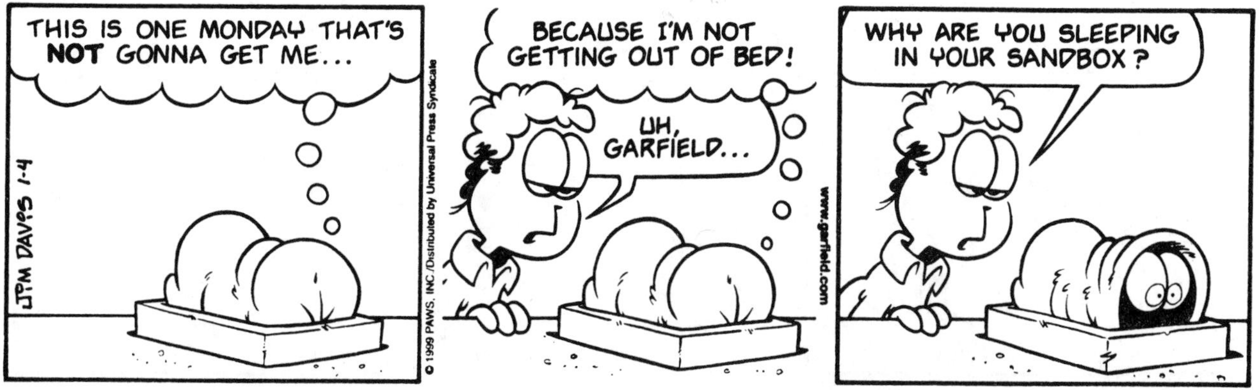
THIS IS ONE MONDAY THAT'S **NOT** GONNA GET ME...
JIM DAVIS 1-4
© 1999 PAWS, INC./Distributed by Universal Press Syndicate
UH, GARFIELD...
BECAUSE I'M NOT GETTING OUT OF BED!
www.garfield.com
WHY ARE YOU SLEEPING IN YOUR SANDBOX?

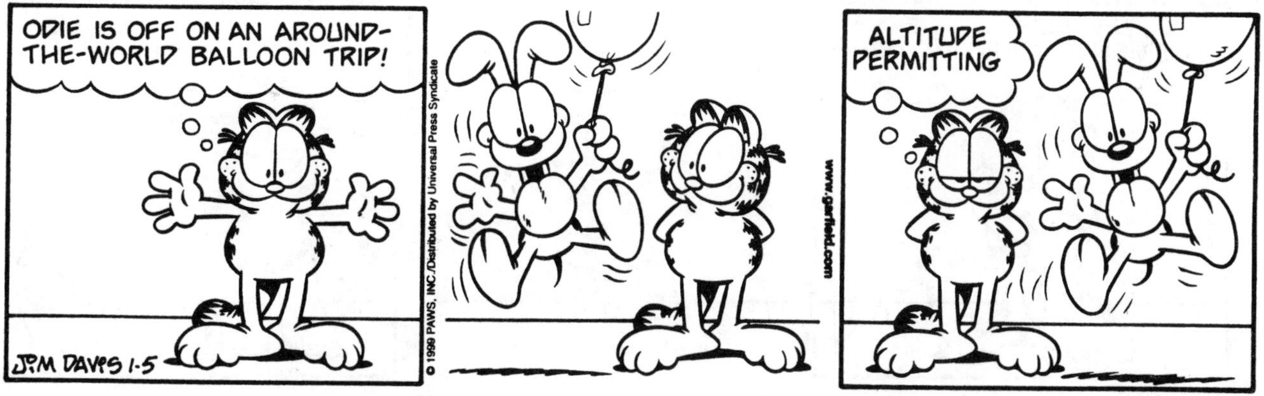
ODIE IS OFF ON AN AROUND-THE-WORLD BALLOON TRIP!
JIM DAVIS 1-5
© 1999 PAWS, INC./Distributed by Universal Press Syndicate
www.garfield.com
ALTITUDE PERMITTING

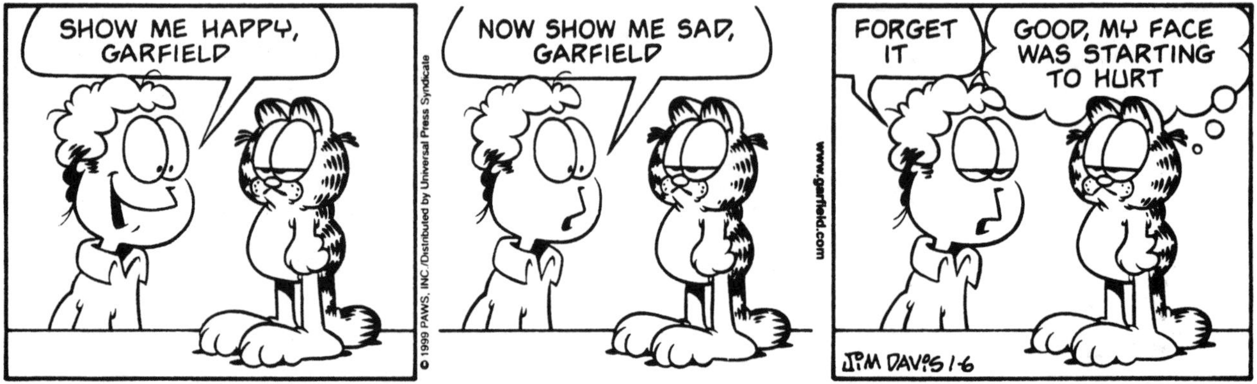
SHOW ME HAPPY, GARFIELD
© 1999 PAWS, INC./Distributed by Universal Press Syndicate
NOW SHOW ME SAD, GARFIELD
www.garfield.com
FORGET IT
GOOD, MY FACE WAS STARTING TO HURT
JIM DAVIS 1-6

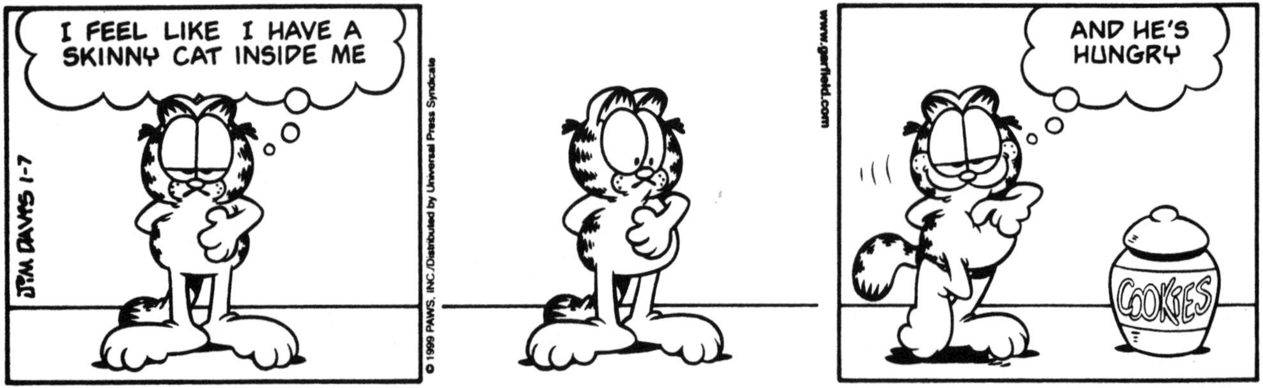
I FEEL LIKE I HAVE A SKINNY CAT INSIDE ME
JIM DAVIS 1-7
© 1999 PAWS, INC./Distributed by Universal Press Syndicate
www.garfield.com
AND HE'S HUNGRY
COOKIES

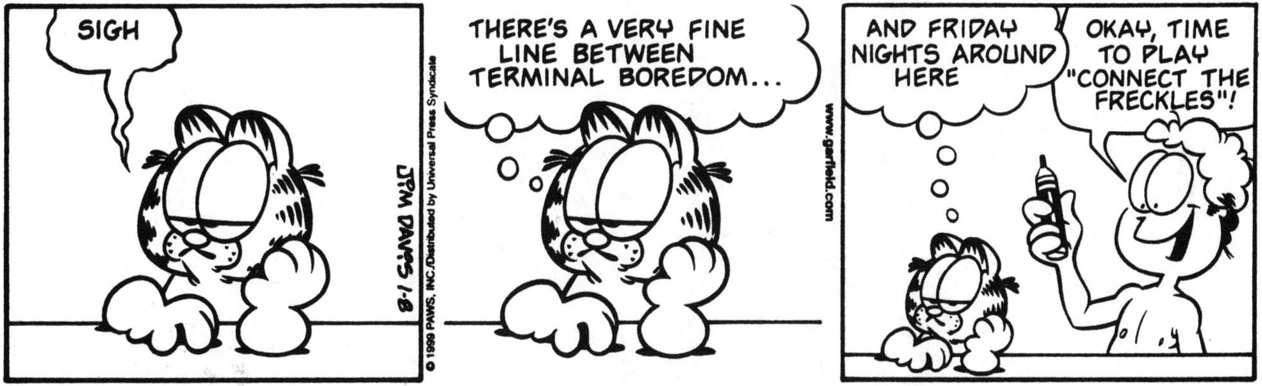
SIGH
THERE'S A VERY FINE LINE BETWEEN TERMINAL BOREDOM...
AND FRIDAY NIGHTS AROUND HERE
OKAY, TIME TO PLAY "CONNECT THE FRECKLES"!
JIM DAVIS 1-8
© 1999 PAWS, INC./Distributed by Universal Press Syndicate
www.garfield.com

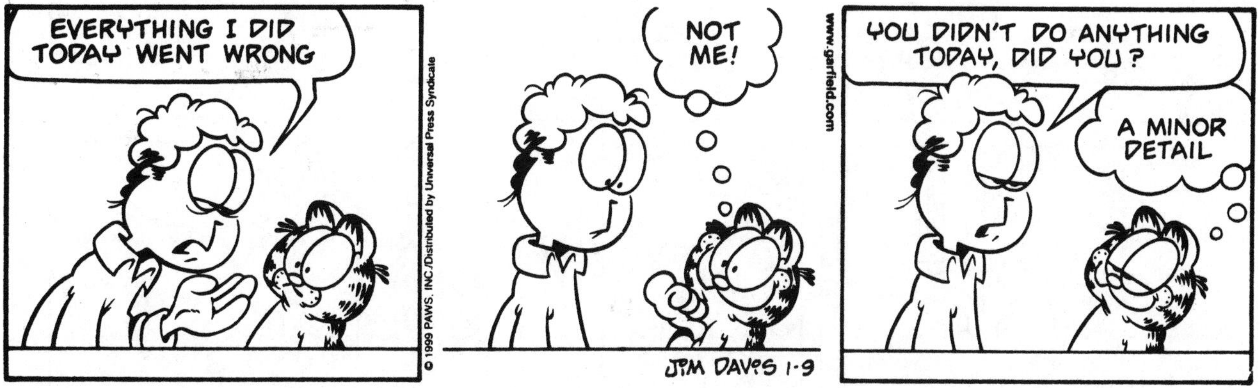
EVERYTHING I DID TODAY WENT WRONG
NOT ME!
YOU DIDN'T DO ANYTHING TODAY, DID YOU?
A MINOR DETAIL
JIM DAVIS 1-9
© 1999 PAWS, INC./Distributed by Universal Press Syndicate
www.garfield.com

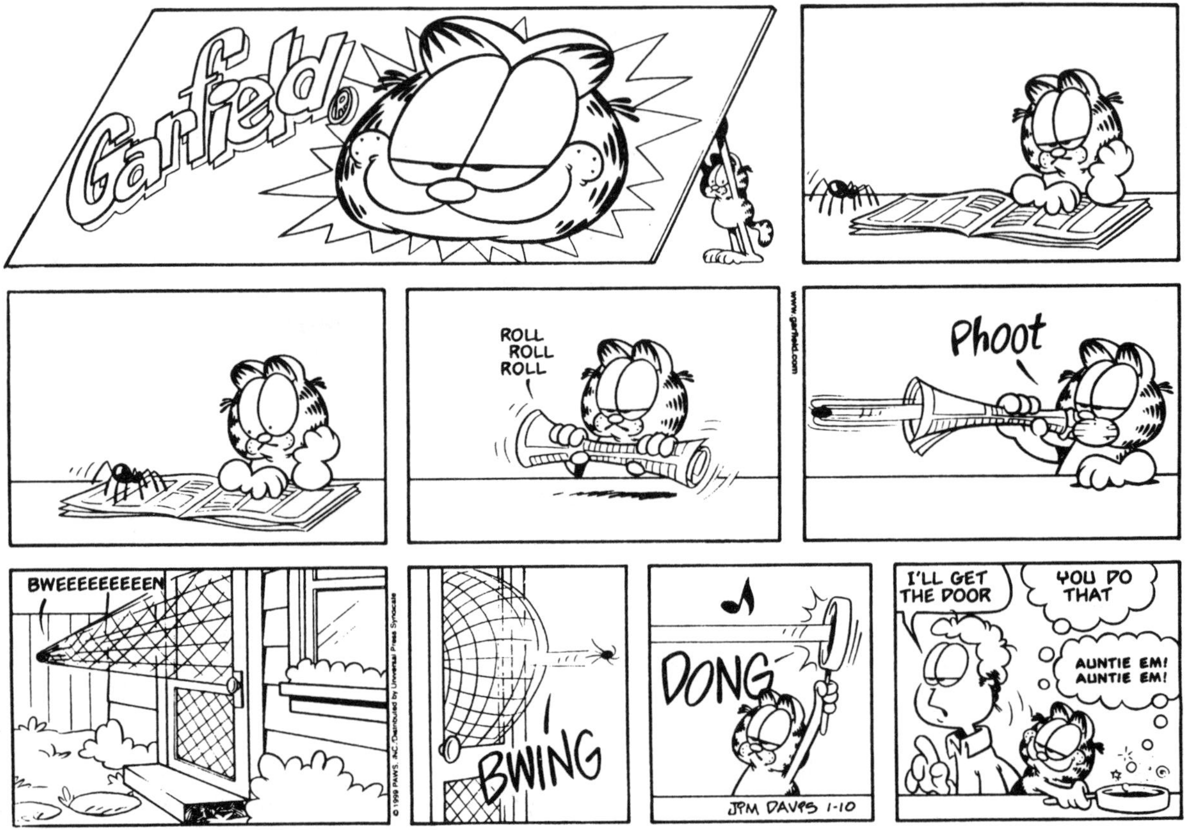
Garfield®
www.garfield.com
ROLL
ROLL
ROLL
Phoot
BWEEEEEEEEEN
© 1998 PAWS, INC./Distributed by Universal Press Syndicate
BWING
DONG
JPM DAVPS 1-10
I'LL GET THE DOOR
YOU DO THAT
AUNTIE EM! AUNTIE EM!

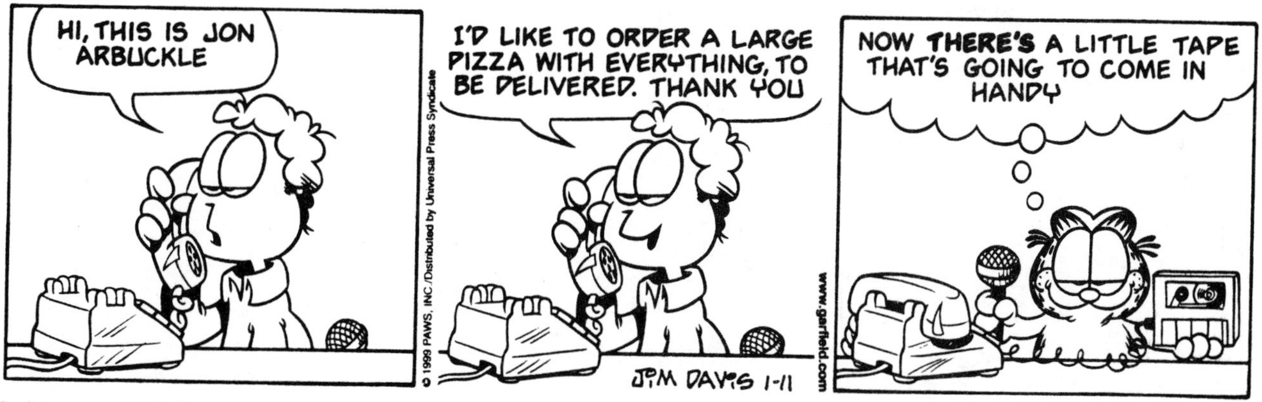
HI, THIS IS JON ARBUCKLE
I'D LIKE TO ORDER A LARGE PIZZA WITH EVERYTHING, TO BE DELIVERED. THANK YOU
NOW THERE'S A LITTLE TAPE THAT'S GOING TO COME IN HANDY
JIM DAVIS 1-11
© 1999 PAWS, INC./Distributed by Universal Press Syndicate
www.garfield.com

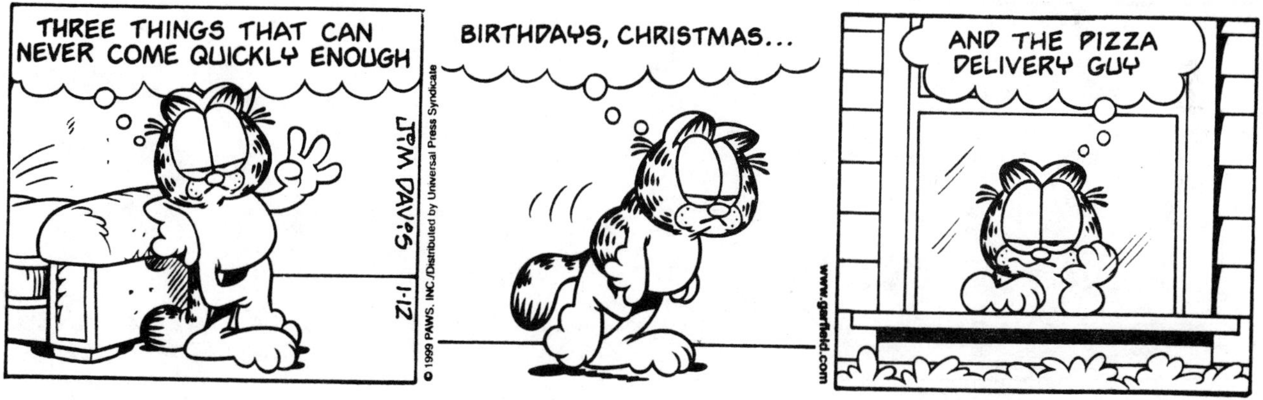
THREE THINGS THAT CAN NEVER COME QUICKLY ENOUGH
BIRTHDAYS, CHRISTMAS...
AND THE PIZZA DELIVERY GUY
JIM DAVIS 1-12
© 1999 PAWS, INC./Distributed by Universal Press Syndicate
www.garfield.com

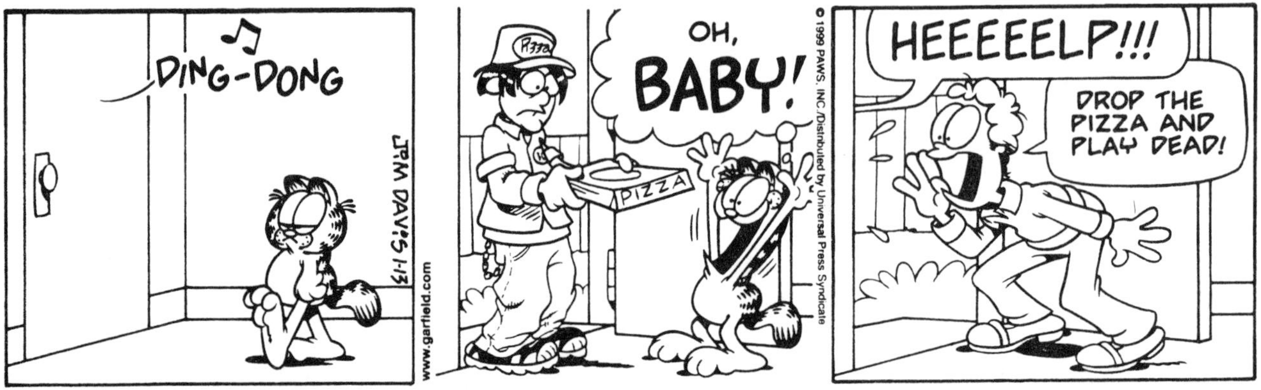
DING-DONG
JIM DAVIS 1-13
www.garfield.com
OH, BABY!
PIZZA
© 1999 PAWS, INC./Distributed by Universal Press Syndicate
HEEEEEELP!!!
DROP THE PIZZA AND PLAY DEAD!

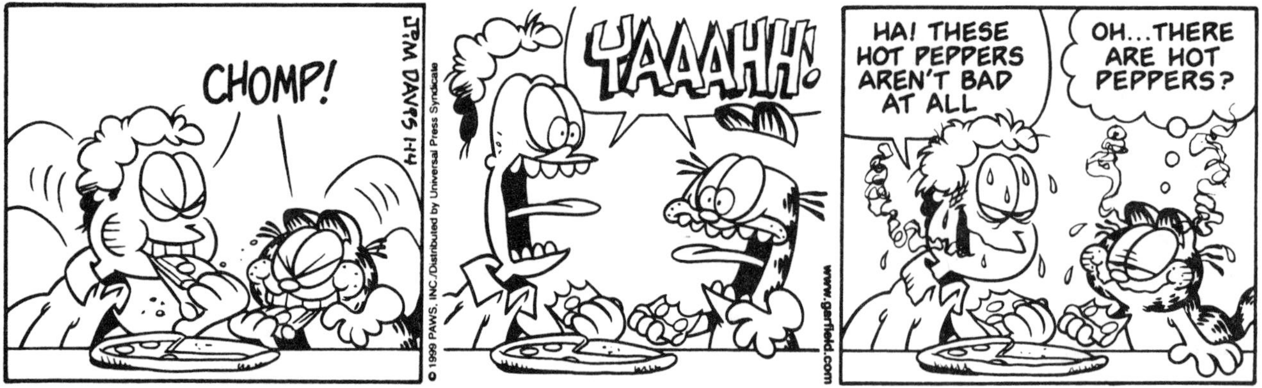
CHOMP!
JIM DAVIS 1-14
© 1999 PAWS, INC./Distributed by Universal Press Syndicate
YAAAHH!
www.garfield.com
HA! THESE HOT PEPPERS AREN'T BAD AT ALL
OH...THERE ARE HOT PEPPERS?

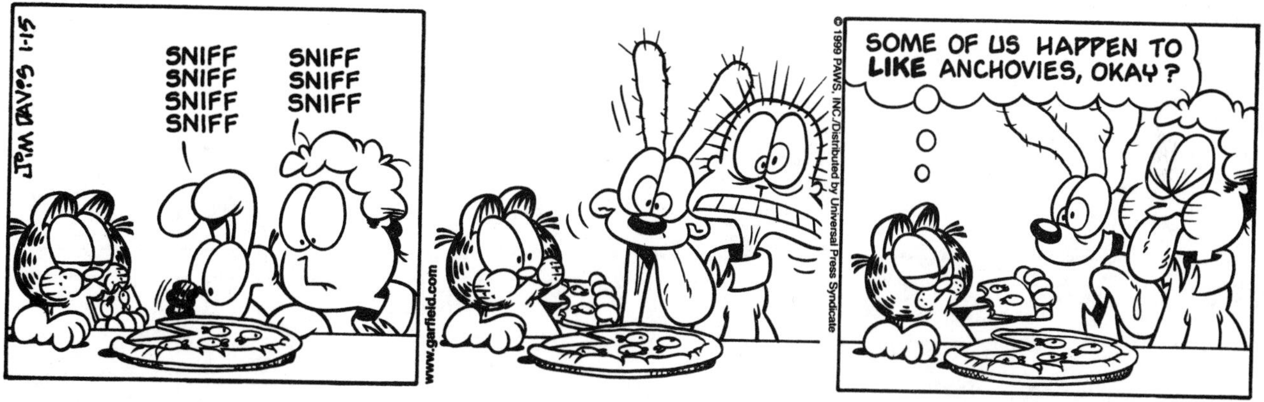
JIM DAVIS 1-15
SNIFF SNIFF SNIFF SNIFF
SNIFF SNIFF SNIFF
www.garfield.com
© 1999 PAWS, INC./Distributed by Universal Press Syndicate
SOME OF US HAPPEN TO LIKE ANCHOVIES, OKAY?

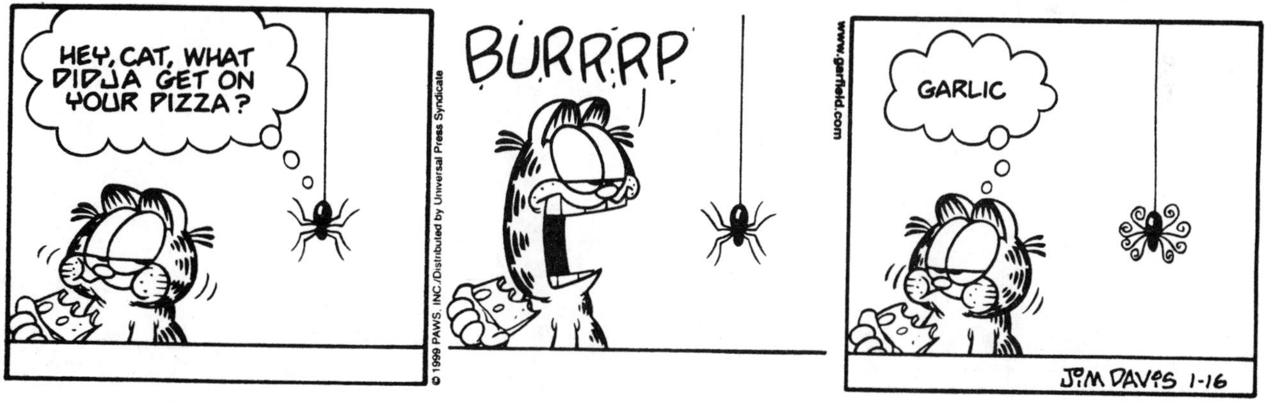
HEY, CAT, WHAT DIDJA GET ON YOUR PIZZA?
© 1999 PAWS, INC./Distributed by Universal Press Syndicate
BURRRP
www.garfield.com
GARLIC
JIM DAVIS 1-16

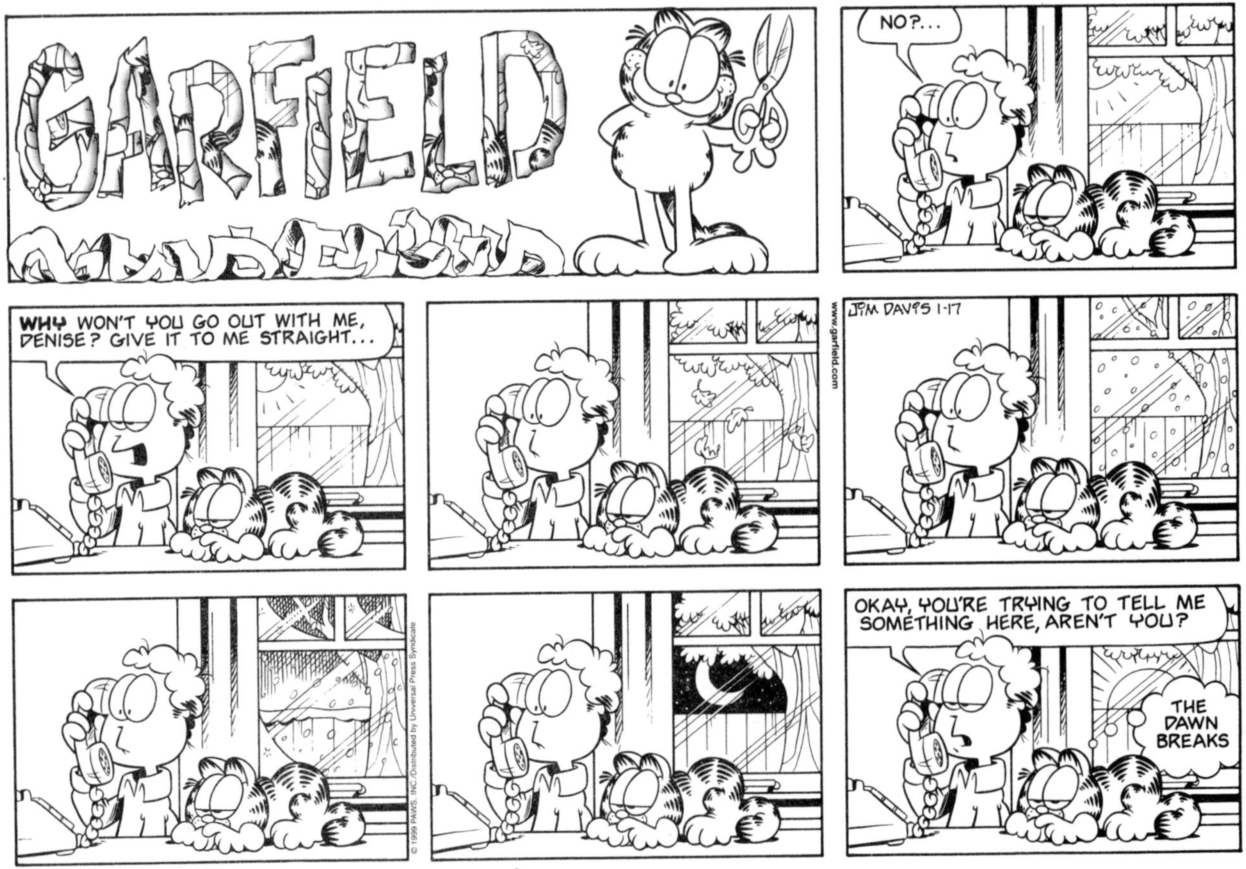
GARFIELD
NO?...
WHY WON'T YOU GO OUT WITH ME, DENISE? GIVE IT TO ME STRAIGHT...
JIM DAVIS 1-17
www.garfield.com
© 1999 PAWS, INC./Distributed by Universal Press Syndicate
OKAY, YOU'RE TRYING TO TELL ME SOMETHING HERE, AREN'T YOU?
THE DAWN BREAKS

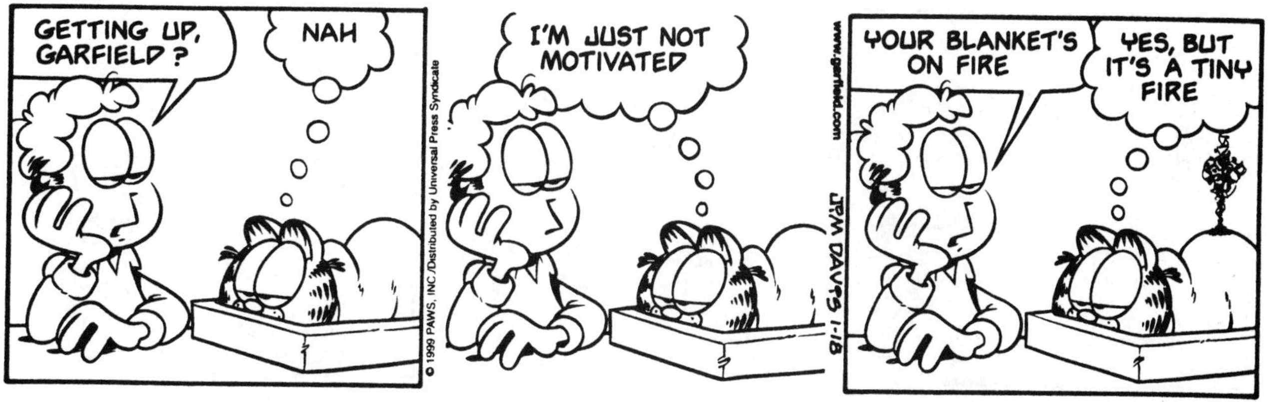
GETTING UP, GARFIELD ?
NAH
I'M JUST NOT MOTIVATED
YOUR BLANKET'S ON FIRE
YES, BUT IT'S A TINY FIRE
© 1999 PAWS, INC./Distributed by Universal Press Syndicate
JPM DAVPS 1-18
www.garfield.com

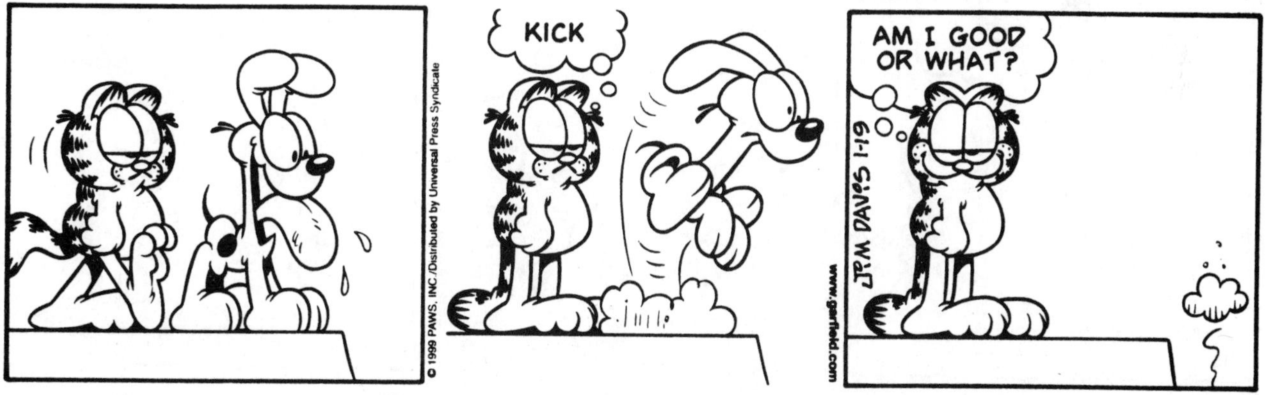
KICK
AM I GOOD OR WHAT?
© 1999 PAWS, INC./Distributed by Universal Press Syndicate
JPM DAVPS 1-19
www.garfield.com

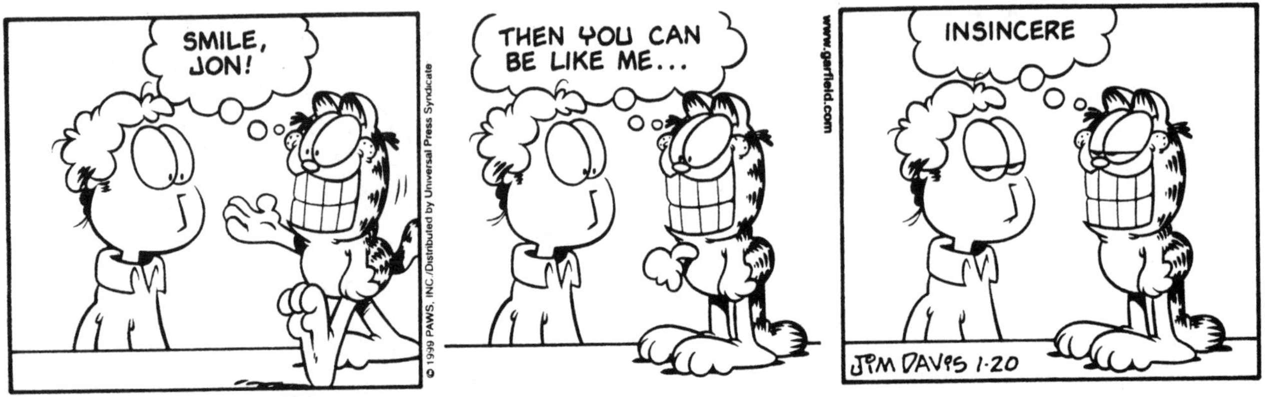
SMILE, JON!
THEN YOU CAN BE LIKE ME...
INSINCERE
© 1999 PAWS, INC./Distributed by Universal Press Syndicate
www.garfield.com
JIM DAVIS 1-20

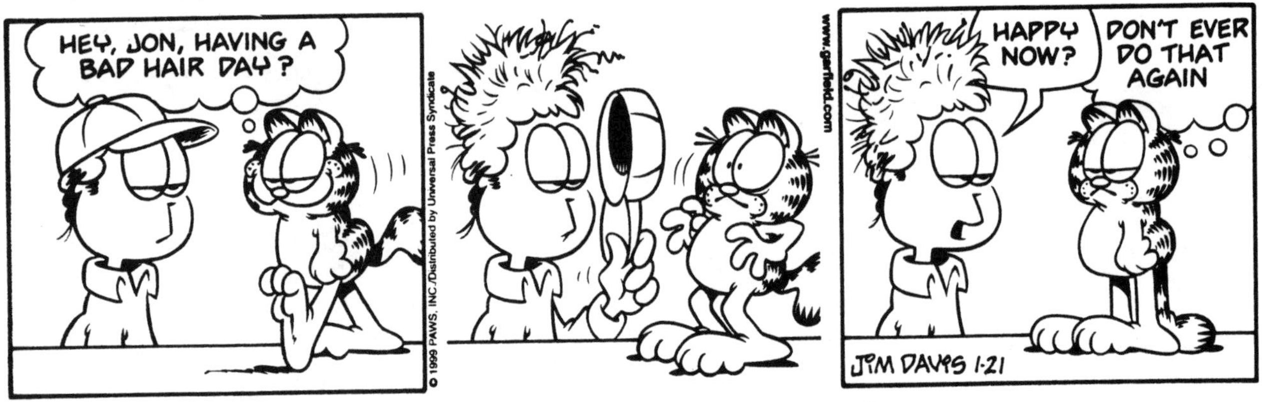
HEY, JON, HAVING A BAD HAIR DAY?
HAPPY NOW?
DON'T EVER DO THAT AGAIN
© 1999 PAWS, INC./Distributed by Universal Press Syndicate
www.garfield.com
JIM DAVIS 1-21

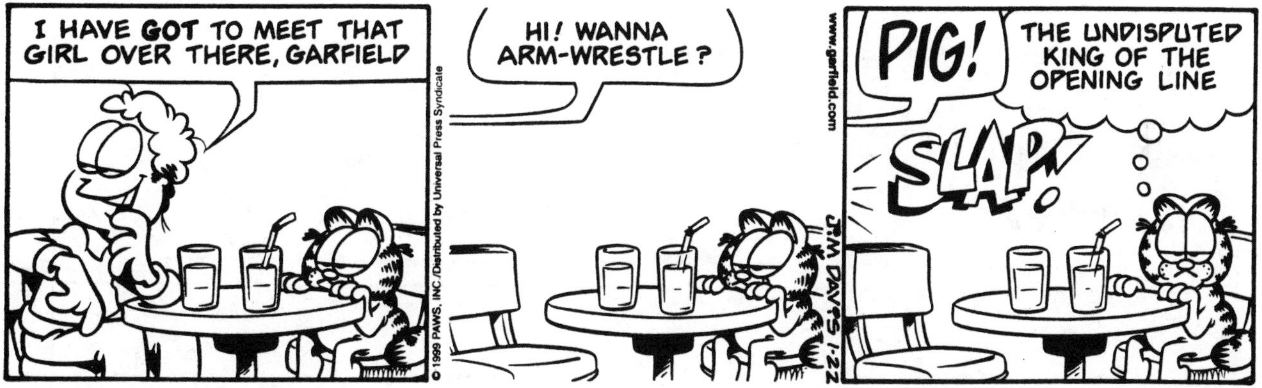
I HAVE GOT TO MEET THAT GIRL OVER THERE, GARFIELD
HI! WANNA ARM-WRESTLE?
PIG!
THE UNDISPUTED KING OF THE OPENING LINE
SLAP!
JPM DAVPS 1-22

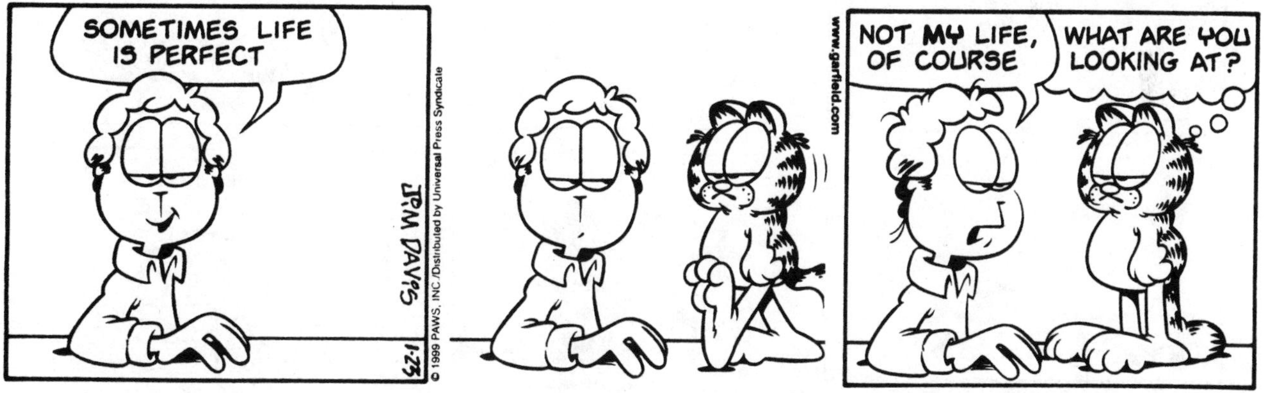
SOMETIMES LIFE IS PERFECT
NOT MY LIFE, OF COURSE
WHAT ARE YOU LOOKING AT?
JPM DAVPS 1-23

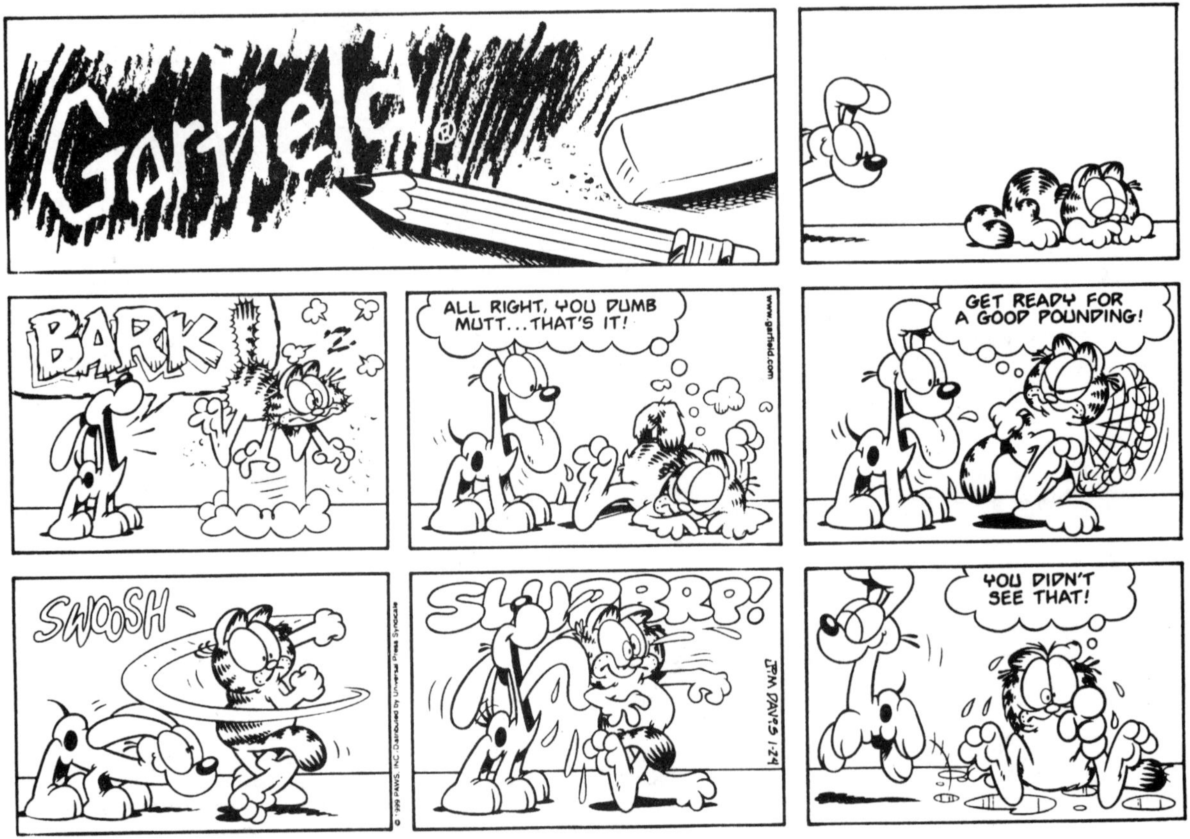
Garfield®
BARK
ALL RIGHT, YOU DUMB MUTT...THAT'S IT!
www.garfield.com
GET READY FOR A GOOD POUNDING!
SWOOSH
© 1999 PAWS, INC. Distributed by Universal Press Syndicate
SLURRRP!
JPM DAVIS 1-24
YOU DIDN'T SEE THAT!

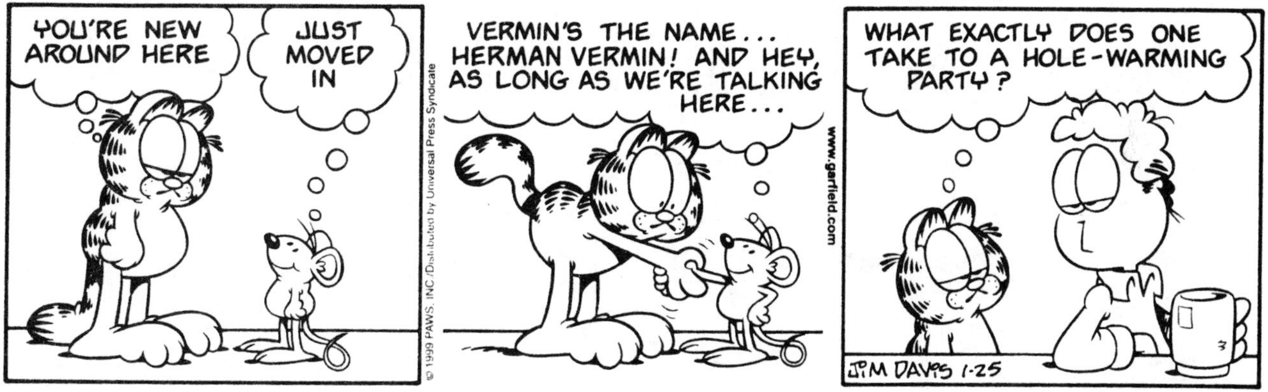
YOU'RE NEW AROUND HERE
JUST MOVED IN
© 1999 PAWS, INC./Distributed by Universal Press Syndicate
VERMIN'S THE NAME... HERMAN VERMIN! AND HEY, AS LONG AS WE'RE TALKING HERE...
www.garfield.com
WHAT EXACTLY DOES ONE TAKE TO A HOLE-WARMING PARTY?
JIM DAVIS 1-25

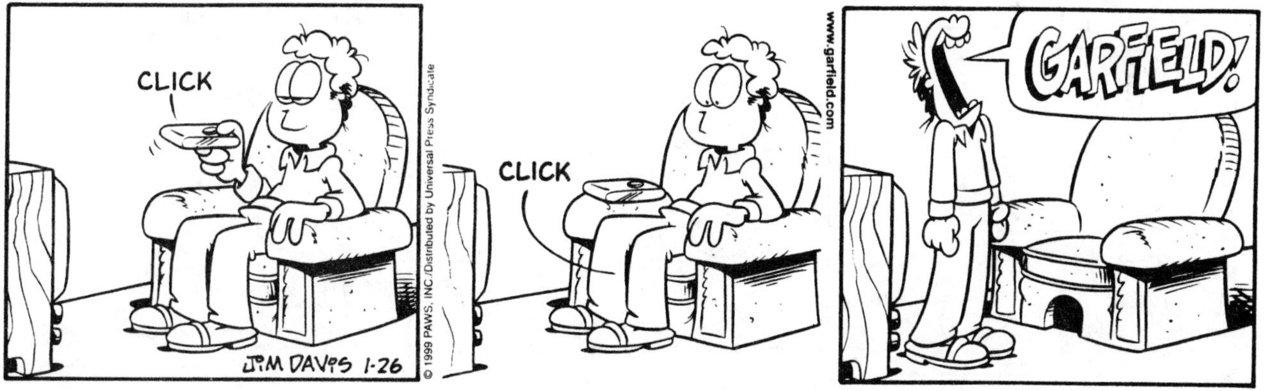
CLICK
JIM DAVIS 1-26
© 1999 PAWS, INC./Distributed by Universal Press Syndicate
CLICK
www.garfield.com
GARFIELD!

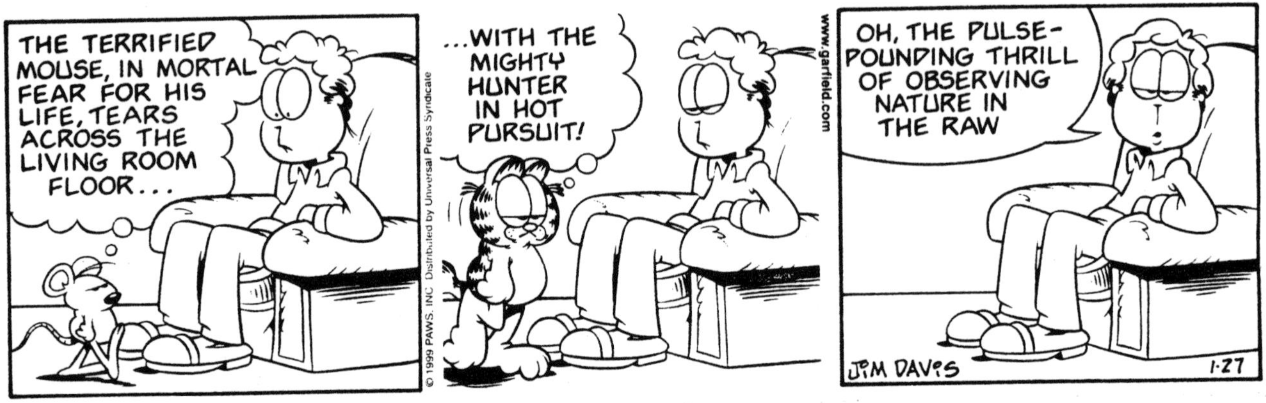
THE TERRIFIED MOUSE, IN MORTAL FEAR FOR HIS LIFE, TEARS ACROSS THE LIVING ROOM FLOOR...
© 1999 PAWS, INC. Distributed by Universal Press Syndicate
...WITH THE MIGHTY HUNTER IN HOT PURSUIT!
www.garfield.com
OH, THE PULSE-POUNDING THRILL OF OBSERVING NATURE IN THE RAW
JIM DAVIS
1·27

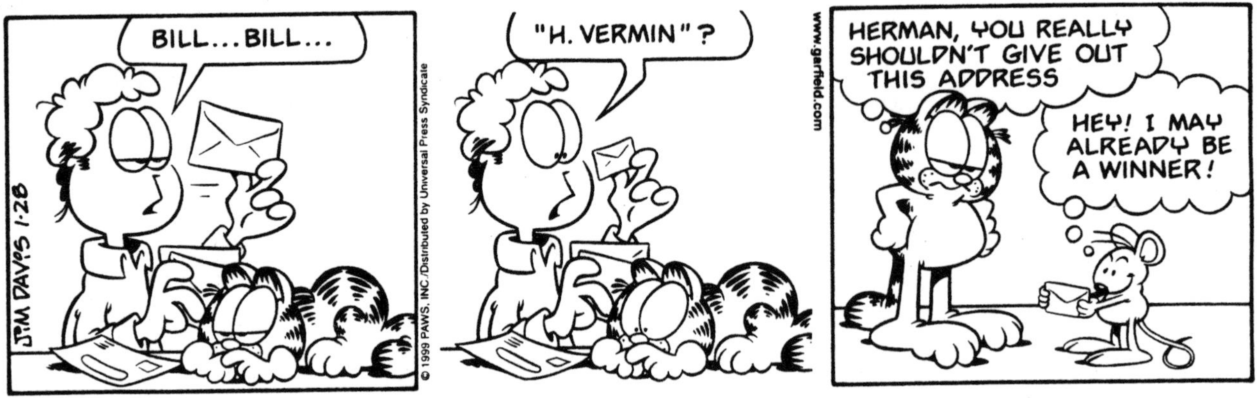
JIM DAVIS 1·28
BILL... BILL...
© 1999 PAWS, INC./Distributed by Universal Press Syndicate
"H. VERMIN"?
www.garfield.com
HERMAN, YOU REALLY SHOULDN'T GIVE OUT THIS ADDRESS
HEY! I MAY ALREADY BE A WINNER!

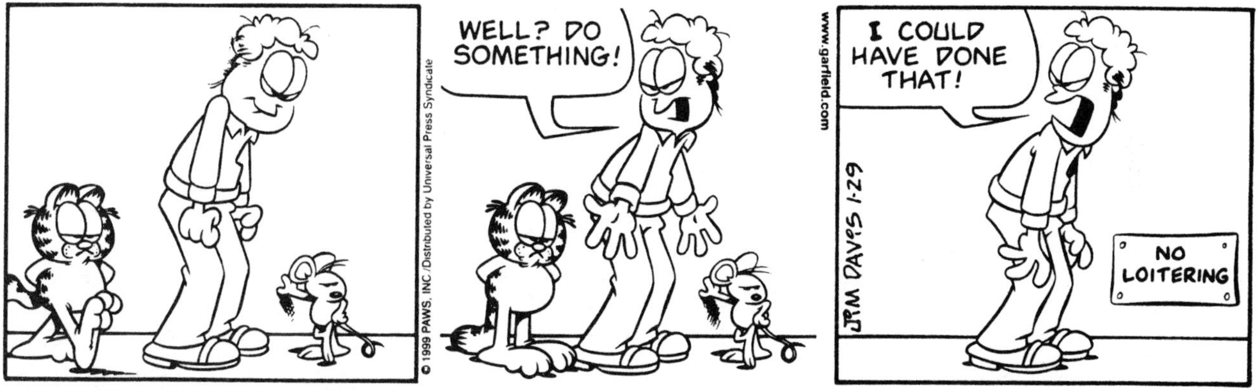
WELL? DO SOMETHING!
I COULD HAVE DONE THAT!
NO LOITERING
© 1999 PAWS, INC./Distributed by Universal Press Syndicate
www.garfield.com
JIM DAVIS 1-29

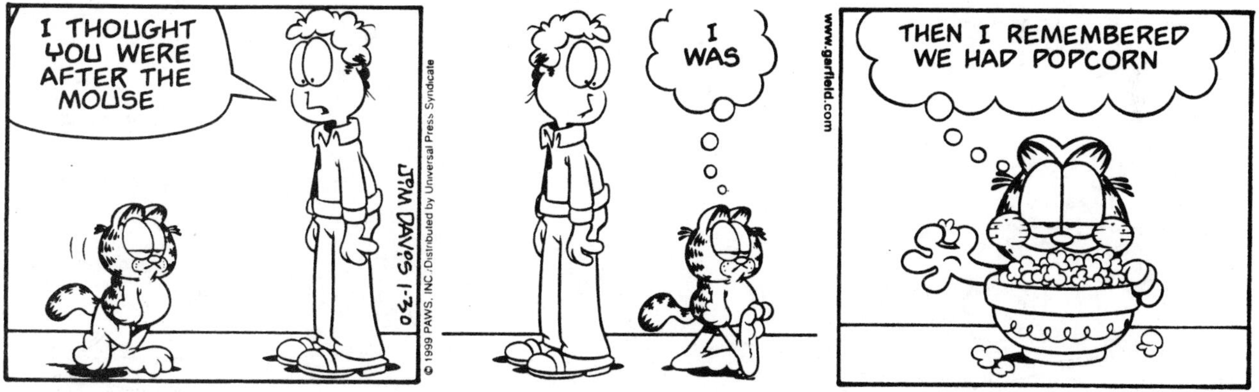
I THOUGHT YOU WERE AFTER THE MOUSE
I WAS
THEN I REMEMBERED WE HAD POPCORN
© 1999 PAWS, INC./Distributed by Universal Press Syndicate
JIM DAVIS 1-30
www.garfield.com

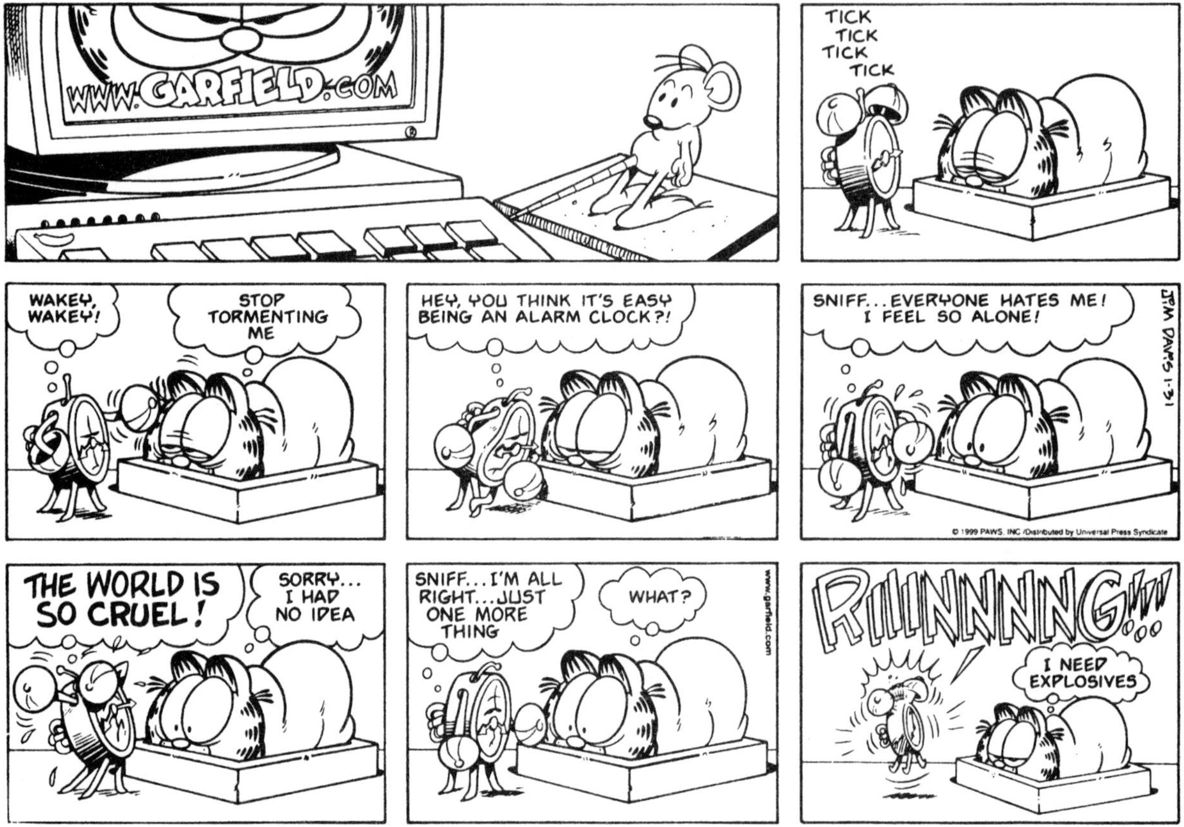
WWW.GARFIELD.COM
TICK
TICK
TICK
TICK
WAKEY, WAKEY!
STOP TORMENTING ME
HEY, YOU THINK IT'S EASY BEING AN ALARM CLOCK?!
SNIFF... EVERYONE HATES ME! I FEEL SO ALONE!
JIM DAVIS 1-31
© 1999 PAWS, INC /Distributed by Universal Press Syndicate
THE WORLD IS SO CRUEL!
SORRY... I HAD NO IDEA
www.garfield.com
SNIFF... I'M ALL RIGHT... JUST ONE MORE THING
WHAT?
RIIINNNNG!!!
I NEED EXPLOSIVES

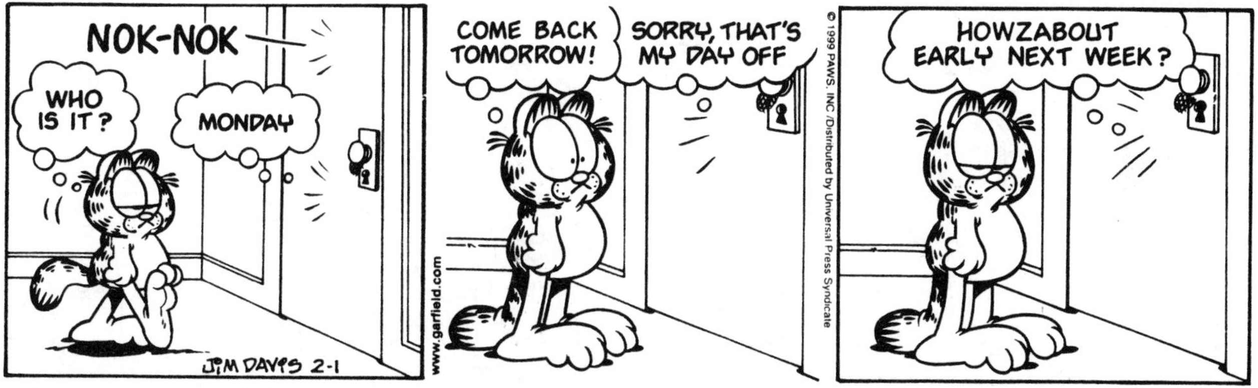
NOK-NOK
WHO IS IT?
MONDAY
JIM DAVIS 2-1
www.garfield.com
COME BACK TOMORROW!
SORRY, THAT'S MY DAY OFF
© 1999 PAWS, INC./Distributed by Universal Press Syndicate
HOWZABOUT EARLY NEXT WEEK?

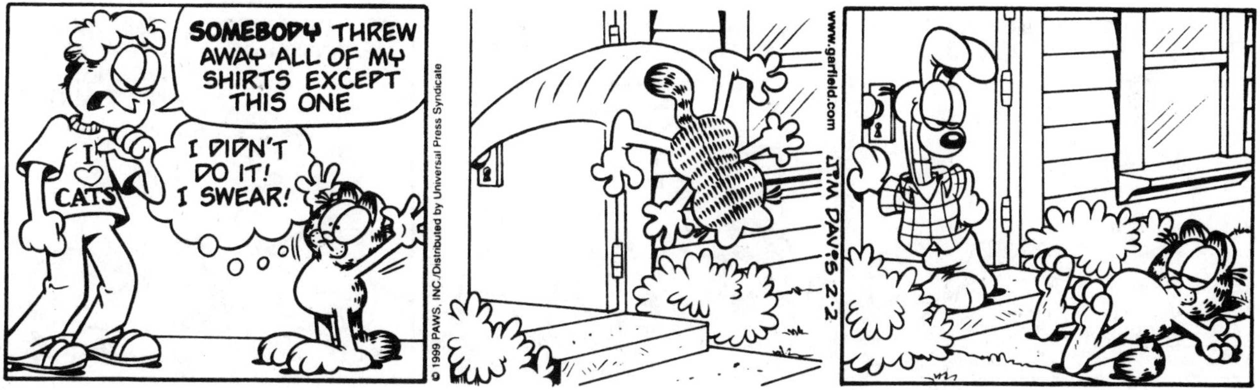
SOMEBODY THREW AWAY ALL OF MY SHIRTS EXCEPT THIS ONE
I ♥ CATS
I DIDN'T DO IT! I SWEAR!
© 1999 PAWS, INC./Distributed by Universal Press Syndicate
www.garfield.com
JIM DAVIS 2-2

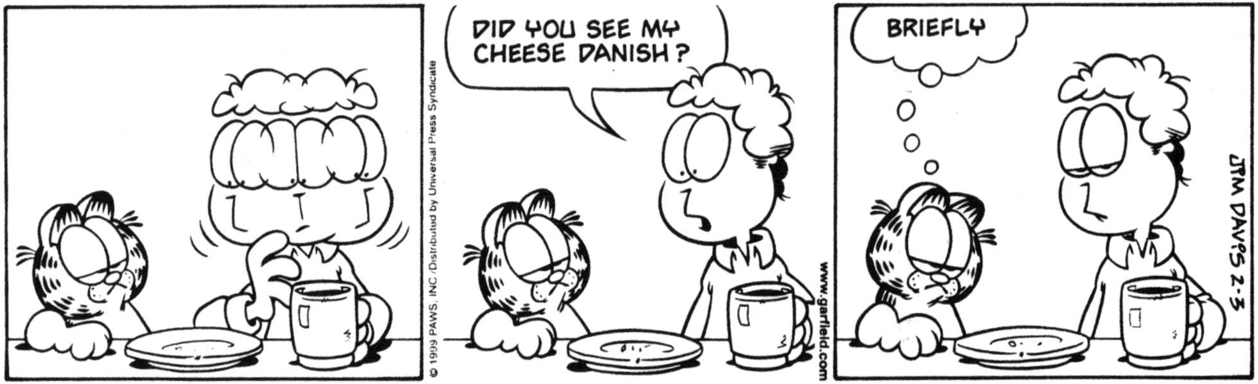
DID YOU SEE MY CHEESE DANISH?
BRIEFLY
© 1999 PAWS, INC./Distributed by Universal Press Syndicate
www.garfield.com
JPM DAVPS 2-3

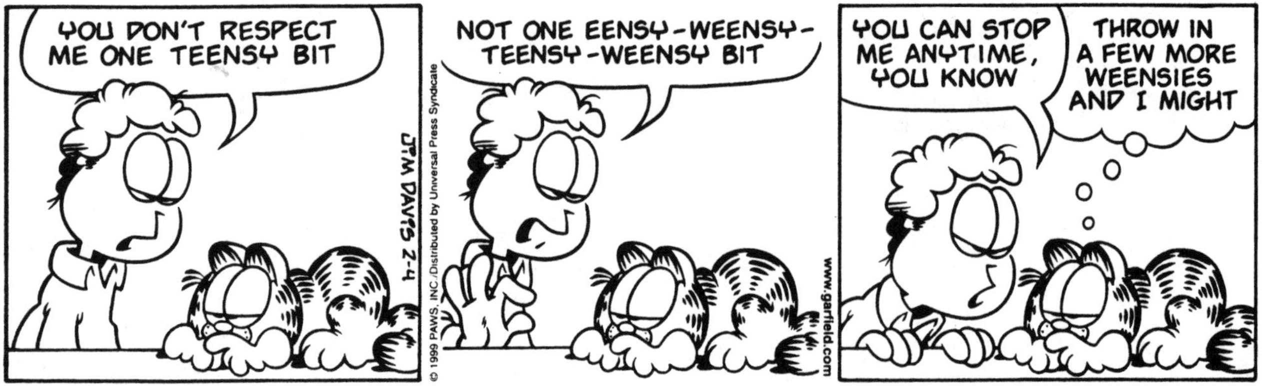
YOU DON'T RESPECT ME ONE TEENSY BIT
NOT ONE EENSY-WEENSY-TEENSY-WEENSY BIT
YOU CAN STOP ME ANYTIME, YOU KNOW
THROW IN A FEW MORE WEENSIES AND I MIGHT
© 1999 PAWS, INC./Distributed by Universal Press Syndicate
www.garfield.com
JPM DAVPS 2-4

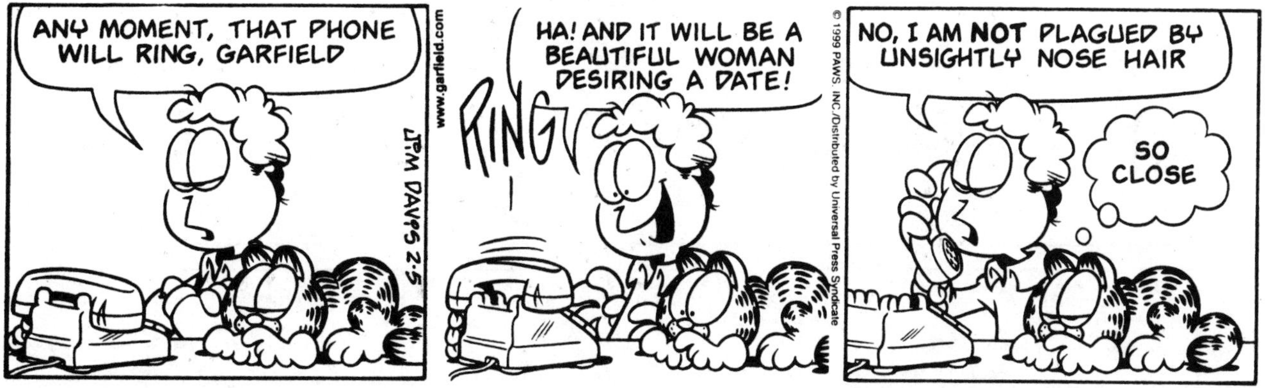
ANY MOMENT, THAT PHONE WILL RING, GARFIELD
JIM DAVIS 2-5
www.garfield.com
RING
HA! AND IT WILL BE A BEAUTIFUL WOMAN DESIRING A DATE!
© 1999 PAWS. INC./Distributed by Universal Press Syndicate
NO, I AM **NOT** PLAGUED BY UNSIGHTLY NOSE HAIR
SO CLOSE

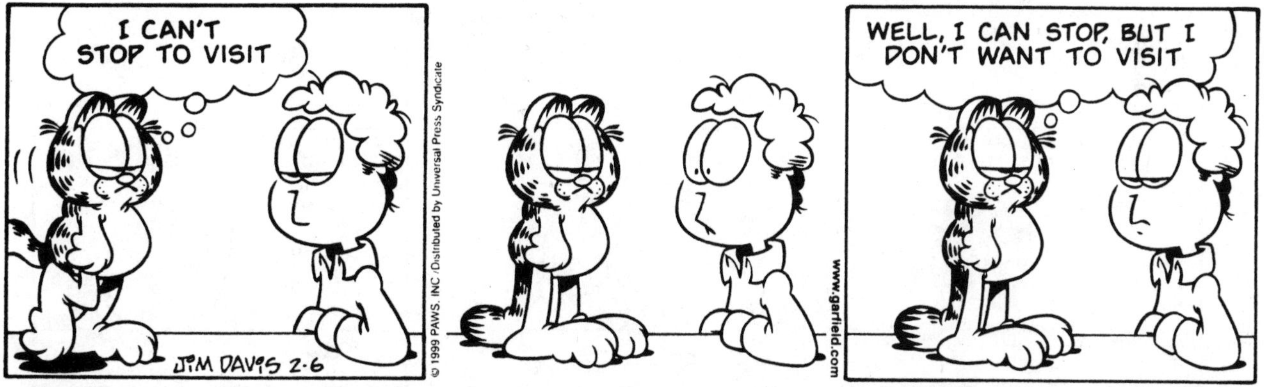
I CAN'T STOP TO VISIT
JIM DAVIS 2-6
© 1999 PAWS. INC./Distributed by Universal Press Syndicate
www.garfield.com
WELL, I CAN STOP, BUT I DON'T WANT TO VISIT

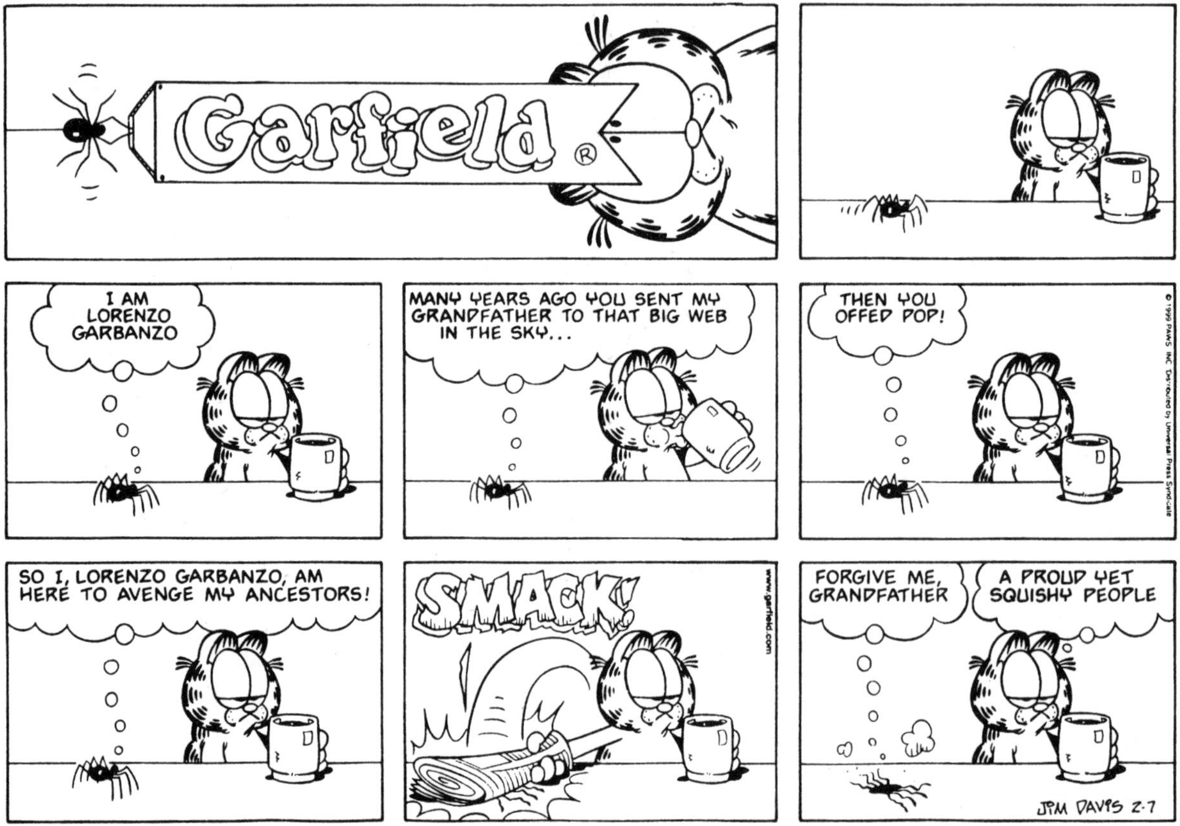
Garfield®
I AM LORENZO GARBANZO
MANY YEARS AGO YOU SENT MY GRANDFATHER TO THAT BIG WEB IN THE SKY...
THEN YOU OFFED POP!
© 1999 PAWS INC Distributed by Universal Press Syndicate
SO I, LORENZO GARBANZO, AM HERE TO AVENGE MY ANCESTORS!
SMACK!
www.garfield.com
FORGIVE ME, GRANDFATHER
A PROUD YET SQUISHY PEOPLE
JIM DAVIS 2-7

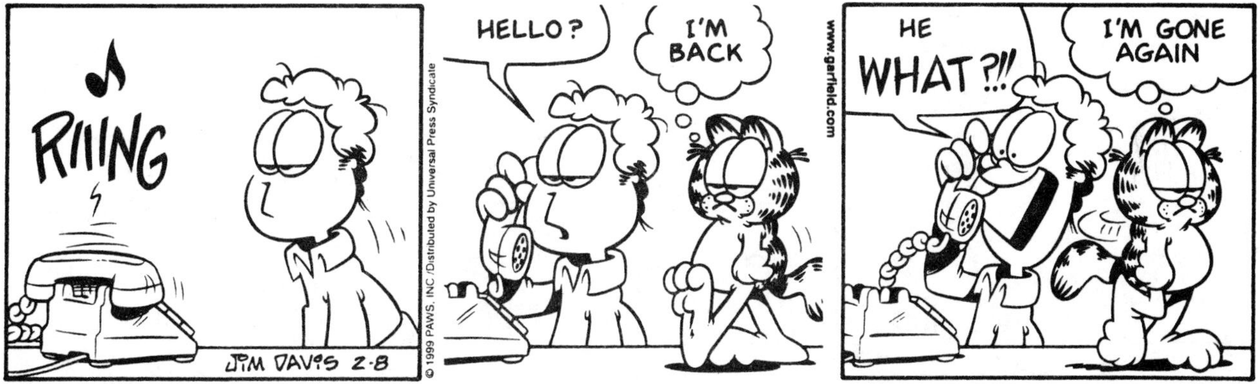
RIIING
JIM DAVIS 2-8
HELLO?
I'M BACK
HE
WHAT?!!
I'M GONE AGAIN

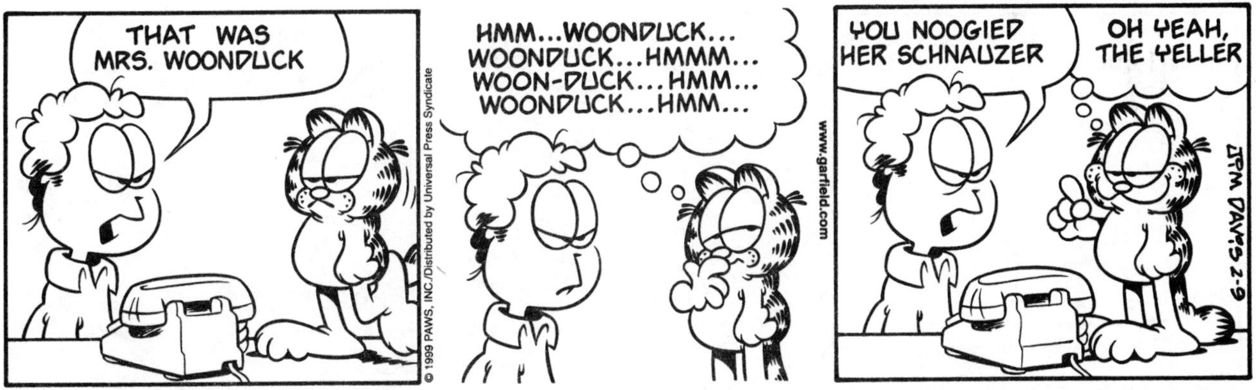
THAT WAS MRS. WOONDUCK
HMM...WOONDUCK... WOONDUCK...HMMM... WOON-DUCK...HMM... WOONDUCK...HMM...
YOU NOOGIED HER SCHNAUZER
OH YEAH, THE YELLER
JIM DAVIS 2-9

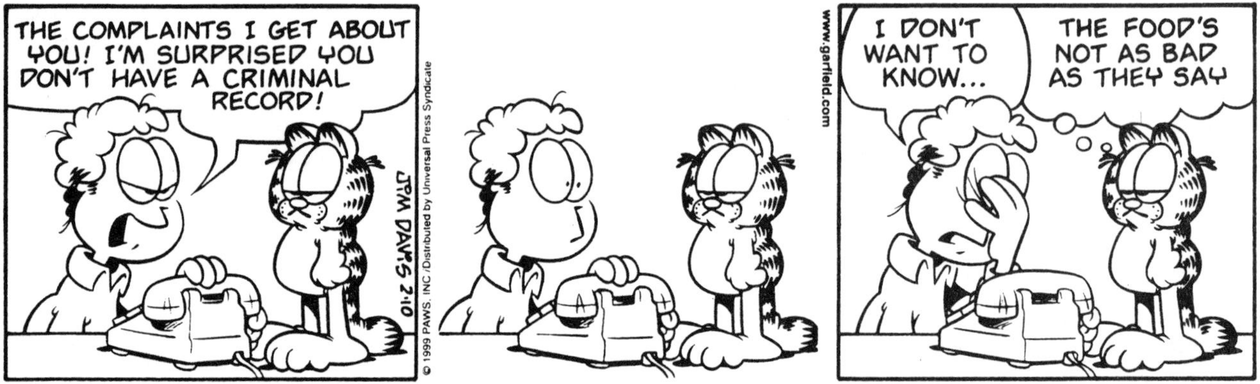
THE COMPLAINTS I GET ABOUT YOU! I'M SURPRISED YOU DON'T HAVE A CRIMINAL RECORD!
JIM DAVIS 2-10
© 1999 PAWS, INC./Distributed by Universal Press Syndicate
www.garfield.com
I DON'T WANT TO KNOW...
THE FOOD'S NOT AS BAD AS THEY SAY

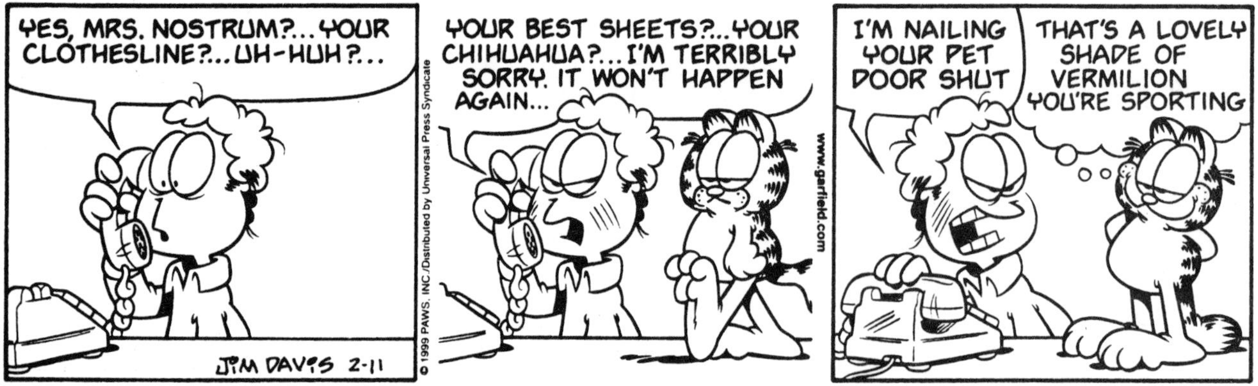
YES, MRS. NOSTRUM?...YOUR CLOTHESLINE?...UH-HUH?...
JIM DAVIS 2-11
© 1999 PAWS, INC./Distributed by Universal Press Syndicate
YOUR BEST SHEETS?...YOUR CHIHUAHUA?...I'M TERRIBLY SORRY. IT WON'T HAPPEN AGAIN...
www.garfield.com
I'M NAILING YOUR PET DOOR SHUT
THAT'S A LOVELY SHADE OF VERMILION YOU'RE SPORTING

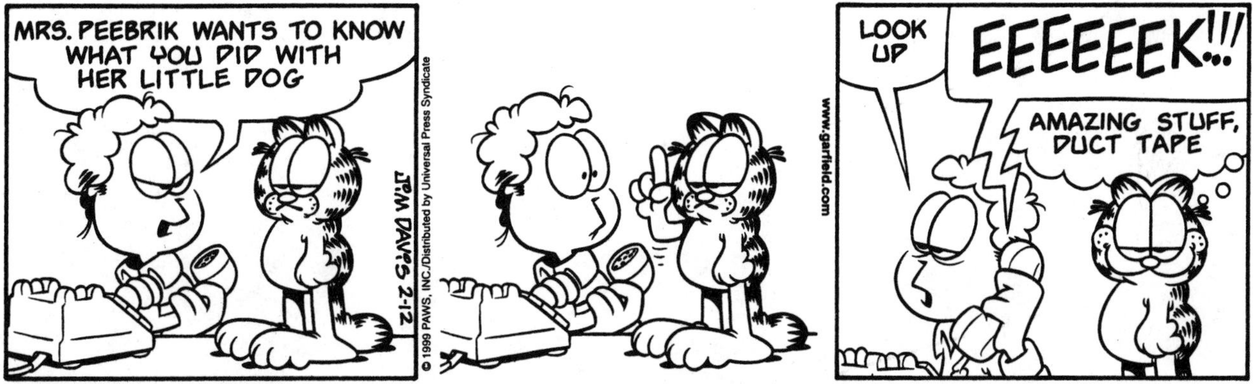
MRS. PEEBRIK WANTS TO KNOW WHAT YOU DID WITH HER LITTLE DOG
JIM DAVIS 2-12
© 1999 PAWS, INC./Distributed by Universal Press Syndicate
www.garfield.com
LOOK UP
EEEEEEK!!!
AMAZING STUFF, DUCT TAPE

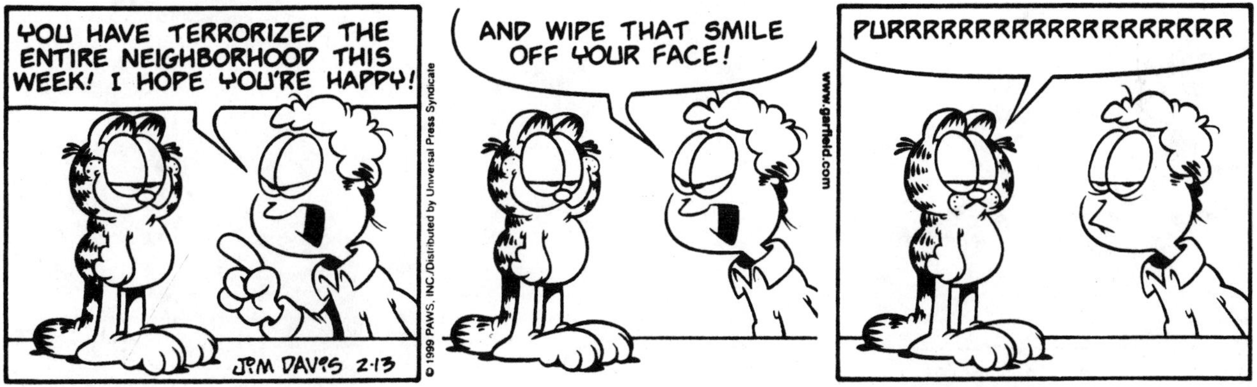
YOU HAVE TERRORIZED THE ENTIRE NEIGHBORHOOD THIS WEEK! I HOPE YOU'RE HAPPY!
JIM DAVIS 2-13
© 1999 PAWS, INC./Distributed by Universal Press Syndicate
AND WIPE THAT SMILE OFF YOUR FACE!
www.garfield.com
PURRRRRRRRRRRRRRRRRRR

REJECTED GARFIELD BOOK TITLES

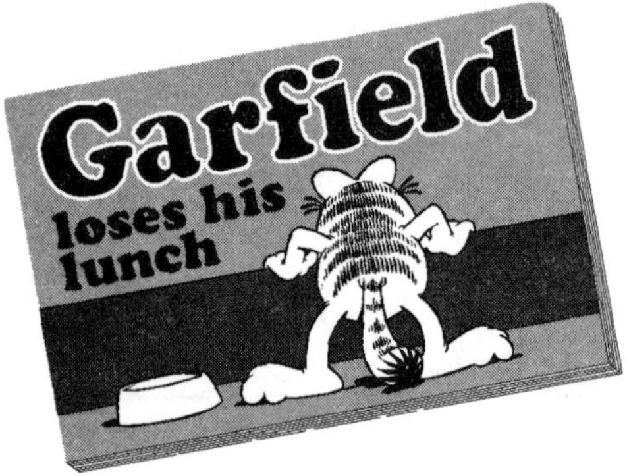
Garfield
loses his lunch

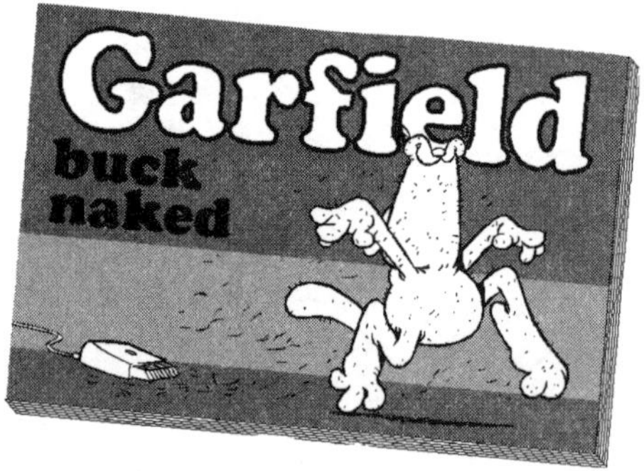
Garfield
buck naked

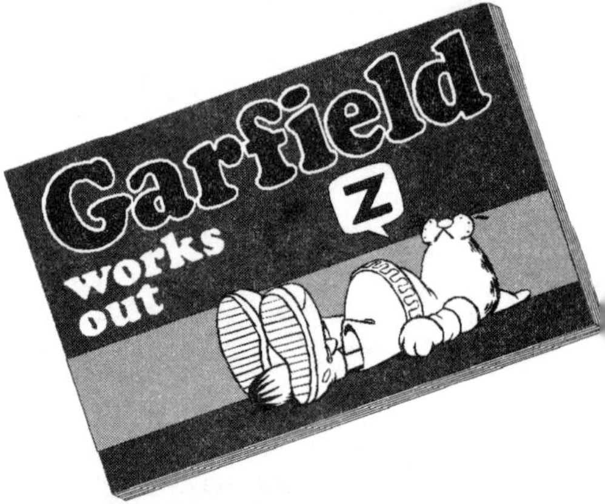
Garfield
works out
Z

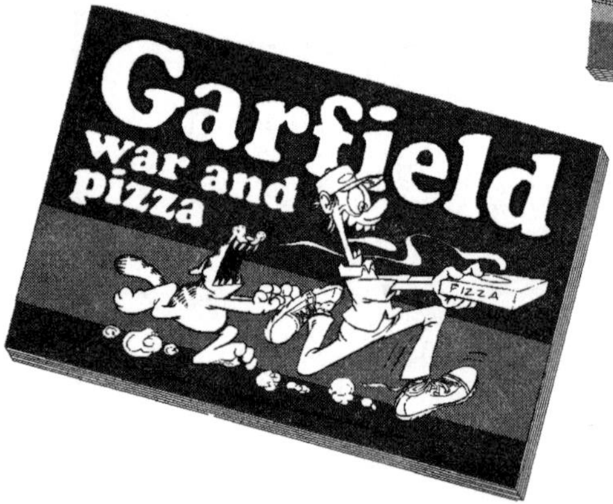
Garfield
war and pizza
PIZZA

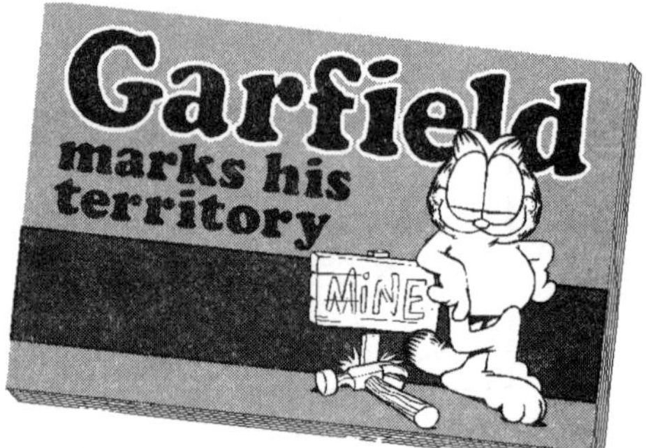
Garfield
marks his territory
MINE

Like to get a **COOL CAT**alog stuffed with great **GARFIELD** products? Then just write down the information below, stuff it in an envelope and mail it back to us...or you can fill in the card on our website - HTTP://www.GARFIELD.com. We'll get one out to you in two shakes of a cat's tail!

Name:
Address:
City:
State:
Zip:
Phone:
Date of Birth:
Sex:

Please mail your information to:

**Garfield Stuff Catalog
Dept.2BB38A
5804 Churchman By-Pass
Indianapolis, IN 46203-6109**

© PAWS

STRIPS, SPECIALS, OR BESTSELLING BOOKS . . .
GARFIELD'S ON EVERYONE'S MENU
Don't miss even one episode in the Tubby Tabby's hilarious series!

__GARFIELD AT LARGE (#1)   32013/$6.95
__GARFIELD GAINS WEIGHT (#2)   32008/$6.95
__GARFIELD BIGGER THAN LIFE (#3)   32007/$6.95
__GARFIELD WEIGHS IN (#4)   32010/$6.95
__GARFIELD TAKES THE CAKE (#5)   32009/$6.95
__GARFIELD EATS HIS HEART OUT (#6)   32018/$6.95
__GARFIELD SITS AROUND THE HOUSE (#7)   32011/$6.95
__GARFIELD TIPS THE SCALES (#8)   33580/$6.95
__GARFIELD LOSES HIS FEET (#9)   31805/$6.95
__GARFIELD MAKES IT BIG (#10)   31928/$6.95
__GARFIELD ROLLS ON (#11)   32634/$6.95
__GARFIELD OUT TO LUNCH (#12)   33118/$6.95
__GARFIELD FOOD FOR THOUGHT (#13)   34129/$6.95
__GARFIELD SWALLOWS HIS PRIDE (#14)   34725/$6.95
__GARFIELD WORLDWIDE (#15)   35158/$6.95
__GARFIELD ROUNDS OUT (#16)   35388/$6.95
__GARFIELD CHEWS THE FAT (#17)   35956/$6.95
__GARFIELD GOES TO WAIST (#18)   36430/$6.95
__GARFIELD HANGS OUT (#19)   36835/$6.95
__GARFIELD TAKES UP SPACE (#20)   37029/$6.95
__GARFIELD SAYS A MOUTHFUL (#21)   37368/$6.95
__GARFIELD BY THE POUND (#22)   37579/$6.95

__GARFIELD KEEPS HIS CHINS UP (#23)   37959/$6.95
__GARFIELD TAKES HIS LICKS (#24)   38170/$6.95
__GARFIELD HITS THE BIG TIME (#25)   38332/$6.95
__GARFIELD PULLS HIS WEIGHT (#26)   38666/$6.95
__GARFIELD DISHES IT OUT (#27)   39287/$6.95
__GARFIELD LIFE IN THE FAT LANE (#28)   39776/$6.95
__GARFIELD TONS OF FUN (#29)   40386/$6.95
__GARFIELD BIGGER AND BETTER (#30)   40770/$6.95
__GARFIELD HAMS IT UP (#31)   41241/$6.95
__GARFIELD THINKS BIG (#32)   41671/$6.95
__GARFIELD THROWS HIS WEIGHT AROUND (#33)   42749/$6.95
__GARFIELD LIFE TO THE FULLEST (#34)   43239/$6.95
__GARFIELD FEEDS THE KITTY (#35)   43673-/$6.95

GARFIELD AT HIS SUNDAY BEST!
__GARFIELD TREASURY   32106/$11.95
__THE SECOND GARFIELD TREASURY   33276/$10.95
__THE THIRD GARFIELD TREASURY   32635/$11.00
__THE FOURTH GARFIELD TREASURY   34726/$10.95
__THE FIFTH GARFIELD TREASURY   36268/$12.00
__THE SIXTH GARFIELD TREASURY   37367/$10.95
__THE SEVENTH GARFIELD TREASURY   38427/$10.95
__THE EIGHTH GARFIELD TREASURY   39778/$12.00
__THE NINTH GARFIELD TREASURY   41670/$12.50
__THE TENTH GARFIELD TREASURY   43674/$12.50

AND DON'T MISS...
__GARFIELD'S TWENTIETH ANNIVERSARY COLLECTION!   42126/$14.95

Please send me the BALLANTINE BOOKS I have checked above. I am enclosing $_____. (Please add $2.00 for the first book and $.50 for each additional book for postage and handling and include the appropriate state sales tax.) Send check or money order (no cash or C.O.D.'s) to Ballantine Mail Sales Dept. TA, 400 Hahn Road, Westminster, MD 21157.

To order by phone, call 1-800-733-3000 and use your major credit card.

Prices and numbers are subject to change without notice. Valid in the U.S. only. All orders are subject to availability.

Name_____

Address_____

City_____ State_____ Zip_____

Allow at least 4 weeks for delivery   3/99